Human Knowledge According to
Saint Maximus the Confessor

Human Knowledge According to Saint Maximus the Confessor

NEVENA DIMITROVA

RESOURCE *Publications* • Eugene, Oregon

HUMAN KNOWLEDGE ACCORDING TO SAINT MAXIMUS
THE CONFESSOR

Copyright © 2016 Nevena Dimitrova. All rights reserved. Except for brief quotations in critical publications or reviews, no part of this book may be reproduced in any manner without prior written permission from the publisher. Write: Permissions, Wipf and Stock Publishers, 199 W. 8th Ave., Suite 3, Eugene, OR 97401.

Resource Publications
An Imprint of Wipf and Stock Publishers
199 W. 8th Ave., Suite 3
Eugene, OR 97401

www.wipfandstock.com

PAPERBACK ISBN: 978-1-62564-574-6
HARDCOVER ISBN: 978-1-4982-8560-5
EBOOK ISBN: 978-1-5326-0850-6

Manufactured in the U.S.A.   OCTOBER 10, 2016

Contents

Preface | *vii*
Acknowledgments | *ix*
Abbreviations | *xi*

1. Saint Maximus the Confessor: His Epoch and His Importance for Byzantine Thought | 1
2. The Human Person as a Knowing Being: Essence, Calling, and Aims | 11
3. Cognitive Faculties and Types of Knowledge | 51
4. Levels of Knowledge | 126
5. Cataphatic and Apophatic Ways of Knowledge | 176

Conclusion | 180
Bibliography | 183

Preface

MAXIMUS THE CONFESSOR (580–662) is regarded as the father of Byzantine philosophy and has been at the center of patristic studies. In recent times, this Byzantine thinker has become an important figure in the fields of philosophy, psychology, anthropology. During the last decade, interest in his work has increased significantly. This book is devoted to the question of human knowledge. Maximus does not investigate the issue in a separate writing; he explores the gnoseological issue from different perspectives in various texts and on diverse occasions. His treatment of this subject can be traced in terms of his use of language borrowed directly and indirectly from the Bible, ancient philosophers, and pre-Christian authors. By incorporating diverse ideas and terms into a great synthesis, he creates a new vision of the major questions of his time.

In the book, the terms "practice" and "theory" are used to signify the practical and contemplative aspects of the soul's activity. Another division is represented by the words "logos" and "tropos," which describe nature and its mode of existing. As the inner principle of existing things, logos also means "reason" (the soul's discerning activity). Furthermore, this word is employed in the biblical sense of God, the incarnate Word. Goodness and Truth are capitalized throughout the book because they refer to the limits of human knowledge in Maximus's *Mystagogia* and thereby, serve as names of the divine existence that are much better than moral and gnoseological expressions. Perichorezis is a complex word that has the meaning of unifying, yet preserving the difference between, the qualities of God's three persons. This term is used also to signify unity between the soul and body that is the essence of the Eucharist.

Maximus the Confessor has long been of interest to philologists because of the complexity and innovative character of his language. For theologians, he is a great defender of Christian truth and doctrine, and in the philosophical realm, he brings ancient language into the Christian sphere of dialogue regarding the Other. A special emphasis in the book is made on the terms describing the "human" situation in the knowing process: heksis and gnomi. Those give way to explaining the paradox of the human existence in this world. Following Maximus's example, quotations are used in different chapters to draw attention on different topics and some of the topics are called more than once in order to be seen from different perspective and in another context. This would allow the path of knowledge to be seen not as an everlasting circle but as a growing spiral (the way apocatastasis is described). In the end what is knowledge if not opening our eyes for reading the Truth that has always been written.

Acknowledgments

THIS BOOK IS A publication of my PhD project that was defended in 2010 at Sofia University "Saint Kliment Ohridski," Bulgaria. Epistemological problems in patristics and especially in Saint Maximus the Confessor have been of main interest in my studies. My aim is to present his understanding of human knowledge in a systematized way (something that is not typical for this author as he is largely unsystematic). Thus the structure of the text is devided into five chapters beginning with the position of human being as a knower and continuing with the sense perception, rational and noetic knowledge—a process that ceases in the mystical union of divine-human communion above discursive reflection and thought.

For my personal and professional development resulting in this monograph, I am grateful to the following persons (in chronological order):

I would like to give thanks to my teachers Tzocho Boiadjiev, Kalin Yanakiev and Georgi Kapriev. To Tzocho Boyadjiev for his lectures and books became the reason for me to study philosophy at Sofia University. To Kalin Yanakiev for his profound knowledge, beautiful lectures and deep interest in my development; for the long dialogues on the topic and not last for the dear friendship. And to my supervisor Georgi Kapriev under whose guidance I became the first scholar with a PhD on Byzantine Philosophy (being an Orthodox woman).

The research on the dissertation topic has been led at De Wulf-Mansion Center for Medieval and Renaissance Philosophy at KU Leuven, Belgium and later at Thomas Institute at Cologne University. I am grateful to Prof. Carlos Steel for his constant encouragement and readiness to help me with discussions (and the translation of parts of Ambigua), to Peter van Deun who gave me the access to the library at the Faculty of Arts, and to Jacques Noret and Carl Laga for the advices and discussions.

Acknowledgments

At Thomas Institute, I would like to thank to its director, Prof. Andreas Speer, for accepting me as a doctoral researcher at TI where I had the opportunity to work with sources from the library. I am grateful for his advices on my work and caring supervision.

This monograph would not have been born without the love and generosity of my teacher and friend—Ivana Noble. Her constant belief in me, thorough supervision and tender friendship during the two years of post doctoral research at Protestant Theological Faculty of Charles University in Prague made it possible for me to write and publish the text of the dissertation.

Thanks to Ivana I met other important persons in my academic life to whom I am grateful too: Aristotle "Telly" Papanikolaou for being always a supportive friend as well as critical reader of my work.

I would also like to thank David Fagerberg for reading the whole manuscript and replicating in conversational manner to the places which did not seem clear enough.

I have been greatly supported from the Protestant Theological Faculty in the face of the dean Doc. Dr. Jindrich Halama from whom I received the financial resources for publishing this text and to whom I am in great debt.

My very special gratitude to the proof reader of this text Joyce Michaels—a great friend and a dedicated person on this project!

I would like to thank my family and to dedicate this book to the loving memory of my grandparents Boyka and Athanas.

Abbreviations

Amb. Io.	Ambigua ad Iohannem
Amb. Th.	Ambigua ad Thomam
Cap. Gnost.	Chapters on Gnoseology
Car.	Capita de caritate
CCSG	Corpus Christianorum Series Graeca
Myst.	Mystagogia
Disput. Pyrr.	Disputatio cum Pyrrho
Opusc.	Opuscula theologica et polemica
Pater	On our Father
PG	Patrologia Graeca
Q. Thal.	Quaestiones ad Thalassium
Qu. Dub.	Quaestiones et dubia
Th. Oec.	Capita theologica et oeconomica

1

Saint Maximus the Confessor
His Epoch and His Importance for Byzantine Thought

INTRODUCTION

All research is, in some sense, a translation of, and a journey through, source material. Yet, at the same time, it is a search for a particular motif in the source material. Answering a major question involves opening a new horizon. In this respect, the result of the dialogue that takes place in this book is not a new discovery. Instead, it is a conversation, an act of rewriting and re-creation, as the work of any person who is reading, rather than writing, may be.[1] The metaphysical position represented in the thought of Saint Maximus the Confessor also follows such a pattern.

"Not speaking for themselves" is a characteristic pattern of medieval writers from Augustine onwards, and continuing this tradition by engaging in a careful reading and critical clarification of his predecessors is an important feature of Maximus's thought. Thus, the challenge facing anyone who wishes to understand Maximus's texts is to read carefully and to "see through" his writings and the ideas expressed therein. Therefore, the necessary condition for fulfilling this objective is not only a reconstruction of the Confessor's personality and of the language he uses. It also entails a clarification of the innovative elements of his thought since he is the one

---

1. The Word of God has been given to humankind to be read and understood. In this sense, all human beings who have been created in the image of God are called to become "readers" of the Word. A knowing human being is someone who is learning how to read God's Word.

who "corrects" the ancient philosophical legacy of Aristotle, Plato, and the Neoplatonists; interprets and clarifies difficult places in the writings of Gregory of Nazianzus or Pseudo-Dionysius the Areopagite; and makes possible the transition from pre-Christian to Christian philosophy (albeit not in a chronological sense) by moving beyond the teachings of Evagrius and Origen.

The accumulation of theological and philosophical works during the fourth, fifth, and sixth centuries and the formation of general theological/philosophical problems, thematic unities, and terminological conventions constitute the foundation of Eastern thought and Byzantine philosophy and theology. Maximus's place in the center of the Byzantine thought as the "father of Byzantine philosophy" confirms the key role of the Confessor's work and personality.[2] His contributions not only had great significance for the cultural history of Byzantium during a particular period of foreign and internal political, social, and religious problems; they continue to have universal value. The descent into the illusory "dolce vita mentality" and the human inclination toward a disunited tropos of existence, as well as humankind's tendency to forget its original mission to unite this world and return it to the creator, necessitates a figure like Maximus, who was orthodox before his successors divided household of God. The witness of such a true believer is critical when numerous heresies threaten the foundations of a way of life that is grounded in the truth of Christ.

At the time of the christological controversies in the seventh century, the physical foundations of the empire were threatened by Arab and Persian forces that made use of the instability which resulted from divisions between the Chalcedonian and non-Chalcedonian (Monophysite) communities. Disputes, which lasted for centuries, regarding the meaning of the Incarnation culminated in two key questions: what kind and how many energies are at work in God the Son and how many wills exist in Christ? This situation and Maximus's involvement in it are aptly described in the following summary:

> The doctrines of monenergism (one "energy" or activity in Christ) and monothelitism (one will which subsumed both human and divine aspects) were instigated by theologians close to the court, particularly the patriarch of Constantinople, as a way of shoring up ecclesiastical unity in a time of political turmoil. With Avar-Slav enemies to the North and Persians and Arabs to the East, the last

---

2. Meyendorff, *Byzantine Theology*, 37.

thing Emperor Heraclius needed was a recalcitrant monk stirring up dissent in Africa and Italy. This was Maximus the Confessor, whose theological obstinacy had a quite unprecedented impact on Heraclius' precarious hold on imperial rule in the declining capital of Constantinople.³Maximus had the support of popes John IV, Theodore I, and Martin I, and he found even more supporters in the West. The power of the West's opposition to the imperial doctrines was demonstrated by the 150 bishops who participated in the Lateran Council that was convened in Rome in 649. Their opposition eventually resulted in Pope Martin 1, Maximus, and his disciple Anastasius being brought to trial on trumped-up charges in Constantinople, where they were condemned to torture and to exile under appalling physical conditions that eventually brought about their deaths.[4]

This backdrop for entering into dialogue with Maximus's thought is necessary for two reasons. On the one hand, the Byzantine thinker's existential situation and spiritual quests have contributed to the central position that he holds in the collective theological, cultural, and historical memory. On the other hand, although scholarly research has been carried out with regard to a number of Maximus's ideas, much of this work has focused on the trinitarian, christological, and anthropological aspects of his teachings.[5] However, in several texts, the issue of human knowledge is discussed in relation to other key themes.[6] In fact, this is Maximus's own approach; he does not devote a separate text to the question of human knowledge. His teachings on this topic are not presented in a systematic way. He takes a stand against the chaos of his age by disclosing the Christian truth in non-systematic rejoinders. His thought is designed to answer the questions of his time.[7] The absence of texts composed in an orderly fashion does not

---

3. Allen and Brownen, *Documents from Exile*, 1.

4. Ibid., 2.

5. Regarding Maximus's trinitarian views, see Piret, *Le Christ et la Trinité* (1983). Regarding his Christology, see Matsoukas, *La vie en Dieu* (1980); Riou, *Le monde et L'Église* (1973); Karayiannis, *Essence et énergies* (1993); Törönen, *Union and Distinction* (2007). Regarding his anthropology, see Thunberg, *Microcosm and Mediator* (1965); Thunberg, *Man and the Cosmos* (1985); Larchet, *La divinisation de l'homme* (1996); Farrell, *Free Choice* (1987).

6. See Völker, *Meister des Geistlichen Lebens* (1965) and Larchet, *La divinisation de l'homme* (1996).

7. Florovsky, *The Byzantine Fathers*, 557; see also Епифанович, Византийското богословие (2008).

diminish the meaning and depth of the powerful synthesis that Maximus creates as he inaugurates the beginning of Byzantine philosophy.

Scholarly considerations of Byzantine philosophy, which had already begun in the eighteenth century, are associated with noteworthy thinkers like Basil Tatakis, Hans-Georg Beck, and Klaus Oehler, as well as with independent academic researchers like Georges Florovsky, John Meyendorff, Dumitru Staniloae, and Kallistos Ware. Maximus' texts are not focused on a specific issue; their aim is to find the reason for—the beginning of—questioning itself. Therefore, the problem of human knowledge is addressed in a large number of his writings. Human knowledge is the place where creator and creation meet. It is the way that the ascent of human beings and the descent of God simultaneously happen in communion with the Logos. Thus, this book represents an attempt to analyze the divine-human relationship that characterizes the movement of knowledge from—and to—unity and communion. Ascertaining the scope, limits, rhythm, and consummation of the parameters of existence is the basic task of every metaphysical quest, of every cognitive act, and of every return to the beginning.

In short, this work is devoted to the synergetic process of divine-human communion, which, according to the father of Byzantine theology and the most ecumenical of the Church Fathers of the seventh century, is an integral part of the knowledge of God that is possible for human beings. Various types of knowledge play an important, but hitherto unexplored, role in Maximus the Confessor's thought, which, in many respects, is both a synthesis and the culmination of the Greek patristic tradition, as well as a successor of pre-Christian thinking and an antecedent of Christian philosophy.

Human knowledge lies at the center of Maximus's works: it consists of an experience of divine presence which reveals the reason and telos of everything that exists and makes humankind's future growth possible. Extension of the limits of created nature and transcendence beyond the given are two of the great tasks that lie before human beings who strive to achieve reunion with their creator. This specific process of attaining knowledge of God becomes a means of becoming human in God through the restoration of human nature to the way it initially existed in the logoi. Hence, the capacity that human beings have to let God enter their universe points to the major aspects of Maximus's anthropology that I will explore. These include the soul-body relationship and a detailed examination of the soul's cognitive capacities, which involve sense perception, rational activity, and the operation of the mind.

These different, but interrelated, parts of the human ascent to knowledge are constitutive of the movement of the trichotomously structured soul, which begins with practical philosophy and is followed by natural contemplation and theology. The two modes of knowledge—positive (cataphatic) and negative (apophatic)—demonstrate the rational and beyond-rational levels of discourse that are operative in human knowledge of God. In the next chapter, these types of knowledge are presented as interdependent and mutually presupposing "modes" that lead to divine-human communion in knowledge. Among the greatest features of Maximus's inventive thought and one of the emphases of this book is his understanding of hexis (ἕξις) and gnomi (γνώμη), which are two of the human preconditions for opening the door to the divine-human communion that occurs as human beings attain knowledge of God. God as Goodness and God as Truth provide the telos, or end, of our practical and theoretical activities. Goodness and Truth reveal the consummation of the knowledge of God that it is possible for human beings to attain. Beyond that lies the mystical experience and real life in Christ that God promises from beginning to end.

LIFE AND WORK

It is difficult to say whether it is extraordinary persons or momentous times that give rise to great ideas. The life, work, and teachings of Saint Maximus the Confessor unfolded during a very interesting age when Byzantium was trying to establish its greatness. Emperor Justinian (527–65) and his great success in the East resulted in the Byzantine Empire being seen as the earthly manifestation of the heavenly kingdom of God. Justinian was the first Byzantine emperor depicted on gold coins holding a sphere and a cross. After his death, the first signs of decline appeared. His successor, Heraclius (610–41), attempted to maintain universal hegemony. Although he was victorious against enemies from the outside (and especially against Persian forces), after losing the eastern provinces, he was unable to cope with the Arabian invasion and the disunity of the empire. During the reign of the next emperor, Constans II (664–68), the status quo remained unchanged.

During the rule of these two emperors, Maximus the Confessor—who never held a high position in the ruling hierarchy—appeared on the scene.

Human Knowledge According to Saint Maximus

He tirelessly stood up for the primacy of truth, regardless of political developments. In other words, while Heraclius and Constans II were busy preserving their universal hegemony, Maximus did not accept the fact that the price for this must be a falsification of the truths of faith that are inherent in doctrine and church practice. The task of the public officials was to preserve the eastern part of the empire where the Monophysites were intransigent opponents of the decisions of the Fourth Ecumenical Council that was held in Chalcedon in 451. After the Council of Chalcedon, Monophysitism primarily spread in Egypt, Syria, and Armenia. At the beginning of the seventh century, there was a religious schism that resulted in the existence of two churches in the Byzantine Empire. These were the Orthodox Church and the unofficial Monophysite Church, which was subject to persecution and was a potential ally of the enemies of the Byzantine Empire. The religious tensions between these two groups were intensified by external political conflicts and internal problems.[8]

Facts about Maximus's life and work received renewed consideration during the last century.[9] One of the most important sources of information is the Greek version of the lives of the saints. The first and second editions of the four redactions of this text that are known to exist have been combined in a single written tradition to which a long and a short version of a Georgian account of the saints' lives has been added. The Greek biography of Maximus's life was composed in the tenth century at the Monastery of Stoudios by a monk named Michael Exabulites.[10] In 1973, Sebastian Brock published a Syriac version of the lives of the saints that dates back to the seventh century. It was written by Georgius of Resh'aina, a disciple of Saint Sophronius of Jerusalem, who remained a Monothelite.[11]

According to the Greek biography, Maximus was born into a rich and influential noble family in Constantinople in 579 or 580. He received an excellent education, pursuing his studies of the Classics between 581 and 601.[12] He may have held a position in the court of Emperor Heraclius

---

8. Regarding the history of the Monophysite heresy and the proceedings of the ecumenical councils, see Карташев, Вселенские соборы (2006).

9. With regard to Maximus's biography, see Sherwood, *Date-List of the Works of Maximus the Confessor* (1952); Larchet, *La divinisation de l'homme* (1996); Louth, *Maximus the Confessor*, 3–18; and Thunberg, *Microcosm and Mediator* (1965).

10. Louth, *Maximus the Confessor*, 4.

11. Larchet, *La divinisation de l'homme*, 8.

12. In the seventh century, a classical education typically began at the age of 6 and continued to the age of 21. It included grammar, classical literature, rhetoric, and, in

between 610 and 613, although this seems improbable. Around 613, he became a monk at a monastery in Chrysopolis, which was located near Constantinople on the shore of the Bosphorus.

In contrast, according to the Syriac biography, Maximus was born to unmarried parents in the Palestinian village Hesfin with the birth name of Moschion. His father was a Samaritan weaver from Sychar, and his mother was a Persian woman who had been a slave. They were cast out by the Samaritan community and went to the Christian priest Martyrios, who baptized them. After the death of his parents in 591, Moschion was sent to an abbot named Pantoleon at Saint Chariton's Monastery. There he was given his religious name, Maximus. In 614, Maximus left for the monastery at Chrysopolis. In 617, a monk named Anastasius became a disciple of Maximus at the monastery near Constantinople. During the Persian onslaughts in 626, Maximus set out by way of Crete and Cypress for North Africa. There, in 632, he met Sophronius, who became his spiritual father. At the monastery of Saint George in Cyzicus, he produced his first writings, which included Letter 2—To John Cubicularius, On the Ascetic Life, The Four Hundred Chapters on Love, and a Commentary on Psalm 59. While there, he also wrote Letters 3, 4, and 10 and a work entitled Questions and Doubts.[13]

During the first five centuries of the current era, an intense clarification of Christian doctrine took place. Although question of the triune God was settled at the First Ecumenical Council with the formulation of the Nicene Creed (which the Orthodox Church calls the Symbol of Faith), christological disputes about Christ's divine and human natures were not resolved until the seventh century. The inquiry about divine-human unity is the most important question that can be rasied about the meaning and telos of human life.

The Monothelite heresy of the seventh century is closely linked to the earlier Monophysite heresy. Although the church had already condemned the Monophysite heresy at the Council of Chalcedon in the fifth century, that position still had many adherents in the sixth and seventh centuries. In the critical seventh century, Monophysitism appeared in a new form as

---

particular, philosophy, which at that time, consisted of arithmetic, music, geometry, astronomy, logic, ethics, metaphysics, and dogmatics. See Larchet, *La divinisation de l'homme*, 8.

13. Larchet, *La divinisation de l'homme*, 12-13.

the Monothelite heresy.[14] In 633, Sergius I, the patriarch of Constantinople, issued a Pact of Union that sought to cultivate peace with the dissenting Monophysites. At the end of the year, in response to Sophronius's protests against this development, the emperor put forth a declaration (*Psephos*) that banned all debate about whether Christ had one or two energies. This marked a transition from Monoenergism to Monothelitism.

In 634, Sophronius became the patriarch of Jerusalem and in his synodical letter, attacked these positions. He maintained that although Christ's two natures have two energies, this does not result in two hypostases. In a letter to Pyrrhus at the end of 633, Maximus interpreted the Psephos in a Dyothelite manner. In 638, Sergius and Heraclius came out with an imperial edict entitled Ecthesis, which professed that there is only one will in Christ. This edict marked the beginning of the disputes that were kindled by the Monothelite belief that because there is only one true God—Christ—who "moves" divine and human wills, there can be only one will, not two, in him. Sergius died in 638, and Sophronius passed away in 639, which was the year that Pyrrhus, the new patriarch of Constantinople, affirmed the Ecthesis at a church council. Maximus debated with Pyrrhus in Carthage, convincing him of the correctness of his views. Then, the two men set out for Rome. The next year, the bishops in North Africa officially rejected the Ecthesis. In a Bull (Typos) issued in 647, Emperor Constans II strictly forbade all discussion of whether there were one or two energies in Christ. At that time, Maximus was in Rome, where he initiated a response. In October 649, the newly chosen Pope Martin I convened the Lateran Council that condemned the Ecthesis, the Typos, and their authors and supporters.[15] The council's documents were prepared with the direct participation of Saint Maximus, who signed the final document as "monk Maximus."

In 653, Saint Maximus and Pope Martin I were arrested, and in 655, they were found guilty of treason and were imprisoned in Byzia and Cherson, respectively. Martin I died the same year. Maximus and two of his followers, who were both named Athanasius, were anathematized by a local council in Constantinople in 658. Maximus was tortured; his right hand and the tip of his tongue were cut off. He was sent far away to the fortress of Schemaris on the southeastern shore of the Black Sea where the nation of Georgia is located today. He died there on August 13, 662. Just twenty years later, his teachings and life achievements were acclaimed by the Sixth

---

14. Лебедев, История Вселенских Соборов, 77.
15. Riedinger, "Die Lateransynode von 649 und Maximus der Bekenner," 111–21.

Ecumenical Council (680–681), and he was canonized. Seventy-four texts of various lengths and fifty letters survive from Maximus's corpus.

His first years in North Africa were a very productive time for Maximus. Between 628 and 630, he wrote texts entitled Ambigua to John; Commentary on the Our Father, and Mystagogia. Questions to Thalassius appeared from 630 to 633, along with Questions to Theotempt scholast and a Commentary on Psalm 59. Maximus's abilities as a theologian and an exegete can be seen in Questions to Thalassius where he develops the tradition of interpreting the Bible that was established by the Alexandrian school. His interpretation of Psalm 59 was written in the same spirit, and his Commentary on the Our Father is also one of Maximus's masterpieces. It is not only an exegetical theological work; it is also a type of mystagogy.[16]

By 634, Maximus had written a text entitled Ambigua to Thomas, which was largely devoted to christological issues and was particularly focused on Christ's natures and energies. During this period, Maximus also wrote Letter 13 and Letter 25. Between 634 and 640, he made use of a special genre of Christian writing that consisted of "centuries," or "hundreds," of "chapters." This genre is the result of an amalgamation of two traditions. On the one hand, its origin may be traced to collections of aphorisms (Apophthegmata) preserved by the first Desert Fathers. On the other hand, it drew upon the aphoristic style used in the philosophical prose of late antiquity by thinkers such as Marcus Aurelius and Porphyry. Evagrius Ponticus was the first author to introduce the genre of the centuries into Christian literature. Maximus used this genre to compose the following works: Four Hundred Chapters on Love, Two Hundred Chapters on Theology and the Economy in the Flesh of the Son of God, and Ten Chapters on Virtue and Vice. His Chapters on Love is an ascetical and ethical text that is the most famous of Maximus's writings and constitutes a true masterpiece.

Maximus's polemical dogmatic writings are of primary importance. In some of these, he engages in debate with the Monophysites and presents his doctrine regarding Christ's two natures (primarily in letters addressed to Peter, the Alexandrian deacon Cosmas, John Cubicularius, the Alexandrian scholastic Julian, and hermits. In other works, Maximus expounds on teachings about the two wills and two energies that are in Christ. His Disputation with Pyrrhus and a dogmatic epistle to Stephen entitled "On the Two Wills of Christ, our God" are of special interest. In addition, the following two works are particularly noteworthy by virtue of their

---

16. See Tollefsen, *The Christocentric Cosmology*, 4–13.

magnitude and content: the well-known Latin translation of the Ambigua (On Various Difficulties in St Dionysius and St Gregory) and Questions to Thalassius.[17] The Ambigua combines two independent texts that were written at different times. One of these is the Ambigua to John, which was translated into Latin by John Scot Eriugena. It is longer and earlier than the other work, which is entitled Ambigua to Thomas. The Second Epistle to Thomas, which was published by Paul Canart in 1964, is considered to be the third part of the Ambigua. These works demonstrate Maximus's theological and philosophical gifts, and have commendable place in the history of Christian theology and in the history of philosophy, insofar as they raise questions that have critical importance for both of these realms of thought.

Maximus's Mystagogia seeks to elaborate on the mystical meaning of liturgy in the spirit of the Corpus Areopagiticum. This book had a great influence on the later Byzantine liturgical tradition. Maximus's method of interpreting scripture is also employed here to explain the Divine Liturgy. This Mystagogia is the first work that was written in the genre of traditional Greek liturgical commentaries (although there are precedents for this sort of text in the Alexandrian and Antiochian schools, as well as in Dionysius's writings, where there are various types of "mystagogies."[18] However, as always, Maximus goes beyond the boundaries of the genre, and his Mystagogia is more like a theological, ascetical, and (at some points) ecclesial work than a commentary on the Eucharist in a strict sense. Without this text, many of the theological aspects of Maximus's thought would be unclear and misunderstood.[19]

---

17. In keeping with established conventions, the titles *Questions to Thalassius and Commentary on the Our Father* will be used throughout this book, even though some scholars prefer *Answers to the Questions of Thalassius*, *To Thalassius*, and/or *Commentary on the Lord's Prayer*.

18. In line with other scholarly works, Pseudo-Dionysius the Areopagite will be referred to as "Dionysius" from this point on.

19. Сидоров, Преподобный Максим Исповедник: эпоха, жизнь, творчество, 7–74.

2

The Human Person as a Knowing Being
Essence, Calling, and Aims

Human Knowledge: Introductory Observations
From Image to Likeness
Knowledge of Good and Evil

HUMAN KNOWLEDGE: INTRODUCTORY OBSERVATIONS

The problem of attaining knowledge of God is one of the most difficult and complicated theological questions considered by the Church Fathers. Maximus is not an exception in this regard; in his cosmological, philosophical, and theological explorations, he devotes special attention to the topic, which is of great importance to us. Human beings have been created to participate in, and to be (re)united with, God.[1] Nevertheless, there is an ontological gulf between the creator and creation that needs to be overcome.

Following Basil the Great and Gregory of Nyssa's critical response to Eunomius's contention that God's essence is knowable, the emphasis on the transcendence, unknowability, and inaccessibility of the divine ousia has been explicitly expressed linguistically.[2] Yet, this divine essence is also the starting point of motion. Although the divine energies are manifestations

---

1. The word "re-ligion" derives from "re-union" or "re-ligare." See Augustine, *Of True Religion* (9), 221.
2. Basil, *On the Holy Spirit*, 83–84.

of the eternal God, their creations are brought forth in time. Thus, in their response to Eunomius, Basil and Gregory affirm that although God is unknowable in essence, human beings can attain knowledge of him through the divine energies and the resultant creations in the same way that every craftsperson can be recognized in his/her art. God's invisible nature—that is, his "eternal power and deity"—has been seen ever since the beginning of the world through knowledge of creation (Rom 1:20).

In his attempts to repudiate the Arians' heretical teachings and their denial of the divinity of the Holy Spirit, Saint Basil focuses his arguments in a particular way. Scripture teaches us that through the Holy Spirit, we become—by participation—like God the Son is by nature. Therefore, insofar as the Holy Spirit deifies us, the Paraclete shares the nature of God the Father and God the Son. Yet, we may ask how the energy of the Holy Spirit leads us to theosis. Here, Basil makes an important distinction. Through his activity, God creates a nature that is different from himself; the creator and creation belong to different ontological orders. When the Holy Spirit descends into the rational, free creation, the end result is not the same created nature. The third hypostasis of God unifies his energies and those of creation in a mutual, perichoretic accord. Thus, the activity of the Holy Spirit has already been identified as a divine-human activity, as this text from Basil's writings indicates:

> We say, for instance, that form abides *in* matter, or that power dwells *in* its recipient, or a certain habit affects a person *in* whom it makes its home, and so on. Therefore, since the Holy Spirit perfects reason-endowed beings, He is present *in* them in the same way Form is present *in* matter. Such a person no longer lives according to the flesh, but is led by the Spirit of God. He is called a Son of God, because he is conformed to the image of the Son of God; we call him a spiritual man. The ability to see is *in* a healthy eye; likewise the Spirit is working *in* a purified soul: Paul prays that the Ephesians' eyes might be enlightened by the Spirit of wisdom [Eph. 1:17–18].[3] The Monothelite heresy provides Maximus with an opportunity to deepen these understandings and to establish the relationship between the theosis of Christ's human nature and the theosis of human beings. In opposition to the Monothelites who see only one will and one energy in the second hypostasis of the Trinity, Maximus presents a coherent account in which God

---

3. Basil, *On the Holy Spirit*, 93.

the Son is entirely human in nature and will and entirely God in nature and will.

Since knowledge is a complex issue in a number of Maximus's works, this chapter will focus on a representative selection of pertinent passages. Maximus's theory of knowledge dispenses with the framework of the subject-object relationship and its insistence that "objectivity" is the way to acquire an object of knowledge. It involves obtaining a state of being in God, rather than possessing knowledge of God's being. The ultimate goal of the pathway of knowing is to be "reborn and recreated in the Spirit."[4] This means that every spiritual creature reaches the perfection of existence through a personal experience of the divine presence in the world. Thus, communion—the restoration of one's relationship with God—becomes a meaningful axis of human life and of every act of knowing.

A crucial aspect of Maximus's gnoseology is the manner in which it refashions the tropos of knowledge as the mediator between the farthest reaches of the divine and the limited capacities of created essences in light of teachings about the Incarnation of the Logos. Love from and to the giver of life lies at the start of the ascent of each individual human nature. Here, the main question is not what Maximus identifies as knowledge, but how he treats this issue.

The Mystagogia and Ambigua were both written between 628 and 630, while Chapters on Love (Capita de Caritate) is a relatively early text composed between 624 and 625. In the first chapter of the Ambigua, Maximus discusses problematic issues raised by the writings of Gregory of Nazianzus, and in Chapters on Love, he develops his own understandings and elaborates on Evagrius's teachings. According to scholarly research regarding Maximus's thought, ideas related to philosophy, theology, and personal experience constitute the foundation of his understanding of gnosis.

The path to knowledge eventuates in a contemplation of divine being that gives rise to the state of being-in-love in and through which participation in God is possible. The Truth in which intellectual activities cease and God is revealed in his essence is attainable by the noetic part of the soul. This occurrence is made possible by the cessation of rational discursive knowledge. The soul enters into mystical unity, participation in the divine energies, and an experiential perception of the divine. In this regard, there are two possible modes of knowing: the rational foundation of the knowledgeable soul and the mystical event of communion. It is only through a

---

4. *Myst.* (5) PG 91 677A.

combination of these two modes of knowing that the last step of human knowledge—the theosis of the seeker of Truth—is achieved.

In Chapters on Love, philosophy (φιλοσοφία) is used solely in the sense employed by the patristic tradition, which understands it as a "love of wisdom" that entails certain ethical and ascetical practices. Yet, in line with Athanasius of Alexandria, Basil the Great, and Gregory of Nyssa, φιλοσοφία is also identified with human striving toward God in Chapters on Love. The distinction between the type of noetic activity that is based on divine wisdom and that of Hellenic philosophy, which is based on human wisdom, is overcome in two respects. This reformulation of the definition of philosophy is a natural consequence of the new horizons that open up for human thought in the Christian milieu. Philosophy is an act of the mind, but as such, it is not opposed to the enlightenment that is given by the Holy Spirit. Even so, a love of wisdom not only changes the content of divine wisdom; it also transforms the wisdom of this world.

In other words, the initial tropos—the love from and to God, which is the main motivating factor in communion with him—turns into a transforming and transcending event that links the practice of the virtues and contemplation of the divine logoi to participation in the divine energies. Thus, although in Evagrius's thought, the final aim of the soul's strivings is the pure mind—which is the state from which it has fallen—for Maximus, spiritual life mirrors the way we love. "As the memory of fire does not warm the body," he declares, "so faith without love does not bring about the illumination of knowledge in the soul."[5]

Elsewhere, Maximus says: "And unless the mind finds something better than these to which it can transfer its desire, it will not be completely persuaded to disdain them. And better than these by far is the knowledge of God and of divine things."[6] "To acquire γνῶσις, πάθος is necessary."[7] Overcoming the passions and disciplining the flesh generally do not have a negative meaning in Maximus's works. Instead, the emphasis is placed on love and its purifying and transformative role. "The soul is pure when it has been freed from the passions and rejoices unceasingly in divine

---

5. *Car.* 1.31.

6. *Car.* 3.61.

7. Actes du Symposium sur Maxime le Confesseur, 1982 "Ἡ ἄνευ πάθους τῶν θείων γνῶσις οὐ πείθει τὸν νοῦν εἰς τέλος κατα - φρονεῖν τῶν προσύλων, ἀλλ' ἔοικε λογισμῷ ψιλῷ πράγματος αἰσθητοῦ."

love," Maximus avows.[8] This is another place where the transformation of Evagrius's teachings can be seen. As we have already noted, the intellectual achievement of a purified mind is not the ultimate goal for Maximus.

Before presenting the stages of knowledge in detail, it is necessary to offer another clarification. Ascetic theology, which gives us a way to attain knowledge of God, is not a "spiritual technique." Reaching knowledge of God is a matter of personal experience, not a speculative exercise. Knowing God means speaking (dialoging) with the One who has made himself knowable.[9] This is knowledge that is above nature, and its final telos is mystical union with God. It is here that participation in the divine energies and the cessation of the mind's activities occur.[10]

In the first century of Chapters on Love, Maximus picks up on the work of Dionysius the Areopagite and Gregory of Nazianzus.[11] Beginning with a quotation, he declares: "And this alone is thoroughly understandable in Him, infinity'; and the very fact of knowing nothing about him is to know beyond the mind's power."[12] In the third century of the same work, Maximus, following up on Evagrius and Dionysius, again emphasizes the unknowability of the divine essence: "The perfect mind is the one that through genuine faith knows in supreme ignorance the supremely unknowable."[13] God is unknowable in His essence, and may only be known in his energies.[14] Thus, the scope of the knowledge that can be attained by the soul's capacities is limited to the province of the divine presence in this world.

In the broader context, the dichotomy that portrays sense perception and noetic activity as two different capacities of knowing that have two different objects of knowledge comes from Plato. Moreover in this tradition, sense perception, the mind, and discursive reason—which serves as a mediator between that pair—constitute a hierarchical system of knowledge in which the sensible and intelligible worlds and the related human capacities are opposed to one another. In the writings of Plotinus and other

---

8. *Car.* 1.34.
9. See Louth, *Maximus Confessor*, 33.
10. *Myst.* (5) PG 90 677A.
11. *Orat.* 38.7, 45.3.
12. *Car.* 1.100.
13. *Car.* 3.99.
14. Κατά τι μὲν γνωστὸν τὸ θεῖον καὶ τὰ θεῖα, κατά τι δὲ ἄγνωστον· καὶ γνωστὸν μέν, τοῖς περὶ αὐτὸ θεωρήμασιν· ἄγνωστον δέ, τοῖς κατ' αὐτό.

Neoplatonists, reason is the power and potency of the soul, but the soul also takes part in sense perception, and, according to Dionysius, can ascend to the level of angelic intellection. This flexibility of the parts of the soul reveals that the different modes of knowing are a continuum of different levels of the One within constitutive noetic activities. In Dionysian and Neoplatonic mysticism, the darkness of the unknown is opposed to the continuum of being, but Maximus emphasizes the unity of the activities of the various capacities of knowing that enable human beings to attain "indivisible and unified knowledge . . . of God, not of divine essence, or hypostases, but only of the fact of His Existence."[15]

The main objective of this book is not to shed light on the specific understandings expounded by Plato, Aristotle, Plotinus, Proclus, and Dionysius. Nevertheless, perusing the history of the development of human thought gives us a clear sense of the continuity of various traditions and helps make our understanding of Maximus's vision more precise. He inherits the structure of the soul's capacities for knowing and the primary levels of knowledge—αἴσθησις, λόγος, and νοῦς—from Aristotle, the Stoics, and Evagrius. However, the Platonic belief that there is a polar opposition between κόσμος αἰσθητός and κόσμος νοητός does not exist in Maximus's thought.

It is not a matter of neglecting the phenomenal world for the sake of the noumenal or of rejecting αἴσθησις when νόησις is attained. Αἴσθησις is a cognitive activity that is directly related to the perception of phenomena (τὰ φαινόμενα). Although it is difficult to differentiate and delineate the spheres of the first two stages of knowledge, Maximus focuses on spiritual discipline and on preparing human beings to ascend from their fallen state. The consequence of such spiritual practices is not only a return to the purified state of mind from which the soul has fallen, as it is in Origen's estimation. As was stated previously, love from and to God spells the beginning of, and gives meaning to, every spiritual quest; the new covenant turns human beings toward that which has been given by God. This is why, following up on Evagrius's teachings regarding prayer and ascetics, Maximus places πρακτική (practical philosophy) at the beginning of spiritual life. Practical philosophy involves returning to God via a path of knowledge that overcomes the passions by practicing the virtues.

---

15. *Amb. Io.* (17) PG 91 1125. οὐ κατὰ τό τί ποτε τὴν οὐσίαν εἶναι καὶ τὴν ὑπόστασιν (τοῦτο γὰρ ἀμήχανον καὶ ἀνεπιχείρητον), ἀλλὰ κατ' αὐτό. [Unless otherwise noted, Louth's translation of the *Ambigua* is used in this book.]

The Human Person as a Knowing Being

In Chapters on Love, Maximus presents a detailed description of the reasons this first stage is necessary for attaining knowledge of God. Thus, he does not neglect human corporeality like Evagrius and Origen do, so that he can open up an incorporeal way to return to divinity. Through virtue (ἀρετή) and contemplation (θεωρία)—which is the next, more perfect stage of knowledge—it becomes possible for human beings to attain a likeness to God.[16] The path of the progressive ascent toward perfection begins with a movement that is a gift from God and passes through ἔρως and ἔκστασις before eventuating in the divine-human communion that is the final aim of gnosis. Eros is the highest stage of human love for God and of divine love for human beings. All virtues are actualized by, and participate in, divine eros. Human beings, who have been purified of their passions and have actualized the virtues are no longer incapable of contemplating the logoi of being during the second stage of spiritual growth. At the end of this ascent is mystical theology where God is "known" in ignorance at the supranatural stage of knowledge.

Natural contemplation (φυσικὴ θεωρία) follows practical philosophy (πρακτική) and is the beginning of theoria. The purified mind is able to contemplate the natural order of things and to understand the "logic" of its inner structure. The mystical ascension "with the Word" that human beings accomplish by contemplating the logoi of things, along with God's descent to and presence in the world, enables theosis to be realized. In Ambigua 10, Maximus describes five modes (τῶν τρόπων) of natural contemplation (φυσικῆς θεωρίας).[17] The second stage in the process of knowing—which involve attaining knowledge of the logoi of creation—is realized through these modalities, which have an essential unity in the Logos. Knowledge of the logoi of everything that exists leads to knowledge of the One who bestows the principle of being. The human mind cannot penetrate the Logos, but through spiritual discipline and efforts to attain gnosis, human beings are transformed. Their tropos becomes a tropos of openness to a vision of God, wherein the Logos is seen in the logoi and the soul passes beyond discursive knowledge by virtue of experiencing unity with God.

---

16. Amb. Io. (10) PG 91 1113A.

17. Steel. (I am grateful to Professor Steel for giving me his translation of Ambigua 10). Also see Louth, *Maximus the Confessor*, 94–153. See also trans. by Maximos Constas, On Difficulties, 151-343.

Thus, the next level of knowledge, theology (θεολογία)—or contemplation of God—is achieved.[18] Here, we meet up with supranatural knowledge where all representations, images, and thoughts coming from the senses, reason, and the mind are transformed.[19] All of the potencies of the soul cease their activities here. Theology is a type of knowledge—or illumination—that is given by grace.[20] At this juncture, Maximus says more about perception, seeing, or having a vision of God.[21] This knowledge is also called "ignorance" since ignorance of God is knowledge that transcends the mind. Thereby, a bridge between the various activities of reason—which passes through visible forms to the principles (logoi) of created existence—reaches those logoi, and in the mind, the many logoi eventuate in one knowledge. This mode of knowing is called "love of wisdom" (φιλοσοφία).

The path to God proceeds through knowledge of the sensible world and contemplation of the divine logoi before it ends in a dispassionate life in truth.[22] Maximus is influenced by his predecessors, but he places knowledge of God on a new footing. The movement toward God passes through a stage of likeness with the One in whose image human beings have been created. Love from and to our creator is the unifying factor that binds the different phases of the process of acquiring knowledge together on the path of human ascent.

FROM IMAGE TO LIKENESS

For after all what is man in nature—all in relation to nothing and nothing in relation to infinity.

—Blaise Pascal[23]

As "a wealth of creation," and "a central point between nothing and all" (σύνδεσμός τις φυσικός), each human being is always a being with a telos

---

18. *Car.* 2.26.
19. *Amb. Io.* (10) PG 91 1113A.
20. *Car.* 3.99.
21. For example, perception is discussed in *Car.* 1.12 and seeing is emphasized in *Car.* 4.58.
22. *Myst.* (5) PG 90 677A.
23. Pascal, *Pensées*, 3.233:38–52.

and a task.[24] Reaching the final cause and persevering at the edge—at the boundary—of existence requires constant effort and results in the perfection of our own nature. Yet, it is also an act that brings human beings closer to God; it is the means by which human beings return to the divine creator. This is why, in a more general sense, knowing human beings are those who have chosen God.[25] To paraphrase Maximus, the knowing person aims at well-being and both reaches and deserves eternal well-being.[26]

As Georges Florovksy notes, the analogical sequence of redemptive activities is communion with God (Incarnation), the constant choice of a pious life, and the incorruptibility of our corporeal nature (resurrection). A knowing person is one who repairs the postlapsarian tropos of human nature. The paradigm of the redemptive return to a blessed state is disclosed by God's descent and Incarnation. The point of the Incarnation is not just to save fallen human nature; it is also intended to fulfill the existential mission of the human creation. Furthermore, this act of descent does not occur because of the fall, but because of the indestructible unity of the divine and human natures, which gives rise to the "entrance of Life in the created being."[27]

In the Ambigua, human beings are given the mission to mediate between the different components of their own nature and are portrayed as realizing universal co-inherence (perichoresis) only through life in Christ. The key to accomplishing this task is rooted in the fact that human nature is created in the image of God and involves the process of likening ourselves to God by making use of the particular inclinations inherent in the gnomic will and choice (γνώμη and προαίρεσις). The dichotomous dyad of image and likeness (εἰκών and ὁμοίωσις) not only plays an important role in Maximus's thought; it constitutes the foundation of the entire corpus of

---

24. *Amb. Io.* (41) PG 91 1305A. See also trans. by Maximos Constas, On Difficulties, 103. Τούτου δὴ χάριν ἔσχατος ἐπεισάγεται τοῖς οὖσιν ὁ ἄνθρωπος, οἱονεί σύνδεσμός τις φυσικός τοῖς καθόλου διὰ τῶν οἰκείων μερῶν μεσιτεύων ἄκροις, καί εἰς ἕν ἄγων ἐν ἑαυτῷ τὰ πολλῷ κατὰ τὴν φύσιν ἀλλήλων διεστηκότα τῷ διαστήματι, ἵνα τῆς πρός Θεόν.

25. Pascal, *Pensées*, 3.233:38–52.

26. *Amb. Io.* (41) PG 91 1308C. See also trans. by Maximos Constas, On Difficulties, 109. [Insofar as human beings did not follow the natural motion toward the immovable beginning (meaning God) that was given to them at the time of creation, but conversely, irrationally, and against nature, were drawn to that which was lower than them – over which they had the task of exerting dominion – they thus misused that which was given to them by nature.] Also see *Amb. Io.* 1392AB: Καί τόν μέν πρῶτον δυνάμεως, τόν δέ δεύτερον ἐνεργείας, τόν δέ τρίτον ἀργίας εἶναι περιεκτικόν.

27. Флоровски П., Восточные Отцы, 572.

patristic literature. It has its origin in Genesis 1:26 and is of central concern to the Alexandrinan tradition, the Cappadocian Fathers, and Origen. Nothing strikingly original or revolutionary new can be found in Maximus's writings on this topic. Nevertheless, he makes a special contribution by putting extraordinary emphasis on likeness in a way that not only directs his readers' attention to purely anthropological aspects of this matter, but places far more stress on gnoseological elements.

The main issues raised by this perspective include the definition of the image, or more precisely, of the nature that has been created in the image; the connection between the divine and human realms; and the way the human mind, will, and body work together during the process of growing toward God's likeness. In most of the Church Fathers' writings, the imago Dei is associated with the mind, or the rational faculty, in degrees that range from virtual identification to the simple assumption that the capacity for thought is an essential aspect of what it means to be made in the image of God.[28] In the Alexandrian tradition, the created image is related to the soul alone. Already in Philo's work, only the highest part of the soul—the nous—is regarded as the image of God, which is an understanding that is also upheld by Christian writers in Alexandria. Modifying this view, the Cappadocian Fathers consider the human being's entire constitution of soul and body to be the image and imitator of God.[29]

Maximus does not identify only the mind or the soul as the imago Dei; he views the whole human being as being the image of the perfect creator. Thus, the creature's task is to acquire a certain similarity to the creator. Another important feature of the human being is the capacity for self-determination that Maximus associates with the natural will when he writes: "Then by the same reasoning, the self-determinative motion [is one of the principles of] the rational [nature]."[30] Thus, the operations of the mind/reason and the actualization of the virtues are both seen as leading human beings to knowledge of God and to deification.

In *Chapters on Love*, Maximus expresses his view: "Every rational nature . . . is made [in] the image of God, but only those who are good and wise are made [in] his likeness."[31] In human beings, both mind (νοῦς) and

---

28. See Williams, *The Divine Sense*. 2007.
29. See Thunberg, *Microcosm and Mediator* (1965).
30. *Disput. Pyrr.* 22.
31. *Car.* 3.25.

reason (λόγος) are closely associated with the image of God.[32] The image and likeness of God are represented by the soul, which is characterized by these two qualities (ἡ λογικὴ τε καὶ νοερα`` ψυχή), and every rational soul is said to be made in the image of God. However, in human beings, the image is primarily related to νοῦς, while the likeness is more closely related to λόγος.[33]

The relationship between image and likeness in Maximus's teachings should be looked at in terms of the distinction between nature and hypostasis that can also be found in Cappadocian texts. Yet, another pair of concepts which raise this issue—namely, the logos of essence and the tropos of existence—is of more interest in this context.[34] It is said that nature is in line with the image and logos, while the hypostasis corresponds to likeness as a mode of existence. On the basis of this discussion, the relationship between image and likeness could thus be regarded as consisting of three dyads and two triads. On the one hand, connections are made between image and likeness, nature and hypostasis, and logos and tropos, and on the other hand, beginning/middle/end and being/well-being/eternal well-being are grouped together. The history of these terms and the various definitions that they have been given are not the main point of concern here, although Maximus's philosophical parlance led some of these characterizations to be reformulated.

The image of God corresponds to the essence, or nature, of human beings, as that was created by God. Hence, the core of this nature consists of qualities, attributes, and faculties bestowed by divine grace. Maximus defines these as "divine attributes" that have been ascribed to human nature, or more precisely, as images of the divine essence.[35] Insofar as the image of God is the logos of human beings, it possesses all of the essential characteristics of human nature, but it also includes that which is ideal, whose potency is in keeping with God's will and should be regarded as the telos of human existence. This amalgamation enables human beings to achieve the middle sphere between that which is given at the beginning and the acquired end. This makes Maximus's conception of the image of God

32. *Amb. Io.* (7). PG 91 1088A.
33. *Amb. Io.* (10) PG 91 1113AC.
34. See Larchet, *La divinisation de l'homme* (1996).
35. These sentences are based on Car. 3.25. Maximus contexts these views in a well-established tradition in which the paradigm (or archetype) of the image is the divine Logos. All of the logoi of created things have their beginning and end in this Logos.

quite dynamic. In fact, for Maximus and some of his predecessors (such as Clement of Alexandria), the image of God is a cluster of capacities that allow human beings to recognize their likeness and to dynamically orientate themselves toward achieving it.

Similarity, or likeness, to God is not applicable to human nature like the image is; instead, it pertains to the hypostasis. While the image of God is part of human beings' natural constitution and is given by the creator without any effort on the part of its human recipients, achieving the divine likeness entails personal participation and, in this sense, is related to the human disposition to will and choose (γνώμη and προαίρεσις). While the divine image reveals the logos of human nature, the likeness reveals a mode of existing (τρόπος). This likeness is composed of the virtues of goodness and wisdom, which are qualities that Maximus discusses in Chapters on Love. Goodness corresponds to virtue (praxis), and wisdom comports to knowledge (theoria). In Ambigua 10, Maximus relates these facets of existence to likeness when he says: "[by] the divine likeness, I understand knowledge and virtues."[36] In Questions to Thalassius, Maximus links praxis to likeness and theoria to the image of God because the image and contemplation are connected to one another through the logoi. The divine image is the logos of human beings, and contemplation enables human creatures to gain knowledge of the logoi.[37]

The relationships mentioned above reveal that Maximus associates being and eternal well-being with the divine image, while likeness is linked to well-being. Although God possesses these qualities and virtues by nature, human beings must acquire them through participation. In this respect, possession of the image of God is "natural," or "by default," while likeness is a fruit of becoming. Pursuing a virtuous life makes it possible for human beings to become imitators of God in accordance with the predispositions of their own will and volition. In other words, although human beings are the image of God by nature, they become God's likeness by grace.[38] Attainment of the acquired state of virtuousness is dependent on the will's disposition toward goodness and its decision to permanently pursue perfection. Maximus's understanding of human beings is integrally related to his perception that actualizing the virtues is a dynamic process, which inaugurates a renewed tropos of human existence and a new *habitus*. Virtue is not a state;

---

36. *Amb. Io.* (10) PG 91 1113D.
37. See Sherwood, *The Earlier Ambigua.* (1955).
38. See Car. 3.25.

rather, it is a process in which the will and the whole body-soul composite follow their inclination toward Christ, who is hypostasized virtue per se. This process constitutes an everlasting path to perfection; "knowing and loving God is a journey to be travelled eternally."[39] Maximus even describes the virtues as the *potential* content of human beings' God-given nature, insofar as each person actualizes these in similarity, or likeness, by means of his/her own effort.[40]

Let us now turn to two of Maximus's predecessors: Gregory the Theologian and Gregory of Nyssa. For these Cappadocians, cultivating the mind's relationship to God occurs through a life of virtue; thus, the mind's activity is perceived to be inseparable from that of the will. For example, Gregory of Nyssa sometimes portrays virtue as a preparatory stage of spiritual life that is antecedent to knowledge of God. Thus, to be virtuous is to resemble divinity. Virtue consists of both a particular kind of knowledge and a mode of right action. The new Adam who has risen with Christ is characterized by gnosis that is acquired through nous. This gnosis is part of the process of restoring the divine image to human nature and of disciplining the passions so that goodness, or well-being, can be achieved.[41]

Thus, the anthropological order is preserved in ethics, philosophy, and ascetical theology: The mind is logically prior to the will and the lower appetites. That is why in one of his orations, Gregory of Nazianzus says that philosophy can open the way to virtue and blessedness.[42] Gregory of Nyssa holds that although the created mind does not reflect the divine essence itself, it does manifest the divine power of wisdom. Similarly, the limitations posed by resemblance dictate the limitations of human reflections on the divine; we apprehend only God's energies or effects. Yet, insofar as are able to become virtuous through ascetic practices, the path of contemplation is opened up, and we can reach knowledge of God.

39. *Gregory of Nyssa: Contra Eunomium.* 2.233. Ludlow Morwenna makes the following observation regarding Maximus's predecessor from Nyssa: "When Gregory talks of the ascent of a soul to God, he is not just meaning the 'vertical' relation of the soul to God as experienced timelessly, for example, in a moment of prayer. Rather, he also means (perhaps he mainly means) the temporal pilgrimage which finishes not in the possession of God (just as Moses never possessed the promised land), but in the eternally growing participation in God."

40. The terms "potentiality" and "actuality" are taken from Greek philosophy and are widely used in translations of, and scholarly articles about, Maximus's work. See Dalmais, *Comentaire du Pater*, 123–159.

41. *Ep.* 32 in Larchet, *Maxime le Confesseur: Lettres* (1998).

42. *Orat.* 25.1, 25.10.

Looking at the moral component from a gnoseological perspective, Maximus declares:

> If the one Word of God is indubitably the essence of virtue in each man, ... every man, participating in virtue with affixed habit, unquestionably participates in God. Now as the beginning, a man receives by participation the natural good with his being; as to the end, he zealously accomplishes his course towards the beginning and source, without deviation, by means of good will (γνώμη) and choice (προαίρεσις) and from God receives deification, adding to the natural goodness of the image, the likeness of the virtues.[43] As was mentioned previously, in addition to the dyadic structures that Maximus employs, there are two triads: beginning/middle/end and being/well-being/eternal well being. The stage of well-being cannot be reached by grace; it must be achieved by personal effort. Thus, the central role of γνώμη and προαίρεσις—and consequently, of the actualization of the virtues—becomes evident. Yet, what does it mean to be virtuous? This question is raised in Ambigua 41, where Maximus concludes that although human beings were made in the image of God, they attain likeness to God only by virtue of the divine grace, free will and by observing the commandments. The logoi of all things—be they past, present, and future—preexist immutably in God. They are brought into being; they develop for good or for evil; and, according to each one's proper disposition, they are ceaselessly compensated for participating in—or for lacking—the perfect state.

Connections between the Cappadocians' views and Maximus's understanding of the higher levels of contemplation merit attention at this point. Gregory of Nazianzus's conception of the mind stresses that the mind and reason (νοῦς καὶ λόγος) are what is godlike within us. From the perspective of potentiality, the nexus of the divine νοῦς and the human mind is the image of God, while from the perspective of actuality, it is contemplation. Contemplation is related to the image of God insofar as it is one of the defining characteristics of human beings; the faculty that gives rise to contemplation and discernment is apropos to the godlike part of the soul. Indeed, only one creature possesses the godly feature of nous. Therefore, it is human beings who are uniquely able to imitate God by engaging in the act of contemplation.

---

43. *Amb. Io.* (10) PG 91 1176D, see also trans. by Maximos Constas, On Difficulties, 285.

Gregory of Nyssa maintains that creation in the image of God, which entails making proper use of the divine gift of likeness, enables human beings to return to God in the final stage of contemplation. According to this Cappadocian father, the image of God does not just exist in the mind; it also involves freedom from sin. Some scholars contend that the divine image is νοῦς καὶ φρόνεσις, along with a whole range of virtues. While it is true that the will is logically dependent on the mind, Gregory's conception does not allow for the possibility that the mind can act apart from a clear capacity to will; nor does it give credence to the idea that the godlike mind can somehow be lacking in freedom.

Although it is the most perfect knowledge of its kind, knowing God through the soul that bears the divine image has the same nature as any other type of rational knowledge. It is inferential knowledge (στοχασμός), rather than direct knowledge of God. Human beings contemplate the soul as an image of God, not as God himself. They are the image and likeness of God primarily by reason of the soul. More precisely, thanks to the soul, human beings possess reason, free will, and supranatural grace.[44]

In the writings of Gregory of Nyssa and Basil the Great, the terms εἰκών and ὁμοούσις are used to express the relationship between the natural and supranatural orders. The word "εἰκών" refers to mind and reason, while "ὁμοούσις" has to do with the resolute will.[45] These emphases demonstrate that we have now passed from the level of essence to the existential plane, where the supranatural realm is given primary consideration. In Questions to Thalassius, Maximus explains at length that the divine skopos is the mystery of Christ which has been hidden since before the foundation of the world. In paragraph 60 of that work, he describes this skopos as an end and explicitly differentiates two orders of being.[46]

Both Gregories derive at least implicit—and sometimes explicit—doctrines of God from the effects that God has on the created order.[47] The foundation of this line of "bottom-up" reasoning is the "top-down" movement of creation that includes the divine initiative whereby God gives rational creatures a way to grasp purely intelligible nature—which is a capacity

---

44. This conclusion appears in a text that is attributed to Gregory of Nyssa, but its authenticity is questionable. See Weiswurm, *The Nature of Human Knowledge* (1952).

45. Das erstes besitzt er einfach durch seine Vernunft, das zweite soll er Erlangen auf Grund freier Willensbestimmung. See, Weiss, Die Erziehungslehre.

46. Q. Thal. PG 90 60–62.1B. Laga-Steel, CCSG, 73, 115.

47. See Williams, *The Divine Sense* (2007).

that enables communion with the Trinity. The theology of the imago Dei is one of the Cappadocians' main themes, which appears most frequently in the work of Gregory of Nyssa. His thoughts regarding the image of God are expounded cogently in a seminal work entitled On the Making of the Human Person, where it is said that the soul is rational. Gregory adds that although the mind which gives the soul this quality operates in rational animals by means of the senses, the mind itself is not part of the body. The body is no more than the outward form of the mind whose needs it serves. Yet, if the body exists to further the mind's ends, what end has been given to the mind?

The opening encomium of this work, which Gregory addresses to his brother Basil, makes it clear that creation in the image of God, which entails making proper use of the divine gift of likeness, enables human beings to end the rational creature's movement away from the uncreated one by returning to God through contemplation. For Gregory, the imago Dei does not just exist in the mind; it also represents freedom from sin. The soul's role as the "governor" of the psychosomatic unity that constitutes human beings means that the mind must be one of its components. Otherwise, it would not be able to discern the good. However, actively choosing the good requires an additional, but closely related, faculty—namely, the will. Every creature who is possessed of reason and mind is meant to be governed by a free will.[48] However, the strong affirmation of the soul's relation to God necessarily raises the question of how the body fits into the Cappadocians' paradigm. Gregory of Nazianzus insists on the body's full participation in spiritual life. Given the inherent differences between body and soul, their unity requires a mediator. Thus, the soul must first be merged with the sensory faculty. However, the connection of the body to the soul is both innate (due to the imago Dei) and moral (in conjunction with the results of human beings' exercise of their will).

The mind is not only the governing principle of the lower faculties; it directs the soul as a whole. Indeed, the soul finds perfection in the intellectual (νοερὸν) and rational (λογικὸν) spheres. Intellectual energies can be dulled and even incapacitated by bodily conditions, but the mind always retains a certain degree of independence. That autonomy is praised for enabling self-determination in relation to God. The soul becomes godlike (θεοειδής) when it resists the downward pull of the worst aspects of

---

48. According to Völker, sin is an error of the mind. See *Maximus Confessor als Meister des geistlichen Leben* (1941).

its nature. In this respect, the imago Dei is characterized as being both a natural endowment and a variable state that is dependent on the personal capacities of specific human beings. Thus, interactions among intellectual capacities, the disposition of the will, and bodily conditions are all connected in the process of awakening and guiding human beings to perfection and deification.[49]

Returning to Maximus the Confessor, in a definitive statement in the Ambigua, he concludes that praxis is implicit in reason (logos). Praxis is linked to the body and manifests virtue. Yet, virtue resides in the sphere mediated by reason. In Ambigua 7, Maximus comments on a passage in which Gregory of Nazianzus uses the phrase "We, who are a portion of God that has flowed down from above"[50] Maximus perceives that here, we are said to be part of God by virtue of the logoi (divine principles) of our being. "However, we are said to have slipped from above because we have not been moved according to that by which we came to be." It is in this fallen state that human beings must acquire a virtuous life and gnosis. In Ambigua 7, Maximus says that the logoi of all beings are preexistent in the Logos and are realized according to God's will and presence in them, although the Logos through whom all creatures proportionately participate in God remains infinitely above. This reference to the proportionality of the process that unfolds according to mind, reason, sense, vital movement or some habitual fitness shows that Maximus is still speaking of the essential order, rather than of the existential, order of grace.

Maximus presents a double-faceted ontological and moral explanation of the doctrine of the logos. When a person's activity is in complete accord with the logos that preexists in God and has no desire for anything other than its own source, that individual will be in God and will not slip from the deity.[51] This mode of being represents a return to, and a reconstitution of, the logos that was normative at the time of creation. Thus, it is evident that the fallen state can be overcome as the natural and supranatural orders interrelate—and a passage from the essential to the existential stage of existence takes place.

Ambigua 41 considers how the fivefold division that characterizes the hypostasis of all created beings can be overcome by analyzing Gregory of

---

49. See Williams, *The Divine Sense* (2007).

50. *Amb. Io.* (7) PG 91 1081C. See also trans. by Maximos Constas, On difficulties, 103.

51. Evagrius and Maximus use the phrase ἐν θέῳ γενήσεται to characterize being in God as the apex of Christian life.

Nazianzus's statement regarding the moment when "nature is restored and God becomes man." Maximus portrays Christ as a paradigm of the transformation of the fallen tropos that characterizes human beings' postlapsarian state. By recognizing the unparalleled virtue of the Logos itself, human beings may reestablish the lost divine-human unity that is implanted in their nature as persons who have been created in the image of God. Thus, the beginning and ending of the human journey interface in such a way that Origen's view of the necessity of apocatastasis is no longer pertinent. The relationship that develops between these points is determined by the activities of human beings themselves as they practice the virtues or fall away from actualizing these.

Maximus perceives that freedom is a sign of the image of God. The goodness of human nature, which is grounded in the fact that it was created in the image of God, is fully realized only when it is put into practice by an act of free will that manifests God's likeness in humankind.[52] Thus, Gregory of Nyssa portrays human creatures carrying out their role as rational beings and presents the mind as a subject of the intellect. This aspect of the mind seems to be especially important to Maximus, insofar as he maintains that since human persons are spiritual beings, it is natural for them to both subordinate themselves to God's Logos and to opt for their irrational components. Thus, in Maximus's thought, the human body is not the locale of the image of God, but it is related to the realization of that image. In this respect, both being and eternal well-being are intended for everyone who has been created in the image of God, and the body is called to share this vocation. The rational soul is obliged to mediate divinity even to the body.[53]

In Chapters on Love 3.25, Maximus develops what he means by image and likeness at some length.[54] He says that the imago Dei is given at the beginning, but likeness to God is acquired through a spiritual process. Maximus views this likeness as a type of imitation of God that includes a manifestation of godly virtues and the whole range of human moral activity. Furthermore, in Ambigua 10, Maximus describes three motions of the human soul that involve the mind, reason and the senses.[55] Each of these faculties performs its own function in relation to the kind of knowledge that it is able to acquire. These movements are interrelated and culminate

---

52. See *Cap. Gnost.* 1.13.
53. *Amb. Io.* (42) PG 91 1348C.
54. *Car.* 3.25.
55. *Amb. Io.* (10) PG 91 1113A.

in the mind's nonconceptual contemplation of God—which is supported by reason and the senses. The development of the godly aspect of human nature manifests the functional reciprocity of the divine-human relationship in which human beings unreservedly move toward God and are ever more grounded in him through the contemplative motion of their minds, even as God simultaneously becomes incarnate within human virtue.

This process of perfection may also be depicted as the outcome of the cultivation of God's likeness in human beings. In Chapters on Love, Maximus makes one of his clearest statements regarding the relationship of image and likeness to God's attributes when he says that "in his goodness," God has imparted to rational beings four divine characteristics by which he "supports, guards, and preserves" them. These attributes are "being, eternal being, goodness, and wisdom." Being and eternal being are allotted to the essence of human creatures and pertain to the image of God in them, while goodness and wisdom are given for the sake of will and judgment and pertain to human beings' likeness to God. The first two attributes are given by nature, and the latter two are bestowed by grace.[56]

In Maximus's thought, likeness is consistently related to the vita practica that issues in a life of virtue. Thus, likeness is linked to human goodness, which is inherently contrary to evil, while image is associated with truth and contemplation, which are regarded as being contrary to falsehood. Human beings are called to add to the natural goodness bestowed by the imago Dei by exercising free choice (προαίρεσις) and to cultivate their likeness to God by practicing the virtues. Thus, persons who make proper use of the three motions of the soul add to the goodness of the divine nature and the voluntary goodness associated with achieving likeness to God. Likeness perfects the divine image that lies at the heart of human nature by completing an unchangeable given of nature with a willed act that is differentiated according to everyone's personal choice and capacity. Acts of divine providence and judgement reveal that God has made human beings in his image through his Incarnation in the virtues. Thus, incarnation also involves a personal appropriation of the presence of the incarnate Logos in the world, and as a result of the role of the virtues, this appropriation includes activities of the body and the senses.

These passages from Chapters on Love and the Ambigua regarding the difference between the image and likeness of God in human beings are powerful expressions of Maximus's conviction that human beings are a

---

56. *Car.* 3.25.

totality of body and soul entrusted with freedom. They also invite the conclusion that the unity conferred by the imago Dei and shared by all people must be weighed against the diversity that characterizes the likeness which is acquired by those who are wise and good.

THE KNOWLEDGE OF GOOD AND EVIL

The Tree of Life and the Tree of the Knowledge of Good and Evil

According to Genesis 2:9, the tree of life is not the tree of the knowledge of good and evil.[57] In paradise, God gave us both the tree of life and the tree of knowledge, along with an order to not eat the fruit of the latter. This raises the question of how these trees differ from each other and how human beings can discern good from evil during the process of seeking knowledge. Maximus answers these questions in an interesting way in a letter to Marinus the Monk, where he emphasizes that "fear of God is the beginning of wisdom."[58] Furthermore, in his reply to Thalassius, he states that although "the tree of life symbolizes wisdom, the tree of [the] knowledge of good and evil does not, nor is said to do so."[59] Expanding on the biblical text, Maximus puts forth an interpretation in which the tree of life is said to represent the intellect/mind (νοῦς), while the tree of knowledge is related to the senses (αἴσθησις). In his *Mystagogia*, Maximus concludes that the final goal of the mind's operation is God as truth and the ultimate aim of reason (λόγος) is God as Goodness.[60]

In Chapters on Love, where Maximus describes the structure of the soul and identifies practices that enable it to move from sense perception to spiritual knowledge, we find a similar polarity between the earthly and heavenly features of humanity.[61] In this biblical passage, an intriguing

---

57. "And out of the ground the Lord God made to grow every tree that is pleasant to the sight and good for food, the tree of life also in the midst of the garden, and the tree of the knowledge of good and evil" (NRSV).

58. The letter to Marinus is found in PG 91 597B–604B.

59. The quotation is from *Q. Thal.* 43, CCSG (293). Unless otherwise notated, translations of this text are the author's.

60. *Myst.* (5) PG 91 674AB.

61. See *Car.* 2.79, where Maximus writes: Εἰκὼν τοῦ χοϊκοῦ αἱ γενικαὶ κακίαι ὑπάρχουσιν, οἷον ἀφροσύνη, δειλία, ἀκολασία, ἀδικία· εἰκὼν δὲ τοῦ ἐπουρανίου αἱ γενικαὶ ἀρεταί, οἷον φρόνησις, ἀνδρεία, σωφροσύνη, δικαιοσύνη. Ἀλλὰ καθὼς ἐφορέσαμεν τὴν εἰκόνα τοῦ χοϊκοῦ, φορέσωμεν καὶ τὴν εἰκόνα τοῦ ἐπουρανίου. Also see *Car.* 2.26, 2.27.

interpretation of what is often considered to be a state of opposition can be seen. Maximus entertains the possibility that the tree of knowledge may actually become a tree of life. In other words, he does not remain bound by the simple notion that there is a diametrical opposition between two trees that symbolizes life and death. Rather, his profoundly christological viewpoint enables him to see the providential possibility of redemption even here. If the tree of life guarantees human beings Truth that is beyond all human activity, That Truth is the divine wisdom that is implanted in human nature by God's Word, or Jesus Christ.[62] The tree of the knowledge of good and evil is located in the dynamic practical sphere of imperfect human creatures—and in that respect, it is diametrically opposed to the tree of life in paradise.

Maximus perceives that this polarity can be overcome by searching for the intellective person inside of us, rather than staying in the realm of the senses like the first Adam did. An intellective human being would be a person of power who does not pursue wrong thoughts and turn those into wrong doings, but who instead follows the Truth.[63] The first Adam would be a sense-bound person who needs to be introduced to the New Adam and brought into a new age. The distinctions that this line of thought draws between theory and practice; contemplation and experience; and the mind, reason, and the senses allows us to see the central role that human beings play in activities that unify the divided hypostases of everything that exists—which includes heaven and earth, the intelligible and the sensible, man and woman, and so forth.[64]

Human Knowledge of Good and Evil: The Realm of Praxis

In essence, knowledge of good and evil is human knowledge of God since the human ethos is an ethos of moral practice. Maximus shows that this correlation is related to the fact that only human beings are endowed with a special type of gnomic will that is able to deliberate and choose between options. This means that people can find their way to well-being or ill-being and to knowledge or ignorance. In other words, they can choose "to be," instead of falling into non-being. Thus knowledge or ignorance of good

---

62. Steel, *Iohannes Scotus Eriugena*, 239–59.

63. *Car.* 1.87.

64. See *Amb. Io.* (41) PG 91 1304D–1305A regarding the possibility of overcoming the five divisions of the universal hypostasis. Also see *Car.* 1.71.

and evil is an ethical type of knowing that represents the practical aspect of human experience; yet, in attaining such knowledge, human beings encounter God as Goodness. Likewise, God as Truth has to do with the efforts of fallen human beings to ascend to perfection and to strive for deification. The process of theosis (or deification) discloses the other side of the process of attaining knowledge; that is, the descent of the divine Logos, which makes human knowledge possible. Through the divine Logos, God becomes accessible to human beings since, in a sense, the entire process of human knowledge that takes place through the logoi coincides with the self-revelation of the Logos itself. The perfection of human nature, which entails participation in trinitarian and christological mysteries, unfolds as the presence of the Logos grows within human beings and a gradual realization of the virtues occurs. These virtues, which result from activities of the soul's practical capabilities, are described in detail in *Chapters on Love*.

Wisdom versus Experience: From "Human Doing" to Human Being

Insofar as it represents the Logos, the tree of life should not be placed in opposition to the tree of knowledge; instead, they should be united with one another. In this regard, Maximus notes that human knowledge is inherently complex and may be muddled by the senses that may give rise to human evil. Thus, the objective of human activity should be to transform the tree of the knowledge of good and evil into the tree of life, or in other words, to nurture the presence of the Logos and truth within human nature. Human knowledge of good and evil is not prohibited by God; the problem comes with its misuse. Human beings want to discern what is good and evil by themselves without first becoming mature in wisdom and acquiring the reason needed for this sort of deliberation. This is the way in which knowledge of good and evil has become part of human experience, and why it is no longer bestowed by God's wisdom as it was before the fall. Here, wisdom is portrayed as being opposed to *peira*, which Maximus defines as "experience."

This pattern may also be seen in the way gnosis is defined by the Church Fathers and by Maximus, in particular. Gnosis is not simply a cognitive faculty and activity; rather, it is an acquired disposition of the soul, or the inclination toward love that Maximus defines as actualized knowledge at the beginning of Chapters on Love.[65] This means that gnosis encompasses the total body-soul composite and mirrors this composite's attitude toward the things that are the object of its knowledge. If, then, the tree of life is the presence of the Logos in human beings, the ultimate aim of the tree of the knowledge, which represents the human experience of good and evil in the postlapsarian age, should be to become the tree of life and to thereby achieve the realization of God's initial plan through the Christ who brings human nature to completion. "Human doing" should become "human being" so that the gift of life that has been given by God will be warranted. A certain degree of openness is necessary for us to receive the gift of life; that gift has been freely given, and our task is to freely receive it. In other words, the gift of life bestows a freedom to be that enables us to reach a level of being that is far above the level of doing. Thus, it might be said that doing should be transformed into being.

Human Knowledge after the Fall

Since Maximus's understanding of human nature is rooted in the Christian conception of history that focuses on creation, the fall, and salvation, it is important to identify the levels of knowledge that are available to human beings before the fall, after the fall, and following Christ's regeneration of human nature. At this point, the focus will be on the second of the *tropoi*, or modes, of existence that characterize human nature as it seeks, with help from above, to reach the final stage of knowledge—deification and union with God—by choosing good over evil. At the beginning of this process lies the Good, which is beyond any qualifications or categorizations; this Good transcends all human intentions, whether they be good or bad.

> The Good that is beyond being and beyond the inoriginate is one, the holy unity of three persons Father, Son and Holy Spirit. It is an infinite union of three infinities. Its principle of being, together with the mode, the nature and the quality of its being, is altogether inaccessible to creatures. For it eludes every intellection of intelligible beings, in no way issuing from its natural hidden inwardness, and infinitely transcending the summit of all spiritual knowledge.[66] Questions immediately arise: how is this goodness

---

65. *Car.* 1.1: 'Love is a good disposition of the soul by which one prefers no being to the knowledge of God.'

66. Th. Oec. in Philoklia, vol. 2, 164.

present to us? How do human beings attain knowledge of it? Does it allow human beings to reach and grasp its meaning?

Maximus inherits a tripartite structure of the soul, which includes the levels of praxis, natural contemplation, and theology, from the Stoics and, more directly, from Evagrius. Natural contemplation and theology constitute the domain of gnosis. This twofold division is also present in the works of Aristotle, Theophrastus, and almost all of the Peripatetics, where philosophy has both a theoretical and a practical aspect (θεωρητικός τῶν ὄντον, πρακτικός τῶν δεόντων). Evagrius defines "praktiké" as "the spiritual method for purifying the passionate part of the soul."[67] Therefore, apatheia, which is a necessary condition for attaining spiritual knowledge, lies at the end of praktiké. The words "praktikos" and "praktikon" have a long history that started when Evagrius gave praktiké a precise technical meaning that later became the classical definition used in Byzantine religious literature.

Plato used "praktiké" and "gnostiké" to distinguish technical and manual arts from political and spiritual acts. Gnostiké requires intelligence. The antithetical relationship between praktikos and theoretikos (rather than gnostikos) is Aristotelian. Nous praktikos and nous theoretikos are differentiated from one another; nous praktikos finds its goal and limit in activity, while nous theoretikos has its limit in the act itself. Theoretical philosophy has Truth as its goal and limit, while practical philosophy involves action and efficiency.[68] Aristotle proceeds to outline practical and theoretical ways of living.[69] In his view, practical life is opposed to theoretical existence. Thus, praktikos has a broader meaning for Aristotle than it does for Plato. In Aristotle's estimation, praktikos not only pertains to the manual arts; it also includes political activity. According to Ammonius, who was an interpreter of Aristotle's work, praktikon has to do with human activities and has its limit, or goal, in a happy life, whereas theoretikon concerns the divine realm and has its limit in the theoretical joy of living. Taken as a whole, the ancient Greek philosophers invariably use the term praktikos to denote manual activity (Plato), any type of activity at all (Aristotle), or social activity in particular (the Stoics).

In contrast, Christian authors often present a religious interpretation of the practical dimension. Origen is the first theologian to maintain that

---

67. Evagrius Ponticus, The Praktikos & Chapters on Prayer, 78.
68. See Aristotle, *Metaphysics*. (2000).
69. Aristotle, *Nicomachean Ethics*, 1095 b, 15–20.

praktikos (vita activa) and theoretikos (vita contemplativa) constitute two successive steps of spiritual growth which are symbolized by the figures of Mary and Martha. This contradistinction is also found in the works of Gregory of Nyssa and Gregory of Nazianzus. However, when these thinkers speak of practical philosophy, they include the religious notion of purifying the body and soul in preparation for divine love. For instance, although Gregory of Nazianzus identifies praxis and philosophy as two planes of life that are often opposed to each other, he perceives that praktikos refers to people who sacrifice their lives for the sake of others. It is quite different for Evagrius who spent his life as un moine: For Gregory, praktiké is a level of monastic life, while for Evagrius, it is subordinate to gnostike. This distinction can be traced back to Philo and Origen. Nevertheless, according to Evagrius, praktike involves exercising the virtues. In principle then, praktiké primarily consists of a battle against inappropriate thoughts (logismoi).[70]

In the first century of Chapters on Love, Maximus shows the course that knowledge should take. He stresses that when the virtues and the mind are actualized on the practical level, genuine knowledge of God, of life in Christ, and of life in Truth and love is acquired.[71] He also writes: "If the life of the mind is the illumination [ὁ φωτισμός] of knowledge and this is born of love for God, then it is well said that there is nothing greater than love."[72] Even if God's essence is inaccessible to human beings, the deity allows people to grow in love and in knowledge of his energies and activities in the world. Human knowledge finds its consummation in divine love. Thus, the human task involves growing in the virtues that represent the hypostasized virtue of Christ the Logos. This is the way practical knowledge develops.

In Chapters on Love 2.34, Maximus asserts that "the reward for the labors of virtue is detachment and knowledge. For these become our patrons in the kingdom of heaven just as the passions and ignorance are the patrons of eternal punishment."[73] With this move from virtue to knowledge, Maximus affirms the interrelationship that exists between the practical and theoretical realms. Previously, Evagrius had made a distinction between

---

70. For more on this topic, see Thunberg, *Microcosm and Mediator* (1965).

71. *Car.* 1.11: "All the virtues assist the mind in the pursuit of divine love, but above all does pure prayer. By it the mind is given wings to go ahead to God and becomes alien to all things."

72. *Car.* 1.9.

73. *Car.* 2.34.

these two levels because purification of the body is different from purification of the mind. However, Maximus does not emphasize actualizing the virtues and disciplining the passions because of the body's separation from soul and mind, but because of their perichoretical unity and interdependence in the christological mystagogia of the Logos. Therefore, even if Maximus retains a threefold structure of knowledge that is based on practicing the virtues, natural contemplation of the logoi, and participation in theology, his viewpoint is very different from that of Dionysius or Evagrius. In Maximus's estimation, these components are only different stages of a single movement toward God. This unifying tendency is a key feature of all of Maximus's teachings, regardless of whether these concern the levels of knowledge or ontological dimensions of the divisions within the universal hypostasis.

Like Evagrius, Maximus makes a distinction between motivation and action.[74] In addition, he distinguishes between virtues of the soul and virtues of the body.[75] Evagrius maintains that at the practical level, we primarily deal with evil thoughts (logismoi), even though our thoughts are generally inspired by angels as well as demons. In commenting on Matthew 15:19 in the Life of Anthony, Evagrius adds that evil thoughts are the source and determinant of all sin. Thus, at the practical stage, the human struggle is directed against demonic thoughts that could bring us to a state of impassiveness. This emphasis is to be found in Maximus, as well as in other early Christian writers, such as John Climacus.

The path to theosis, or deification, which ends with the acquisition of knowledge, begins at the practical level where it is necessary to discipline one's thoughts about personal dos and don'ts in order to acquire the habit of goodness and to arrive at being instead of nonbeing. In this regard, Maximus says: "Do not misuse thoughts, lest you necessarily misuse things as well. For unless anyone sins first in thought, he will never sin in deed."[76] Regarding the vices of body and soul, Maximus also warns that compromises can be made when the virtues are being practiced on the bodily level; however, when it comes to virtues of the soul, no excuses should be made.[77]

In the third century of Chapters on Love, Maximus briefly presents a comprehensive picture of knowledge by developing two pivotal ideas. In

---

74. *Car.* 2.35, 3.48.
75. *Car.* 2.57.
76. *Car.* 2.78.
77. *Car.* 2.57.

3.44, he concludes that "the virtues separate the mind from the passions; spiritual contemplation [πνευματικαὶ θεωρίαι] separates it from simple contemplations [νοημάτων]; then pure prayer sets it before God himself."[78] Furthermore in 3.45, he states that "the virtues are related to the knowledge of creatures, knowledge to the knower, the knower to the one who is known in ignorance and whose knowing transcends knowledge."[79]

Evil is associated with the use of the senses. Following their lead shows that the thinking faculty—which contains both simple and compound thoughts—has already been defeated by sensual images. Simple thoughts are without passion.[80] The mind receives passionate thoughts from the senses.[81] On the basis of this deduction, Maximus makes a distinction between earthly and heavenly human beings. In addition, he defines ignorance as a vice of the soul and equates knowledge with virtue.[82] Moreover, he continues to assert that misuse of the soul's faculties is the reason for sin and its consequences, which he identifies as ignorance and folly (ἀγνωσία καὶ ἀφροσύνη). In Maximus's estimation, such misuse (παράχρησις) occurs when the mind fails to cultivate its natural powers.[83]

This summary invites the conclusion that actualizing the virtues at the practical level enables us to attain gnosis and to contemplate the divine ideas, intentions, and principles which lie within the logoi of everything that exists, even though these are hidden from human sight in this postlapsarian age. The fact that Maximus places considerable emphasis on the positive aspect of this experience is revealed by the words that he uses to speak of the levels of gnosis; his writings are more focused on fighting for a life of virtue in Christ than on fighting against something.

In order to show that his perspective is ontologically grounded, Maximus turns to the epistemological sphere. In this regard, he asserts that "just as evil is privation of good and ignorance that of knowledge, so is nonbeing the privation of being—but not of being properly so called, for it

---

78. *Car.* 3.44. McFarland uses the term "conceptual images" for νοημάτων. See "Apophatic Christocentrism," 200–14.

79. *Car.* 3.45.

80. *Car.* 2.84.

81. *Car.* 2.74.

82. *Car.* 3.27.

83. *Car.* 3.3. Καὶ τῆς μὲν λογιστικῆς δυνάμεως παράχρησίς ἐστιν ἀγνωσία καὶ ἀφροσύνη. . . . Χρῆσις δὲ τούτων, γνῶσις καὶ φρόνησις, ἀγάπη τε καὶ σωφροσύνη.

has no contrary—but of true being by participation."[84] According to this statement, ignorance is a vice of the rational soul and may be ontologically defined as nonbeing. Here, a central component of Maximus's understanding of the human will emerges. In Chapters on Love 3.27, he adds: "To existence is opposed nonexistence, to the aptitude for goodness and wisdom is opposed vice and ignorance. For them to exist forever or not to exist is in the power of their maker. To share in his goodness and wisdom or not to share depends on the will of rational beings."[85]

In 3.24, Maximus states that "a nature endowed with reason and understanding participates in the holy God by its very being, by its aptitude for well-being (that is, for goodness and wisdom), and by the free gift of eternal being. In this way it knows God." In the next paragraph, he adds that of "the four divine attributes" of being, eternal being, goodness, and wisdom that God has given to human beings, "the first two of these he grants to the essence, the second two to its faculty of will, . . . and to the volitive faculty, he gives goodness and wisdom in order that what he is by essence, the creature might become by participation."[86] These assertions encapsulate the entire course of human knowledge, which begins at the practical level with the cultivation of virtue. This activity enables the next step, which involves the contemplation of God and the logoi, which represent God's desires and goals for each being's growth. This ultimately leads to the theological realm (which Aristotle might call poetics), where we are open to gift of God' grace, which enables us to embrace divine knowledge and to enter into mystical union with God in a state of ekstasis.

Gnoseology is not simply a theory about the workings of the mind, or rather, the mind is not only an intellective, thinking power. Thus, Kevin Corrigan says:

> Mind is a complex thing. Already in [the] fourth century the mind includes the ordered feeling (the heart [καρδία] within mind) as part of its concrete activity. *Praktike* opens the self up beyond preference and passion to the reality of all created things. So if *praktike* is the threshold of cognitive psychology, *gnostike* is the method of empirical science. Body is co-extensive with soul, in the sense of [being an] indispensable means of purification it has an implicitly intelligible nature, on the one hand; as the locus of passions, on

---

84. *Car.*3.29.
85. *Car.* 3.27.
86. *Car.* 3.24, 3.25.

the other, together with the soul's passible parts even the soul can experience a kind of death insofar as it becomes entrapped by its own web of desire and this is called a vice of the soul. For this, one has to "separate" the soul from the body or flesh that is from attachment to passion. The significance of the separation motif, a motif both Platonic and scriptural, has been lost in modern scholarship which mistakenly regards it as Platonic dualism. Separation of soul from its uncritical slumber of the body, however, is the precondition for authentic integral relation or, in Christian terms, for intelligent incarnational living.[87] Therefore, for Maximus, thinking is not simply brainwork that delivers a sterilized definition at the end of the process of knowing; rather, it actively engages the whole composite of body and soul in overcoming the fall of the first Adam and moving toward the second Adam, the divine Logos, and life and love in Christ. This means that gnosis is closely related to the whole gamut of human existence and has ontological dimensions. In the third century of *Chapters on Love*, Maximus concludes that since everything that comes from God is good, evil is just a privation of the good. It is a lack of goodness that represents an imperfection in the effort to be good.[88] Evil does not exist as a power opposed to God. Thus, in 2.82, Maximus says that evil "is nothing other than carelessness of the natural functioning of the mind . . . which is the mistaken use of thoughts on which follows the misuse of things.[89]

In *Chapters on Love* 2.25, Maximus once again describes the path that leads to knowledge: We gain knowledge through faith, and that knowledge gives rise to love for God.[90] Here, faith is identified as a precondition of knowledge, while in chapter 5 of the *Mystagogia*, Maximus says that faith (πίστις) comes at the end of escalating steps of praxis. Yet, he also maintains that love is the chief way in and through which we are able to know

---

87. Corrigan, *Mind, Soul, and Body*, 122–124. Corrigan's assertion that the soul can experience death also appears in the work of the late Byzantine father Gregory Palamas. See, for example, Grégoire Palamas, *Défense des saints hésychastes* (1973).

88. Basil describes evil as a brief lapse of attention. See "God Is Not the Cause of Evil," 65–80.

89. *Car.* 2.82. ἥτις ἐστὶν ἡ ἐσφαλμένη χρῆσις τῶν νοημάτων, ᾗ ἐπακολουθεῖ ἡ παράχρησις τῶν πραγμάτων. "Thoughts" is translated as "conceptual images of things" in *Philokalia*, 79.

90. *Car.* 2.25: Μισθὸς τῆς ἐγκρατείας, ἡ ἀπάθεια· τῆς δὲ πίστεως, ἡ γνῶσις· καὶ ἡ μὲν ἀπάθεια τίκτει τὴν διάκρισιν· ἡ δὲ γνῶσις, τὴν εἰς Θεὸν ἀγάπην. (The reward of self-mastery is detachment and that of faith is knowledge. And detachment gives rise to discernment while knowledge gives rise to love for God.)

anything at all. At the beginning, we have an intention to do something, which is completed when we actually follow through. Already at this stage, we may use our free will to move toward God or to fall away from him. Things that exist outside of our minds are not under our control, but their lasting impressions on our minds enable us to make either good or bad use of them.[91] The soul's faculties and the organs through which we make contact with our surroundings are good in and of themselves, but their proper use or misuse may turn us into good or evil persons.

In *Chapters on Love*, Maximus maintains that ignorance is a passion of the soul.[92] He also asserts that "passion is an impulse of the soul that is contrary to nature."[93] In the first century of that text, Maximus associates passion with earthly things and interprets Paul's writings to mean that the earth is the will of the flesh. He also maintains that Paul uses the word "passion" to refer to impassioned thoughts.[94] In the second century, Maximus concretely states that practicing the virtues only frees the mind from debauchery and hatred; it is spiritual contemplation that releases it from forgetfulness and ignorance. In addition, in *Chapters on Love* 2.67, he says that God allows us to be assailed by demons so that we can discriminate between virtue and vice (or good and evil).[95] Elsewhere, Maximus asserts that a mind which has succeeded in the active life advances in prudence, while a mind that has prospered in the contemplative life excels in knowledge.[96] The task of the active mind is to bring struggling human beings to a discernment of virtue and vice, and it pertains to the contemplative mind to direct participatory souls toward the principles of incorporeal and corporeal things.[97]

Maximus understands the categories of good and evil in a practical, experiential way. He says that "it is on the basis of whether we make use of things rationally or irrationally that we become either virtuous or wicked."[98] This means that good and bad are not characteristics which belong to

91. *Car.* 2.73.
92. *Car.* 1.67.
93. *Car.* 3.16.
94. *Car.* 1. 83.
95. *Car.* 2.67.
96. *Car*, 2.26. Πρακτικὴν μὲν ὁ νοῦς κατορθῶν εἰς φρόνησιν προκόπτει· θεωρητικὴν δέ, εἰς γνῶσιν.
97. *Car.* 2.2.
98. *Car.* 1.92.

things themselves; they result from human beings' use or misuse of them. In *Chapters on Love* 2:73, Maximus similarly states: "Things exist outside the mind while thoughts about them are put together inside. Therefore on it depends either their proper or improper use, for the abuse of things follows on the mistaken use of thoughts."[99]

In the final section of the first century of *Chapters on Love* (1.96–100), Maximus describes the stages of knowledge that progress from the actualization of the virtues through natural contemplation to unlimited union with God by referring to Gregory of Nazianzus and Dionysius.[100] "Love," he says, "is a good disposition [διάθεσις] of the soul by which one prefers no being to the knowledge of God."[101] As Andrew Louth notes, Maximus thus transforms the Evagrian model, which views love as a state (στάσις), to a more dynamic paradigm in which love is seen as being a disposition of the soul (διάθεσις ψυχῆς).[102] The whole process of attaining knowledge involves acquiring such a disposition and making it a *hexis* (habitus) of the soul.

This becomes possible only when we turn away from everything that distracts us from the mode of existence that may aptly be called being-in-God and avoid everything that strengthens the earthly, rather than the heavenly, person inside of us. The part of the soul that is responsible for this is reason—the logos that operates within the dichotomies of good and evil and virtue and vice—because its final goal is God, conceived of a Goodness, as well as the actualization of virtue and the attainment of life in Christ, who is hypostasized virtue. This is where epistemology and ontology meet and is what Maximus means by the tripartite structure of being, well-being, and eternal well-being. The only component of this triad that is dependent on human will is well-being; the other two are bestowed by the grace of God.

> [The human being] comes to be in God through diligence when he has not corrupted the rational principle of his being that preexists

---

99. *Car.* 2.23.

100. The tripartite schema that Maximus describes here follows the Evagrian model, which is a continuation of the Stoic division of philosophy into three parts. (Philosophiae tres partes esse dixerunt et maximi et plurimi auctores: moralem, naturalem et rationalem.) Seneca, "Moral Letters to Lucilius," 89:9. See also the prologue to Origen's commentary on the Song of Songs, where he replaces practice with ethics. He writes: "Practice is the spiritual method that purifies the passionate part of the soul." Évagre le Pontique, *Traité Pratique*, 39.

101. *Car.* 1:1.

102. See Louth, *Maximus the Confessor*, 1996.

in God. He is also moved in God according to the rational principle of well-being that preexists in God, being actualized through the virtues. Finally, he lives in God according to the rational principle of eternal being that preexists in God.[103] Thus, well-being is attained by virtue of the soul's movement toward the Goodness of the Logos. It is realized by detachment from the passions, which, in this context, may be interpreted as occurring when someone who is passive with regard to the temptations of the mind and flesh becomes an "active person."[104] Such a person realizes the virtues by putting them into action. This conception goes a step beyond Evagrius's model where impassiveness is an acquired state. It introduces the dynamic idea of self-formation. Well-being itself is not a status; it is a never-ending goal for which human beings may strive. In a sense, well-being is the tropos of authentic human beings, characterized by realized potential. Thus, as was stated previously, human doing becomes a way of being that involves a habitus of life in Christ, of a disposition to love, and of being human in the likeness of God.

If reason (λόγος) has to do with things and our perception of them, the mind has a broader range of activity. It receives images, representations, and "passionate thoughts . . . from sense experience, temperament, and memory," as Maximus says in *Chapters on Love*.[105] Elsewhere, he adds that "our mind is in the middle of two things, each one active at its own work, the one at virtue; the other at vice. . . . The mind has the power and strength to follow or oppose the one it chooses."[106] Here, the influence that Gregory of Nyssa's emphasis on free will has had on Maximus is evident, but within the broader scope of the mind, the Confessor also includes the virtue of virtues: love. He thereby subordinates virtues of the body to virtues of the soul and mind.

As was noted above, a failure to practice bodily virtues may be excused, but the soul's virtues are a necessary habitus for it; love, in particular, should be a habitual virtue of the human soul. In this regard, Maximus writes: "All bodies are by nature without movement. They are moved by a soul, whether rational, irrational, or insensitive."[107] The rational element

---

103. *Amb. Io.* (7) PG 91 1084B2–7, trans. Lollar, *To See Into the Life of Things*, vol. 2, 229.
104. Here, I prefer Berthold's translation of praktikos as an "active man."
105. *Car.* 2.74.
106. *Car.* 3.92.
107. *Car.* 3.31.

includes reason and understanding. Therefore, the whole process of actualization depends on whether the soul lets itself move toward well-being within the Logos or succumbs to the turmoil of the passions; whether it ascends to the virtues, which are the embodiment of God, or falls into vice.

According to Maximus, "evil is the noetic soul's forgetfulness of what is good according to nature."[108] In Questions to Thalassius, he also identifies evil as ignorance of our maker.[109] Elsewhere, he declares that "evil is an irrational movement of the natural energies, through a mistaken judgment, to something other than their end."[110] These citations demonstrate that evil does not exist as an absolute essence; rather, it is a privation of the good. Therefore, human beings who choose evil demonstrate a lack of good will and a dearth of disciplined persistence in the goodness that Maximus identifies as a godly mode of being. "The mind is like a sparrow that is bound to the earth when it is ruled by the passions, but when it is free of these, it flies to God in contemplation."[111] The mind is the light of spiritual knowledge, which "is born of love for God."[112] In Chapters on Love 4.86, Maximus resumes his argument: "Love and self-mastery free the soul from passions; reading and contemplation [ἀνάγνωσις καὶ θεωρία] deliver the mind from ignorance; and the state of prayer places it with God himself."[113]

Thus, Maximus's sketch of the path to knowledge is completed, proceeding from love as a "good disposition of the soul" that we learn to acquire, through the faculties and activities of the soul that pave the way to knowledge, to the mind that is able to contemplate God as Truth.[114] This pattern reveals that not one single activity of the composite of mind, soul, and body is or should be self-centered or self-initiated. The divine intentions mediated by the logoi are ideas that God has implanted in created beings. Henceforth, the role of those who are endowed with reason is to make a willing choice to live in Christ. In other words, the task of human beings is to bring the logoi to the Logos; to actualize the virtues on the practical level until they become Virtue; and, ontologically speaking, to

---

108. *Th. Oec.* 1:57.
109. *Q. Thal.* (Introd.) PG 90 253AC. Laga-Steel, CCSG, 29.
110. Berthold, *Selected Writings*, note 73, 91.
111. *Car.* 1.85.
112. *Car.* 1.9. The image of light is suggested by these words: Εἰ ἡ ζωὴ τοῦ νοῦ ὁ φωτισμός ἐστι τῆς γνώσεως.
113. *Car.* 4.86.
114. See *Car.* 1.1, where love is identified as a good disposition of the soul.

choose well-being. This undertaking is initiated by the creator, but whether the human will chooses well-being instead of ill-being lies in the realm of human activity and human freedom. During the process of moving toward knowledge, descending agape love is united with ascending erotic inclinations. In other words, all knowledge is possible only in, through, and for the love of God. Thus, I would propose that Maximus sees the task confronting human beings as involving the unification of the tree of knowledge and the tree of life—or the subordination of the former to the latter.

In Questions to Thalassius 43, Thalassius asks, "if . . . wisdom is the tree of life and the work [ἔργον] of . . . wisdom is to discern between good and bad, why [do] they differ from each other?"[115] Maximus replies that there is an enormous difference between the trees. Apparently, the tree of life does not include death; thus, whatever is not a tree of life is subject to death. Furthermore, the attributes of wisdom are mind and reason (νοῦς καὶ λόγος), while the attributes that are characteristic of the opposite state of being are irrationality and sensibility (ἀλογία καὶ αἴσθησις).[116] With respect to differentiating between good and evil and between pleasure and pain, the tree of wisdom is not, and cannot, be the composite structure of the human mind and body because wisdom stands beyond good, evil, pleasure, and pain. According to Maximus, that is why the trees of life and knowledge are not equal, and cannot be mistaken as such. As a result, we cannot claim that it is possible to return to a perfect state, to the state of life-as-wisdom. To suppose that would be Origenism. Thus, another place where Origen's views are modified becomes evident. Human beings do not return to their once lost status; instead, they overcome the duality of the tree of knowledge so that they can rest in a state of everlasting wisdom.

Although the tree of life and the tree of knowledge are in opposition to one another in paradise, the telos of true Christians is to turn the tree of knowledge into the tree of life. Maximus asserts:

> Death is, properly speaking, separation from God, and "the sting of death is sin." In taking it on, Adam was banished at once from the tree of life, from Paradise, and from God, whereupon there followed of necessity the death of the body. On the other hand life is, properly speaking, the one who says, "I am the life." By his death he brought back to life again the one who had died.[117] Maximus

---

115. See Q. Thal. (43) PG 90 409A. Laga-Steel, CCSG, 293.
116. Ibid.
117. Car. 2.93.

says: "Many of us talk, few of us act."[118] Yet, every human being must act in order to become a being in Christ and to accomplish his/her God-given task within the guaranteed state of everlasting well-being. Human beings are endowed with a dynamic system of choices that are kept in the creator's loving care, but it remains for them to decide between being in the likeness of the creator and existing as broken creatures. Free will underlies the central role that human choice plays in this gnoseological schema, which focuses on the triad of creation, fall, and deification and differentiates between being, well-being, and eternal well-being. In Chapters on Love, the congruity between these two ontological paradigms is presented in relation to a third triad concerning nature, choice, and grace that derives from them. The microcosm's position as a mediator between the created and uncreated spheres determines the rebirth and regeneration of human nature, insofar as personal choices invariably lead people to the realm of divine perfection or to the opposite pole of nothingness.

In the very first paragraph of the first century, it is said that "love is a good disposition of the soul by which one prefers no being to the knowledge of God."[119] Ascetical theology may be described as a "cutting off the passions" or a separation from the world. Yet, Louth contends that "Maximus does not play down this negative side, but he supplements it with a positive emphasis on the importance of deeper and purer love: 'A pure love is one freed from the passions and constantly delighted by divine love.'"[120] Maximus warns that "unless the mind finds something better than [the passions] to which it can transfer its desire, it will not be completely persuaded to disdain [earthly things]."[121] The way to theosis is opened up by practicing virtue and resisting the fall into vice. This involves distinguishing between the activities of the good will that directs the soul's highest part (νοῦς) to God and the evil will that diverts human beings from well-being.

In paragraphs 1.24, 1.25, 2.32, and 2.33 of Chapters on Love, Maximus explicitly describes the difference between the good and evil wills in terms of the rational (eulogos) or irrational (alogos) use of things. Then, the Confessor asks: "What then is evil? Evidently, it is the passion of the natural representation [φύσιν νοήματος], which does not have to exist in

---

118. *Car.* 4.85.
119. *Car.* 1.1.
120. Louth, *Maximus the Confessor*, 40. The embedded paraphrase is from *Car.* 1.34.
121. *Car.* 3.64.

our use of representations [τα νοήματα] if the mind is watchful. Passion is a movement of the soul contrary to nature, either toward irrational love or senseless hate of something or on account of something material."[122] In Questions to Thalassius, evil is described as "an irrational movement of the natural energies to something other than their end as a result of mistaken judgement."[123] Evil is characterized as an irrational fall into nothingness, rather than as the natural energies' hesitant movement toward perfection.

Taken together, these statements and the preceding affirmations of the choice that human beings have to use the will in good or evil ways—after distinguishing (διαίρεσις) between these opposite tendencies—point to the interrelationship between nature and grace. This connection is evident in the ascent of the fallen nature to the perfect state of contemplating the divine Logos by choosing good over evil and practicing the virtues. The fact that this specific choice lies at the heart of the well-known doctrine of being, well-being, and eternal being is evident when Maximus writes:

> The total logos of the whole coming to be of rational beings is seen to have that of being, that of well-being, and that of eternal being; and that of being is first given to beings by essence, that of well-being is given to them second by choice, as self-moved, and that of eternal being is bestowed upon them third, by grace.[124] The main point here is that human creatures must be able to increase their participation in their source. This is made possible also by the logos of well-being, which Maximus associates with choice. In the aforementioned triad of nature, choice, and grace, nature and grace are pure gifts of God in which human creatures have no concrete involvement. The difference between these gifts is that eternal being, or deification, can come only after well-being, which is dependent on each creature's own freely chosen course. Maximus presents this conception in Chapters on Love 3.24–27, where he explains it in terms of the creature's progression from image to likeness:

> In bringing into existence a rational and intelligent nature, God in his supreme goodness has communicated to it four of the divine attributes by which he maintains, guards, and preserves creatures:

---

122. *Car.* 2.15.

123. *Q. Thal.* (Introd.) PG 90 253B. Laga-Steel, CCSG, 29; also see *Amb. Io.* (42) PG 91 1332A.

124. *Amb. Io.* (65) PG 91 1392A. See also trans. by Maximos Constas, On Difficulties, 277.

being, eternal being, goodness, and wisdom. The first two of these he grants to the essence; the second two to its faculty of will; that is, to the essence he gives being and eternal being, and to the volitive faculty he gives goodness and wisdom in order that what he is by essence the creature might become by participation. For this reason he is said to be made to the image and likeness of God.[125] Like many of the Church Fathers, Maximus perceives that the imago Dei is related to nature and creation, while humankind's likeness to the divine has to do with grace and deification.

Elsewhere, the Confessor maintains that "for them to exist forever or not to exist is in the power of their maker. To share in his goodness and wisdom or to not share depends on the will of rational beings."[126] Human beings have been granted a logos by which they may be part of God, but they have failed to appropriate that gift and to move toward their logos. Thus, they have fallen toward nonbeing. Because human creatures have failed to be part of God by moving against their logoi, by choosing not to obey the commandments, and by misunderstanding what it means to become like God, the only way they can ascend is by moving toward God in a participatory way. Before the fall of humankind, there was no need to distinguish between good and evil by means of knowledge because the difference between them was clear. The good consisted in obedience, and evil resulted from disobedience to God. However, after the fall, human nature could be deified by choosing to practice virtue and as a result of divine grace.

A text that particularly influenced Maximus's understanding of knowledge in this case was Gregory of Nyssa's De opificio hominis. There, a distinction is drawn between knowledge (gnosis) defined as skill (episteme) and discernment. Thus, a differentiation is made between objective (scientific) knowledge and knowledge that is "a disposition towards what is agreeable."[127] This disposition opens up a way of knowing that includes desiring the object of knowledge. Here, knowledge (gnosis) has a different meaning than discursive reasoning and rational contemplation. As we will see later, this is the case because, as Carlos Steel notes, it is impossible for evil to subsist alone.

---

125. *Car.* 3.25.

126. *Car.* 3.27.

127. Gregory of Nyssa, *De opificio hominis* XX.

It only exists as [a] parasite upon the good. . . . Evil can never appear by its own self, manifesting its own nature. It must always be disguised under the form of some good, covered with beautiful blossoms, colored, perfumed, and appearing attractive. For if evil were not clothed with some form of beauty, it would never seduce and attract the desire towards it.[128] Gregory begins by making it clear that knowledge (γνῶσις) is not the equivalent of rational thought (ἐπιστήμη) and must also be distinguished from discernment (διάκρισις). The ability to discriminate between good and evil belongs to "the spiritual man," to use Paul's phrase (I Cor 2:15). Thus, as Steel observes, gnosis does not have

a purely cognitive sense, but indicates a positive, affectionate disposition of the mind towards things or persons we favor. This γνῶσις is further specified as the knowledge "of good and evil." As Gregory explains, good and evil must be taken jointly as a whole: they are not two clearly distinguished objects of knowledge, but a "concretion" (ἀνάκρισις) or a "mixture" of the two contrary qualities.[129] After the fall, Adam, the representative prototype of human nature, became the representative prototype of fallen nature because he turned his faculties away from their natural movement toward God, yielded his spirit to sensory experience, and sought his well-being in the sensible realm. As a result of this original sin, human beings lost their inner harmony, which had derived from their unity with God. Following the regeneration of their human nature in Christ, human beings must take up an ascetic life of contemplation. Just as God has adopted human nature, human souls must adopted divine nature. Having been created in the perfect image of God and having a partial resemblance to him, human beings can elevate this partial resemblance to complete resemblance, or perfection. To attain life in God, one needs to practice asceticism and to observe certain virtues.

In paragraph 25 of the second century of Chapters on Love, Maximus declares that "the reward of self-mastery is detachment [apatheia] and that of faith is knowledge. And detachment [apatheia] gives rise to discernment while knowledge gives rise to love of God."[130] This suggests that the ability to distinguish between good and evil is acquired by practicing virtue at the first stage of seeking knowledge. The battle against the passions goes on at

128. Steel, "The Tree of Knowledge of Good and Evil," 245.
129. Ibid.
130. *Car.* 2.25.

two levels: through praxis and, more importantly, in the context of theoria. This means that the struggle against evil thoughts is twice as difficult and intense as the fight against evil actions. Ultimately, we arrive at the perfect mind, which "is the one that through genuine faith supremely knows in supreme ignorance the supremely unknowable, and in gazing on the universe of his handiwork has received from God comprehensive knowledge of his Providence and judgment in it, as far as allowable to men."[131]

Adam's Fall and Human Beings' Meditating Function in the Universe

Because Adam enjoyed knowledge (γνῶσις) beyond the sphere of purely natural contemplation, he was passionless by grace, free from needs produced by outward circumstances, and inherently wise. Yet, he does not return to a realm of mystical enlightenment or to knowledge itself (gnosis). His return involves something beyond that: union with God in love. This section will focus on the theme.

By virtue of their very existence and their modes of cognition, human beings find themselves mediating between extremes, such as the intelligible and sensible; heaven and earth; and the male and female. According to Maximus, these extremes in the fragmented universal hypostasis find their unity in the human being. Thus, the greatest tasks facing humankind involve mediating between God and creation; re-creating the world after the paradigm of Christ; and transforming humankind's fallen state of being into a supremely human mode of being in Christ.

An important feature of Maximus's view of the position of human beings before and after the fall is related to the revised understanding of the beginning and end that he expounds in his considerations of apocatastasis. He alters the Neoplatonic Origenist view that the beginning and end are identical. The human ascent toward—and return to—God cannot be regarded as a return to a previous state. The return to paradise entails overcoming the "fourth division" between paradise and the inhabited earth. Human nature that has been restored to the divine Logos is called to enter into deeper communion with God. Yet, the divisions between the intelligible and the sensible worlds and between created and uncreated nature still exist. Thus, Maximus says:

131. *Car.* 3.99.

> Manifold is the relation between [intelligible minds] and what they perceive and between [the] senses and what they experience. Thus the human being, consisting of both soul and sensible body, by means of its natural relationship of belonging to each division of creation, is both circumscribed and circumscribes: through being, it is circumscribed and through potency, it circumscribes.[132] Maximus indicates that this potency is inherent in the human intellective capacity. Human beings are circumscribed because their nature is composed of both an intelligible and a sensible aspect, and they circumscribe because they are able to embrace these two levels of reality with their minds and senses. The unity within individual members of the human race is represented as an overcoming of the division between paradise and the inhabited earth. Thus, if the process of unification is understood ontologically, the existence of humankind as a whole and of individual persons will ultimately coincide. However, if the process is understood in a purely epistemological sense, the existence of humankind and of individual persons will necessarily be united. Eriugena "comments on Maximus's remarks [in the Ambigua] that the intelligibles and the sensibles (the second division) are unified 'in respect [to] knowledge and ignorance.'"[133]

There are different approaches to the division between created and uncreated nature. Under the rubric of "double creation," one of these differentiates between ideal and corporeal human beings, or to use Paul's words, between our inner and outer natures (2 Cor 4:16). According to this schema, the ideal being is identified with the soul and is particularly associated with the mind. Yet, insofar as a division of the sexes was not part of God's original plan for creation, sensual lust and pain were not created along with human nature. Thus, I am not convinced that Maximus neglects interpersonal relationships by replacing the ego and the existence of the other with God's presence. Human beings have the capacity for a different kind of lust—for a spiritual type of pleasure—that is in keeping with nous. However, they misuse this capacity and immerse themselves in the sensible world.[134] Maximus does not support the theory of the double creation; instead, he emphasizes that human beings misuse their capacity for true pleasure.

132. *Amb. Io.* (10) PG 91 1153A.

133. Gersh, *From Iamblichus to Erigena*, 255 in reference to Eriugena, Periphyseon, 11.530A.

134. See Q. *Thal.* (61) PG 90 625A. Laga-Steel, CCSG, 85.

3

Cognitive Faculties and Types of Knowledge

Sense Perception: Introductory Remarks
    Knowledge through Sense Perception and "the Sense of the Mind"
    Experiential Knowledge

SENSE PERCEPTION: INTRODUCTORY REMARKS

This chapter will focus on the role that sense perception plays in Maximus's understanding of human knowledge. In it, I will seek to demonstrate the positive value that the senses and sense perception has for human beings' participation in the divine energies following their descent. Moreover, since, in Maximus's parlance, the word "perception" signifies both the first stirrings of gnoseological activity and the final stage of knowledge (that is, participation in, and unity with, the divine energies), I would like to begin by proposing that the opposition between discursive knowledge and direct contemplation—which, in the broader context, reflects the difference between philosophical and theological concerns—is external to Maximus's holistic system of thought.

Human knowledge is a process of acquiring self-unity through union with God, or in divine-human communion. This endeavor requires the engagement of all of the capacities of the soul and body in pursuing the goal of life, which is being-in-Christ. The perichoresis of the human composite of soul and body results in the unification of the soul's faculties in the knowledge of God. In Maximus's work, this epistemological unity has ontological dimensions. The phenomenological unity of human beings, which the Confessor describes as the overcoming of the fragmented universal hypostasis by means of Christ's hypostasis, requires the unity of the soul's various faculties, movements, and acts on the ontological plane.[1] Divine-human communion is the bridge that overcomes the ontological gap between the creator and creation. One of Maximus's main contributions to revising the Dionysian ontological schema lies in his revisioning of ontological and epistemological categories in the hierarchy of being. Instead of calling for a progressive rejection of lower dimensions by superior ones, Maximus integrates all aspects of existence into a single synthesis. The whole human being becomes a perichoresis of capacities, a dialogue between the differences that underlie human "part-icipation" in the divine-human discourse. In this paradigm, the superior faculty embraces the acts of the inferior one as its own.

Sensory phenomena activate the process of seeking knowledge only when perception is rightly orientated toward the nature (logoi) of things. This means that a decisive aspect of perception is its "logicization," its ratiocination, and its dependence on the human inclination to be in Goodness and Truth (which are two names for God that represent the final attainment of human praxis and contemplation, respectively). This insight enables Maximus to overcome the Platonic division between the sensible and intelligible worlds. Likewise, he "rewrites" the severance of the human composite that distinguishes Evagrian and Origenist teachings in which the soul is freed from the body when knowledge is achieved. In the first case, Maximus emphasizes that the perception of visible, sensory things discloses their inner, intelligible, perceiving logoi, while in the second instance, he unifies psychological acts of knowing by incorporating all such activities into a single path that leads to union with the divine energies.[2] In this respect, he writes:

> If it [the soul] uses the senses properly, discerning by means of its own faculties the manifold *logoi* of beings, and if it succeeds in wisely transmitting to itself all the visible things in which God is hidden and proclaimed in silence, then by the use of its own free choice it creates a world of spiritual beauty within the understanding. This it does by combining the four general virtues with each other as if they were physical elements, so as to form from

---

1. See *Amb. Io.* (41) PG 91 1305C.
2. See *Amb. Io.* (10) PG 91 1113B.

them a world completely constructed in a spiritual and intellectual way.³ When viewing Maximus's thought as a philosophical system, we need to bear in mind the specific connotations that the word "philosophy" had in the sixth century. At that time, it referred to the "external" wisdom of Hellenistic philosophy, but even more significantly, "philosophia" became a term that described activities which were oriented toward the divine presence in this world (i.e., the divine economy).⁴ A second premise here is that Maximus's ideas must be explicated in terms of his particular system of thought and must not be taken out of context. Maximus invariably develops his ideas in reference to concrete examples. Thus, the topic of knowledge gives us a vision of his psychology, anthropology, and gnoseology. The process of acquiring knowledge—which begins with sense perception and ends with the mind's contemplation—does not mirror the diverse stages of the journey to perfection, as much as it reveals the unity of the sensible and intelligible realms. Human beings mediate between the sensible and intelligible spheres as they participate in constant spiritual growth.

Two issues constitute the framework of the following analysis. One of these concerns the place that sense perception holds in Maximus's gnoseology—which may serve as the core of his entire system. The other involves investigating the way in which patristic philosophy works with ancient concepts and languages in the medieval setting. In Maximus's holistic system, sense perception is a "composite" motion of the soul, which is affected by external things.⁵ Yet simultaneously, this motion enables the mind to penetrate the logoi of things doing the final stage of contemplation. In this regard, the relationship between body and soul, the interaction between the sensible and intelligible realms, and the connection between contemplation and praxis may disclose the pulse of this system of thought. In other words, an exhaustive examination of the various capacities of knowledge, which begins with the external senses, deepens with the actualization of the virtues, and eventuates in the mind's never-ending contemplation of the

---

3. *Amb. Io.* (21) 1248C-D, trans. Bradshaw, note 45, 9–22.

4. "Οἰκονομία" means "economy" in the sense of managing a household. Two passages in the New Testament use this word to mean "service" (Lk 16:2, 1 Cor 9:17). Elsewhere, in the New Testament and the writings of the Church Fathers, this term is understood in a deeper spiritual and theological sense. (See Col 1:25; Eph 1:10, 3:2, 3:9; and Stoiadinov, Божията благодат, 78.

5. *Amb. Io.* (10) PG 91 1113A.

truth, may reveal the final cause and absolute unity of human knowledge and existence.

The Unity of Sense Perception

Sense perception is part of the process of acquiring knowledge which may be seen as an overcoming human ignorance. The senses represent the final stage of the course of knowledge because they are a necessary condition of the path of knowledge once Goodness and Truth have become the final causes of human perfection.[6] In developing his views of the soul's structure and functions, Maximus correlates Goodness with the practical part of the soul and Truth with its contemplative aspect.[7] It is quite important to emphasize the relationship between body and soul that characterizes human perception and to highlight the body's participation in human perfection. Accordingly, Lars Thunberg notes that "the coexistence of body and soul is in the first place for Maximus part of his refutation of Origenism in which the preexistence of the soul was a predominant element."[8] Maximus does not set himself apart from the early Christian philosophers by insisting on the unity of human beings and their creation as a perichoresis of soul and body, although one of the features of his philosophy consists of an elaboration of this theme.

Prior to Maximus, the positive worth of the body and its resurrection is discussed in writings by Gregory of Nyssa and Basil the Great, who both, to some degree, affirm the Stoic view that since bodies and souls consist of distinctive elements, the same body can be rejoined to the same soul following their resurrection. In response, Maximus merely adds that none of the soul's abilities and no bodily characteristics are evil. Their misuse, which stems from ignorance, is the only reason for evil and the falling away from perfection that Maximus seeks to counter with a path of knowledge where the senses, reason, and the mind lead human beings back to Goodness and Truth. Knowledge begins with sense perception and continues with higher stages of reasoning and the operation of the mind until it eventually reaches the mystical ekstasis that is beyond all types of knowledge in the "darkness of [the] unknown."[9] Maximus views the created world

---

6. See Plotinus, *Enn.* VI.9.3 and Dionysius, *On the Divine Names*.
7. *Myst.* (5) PG 91 673.
8. Thunberg, *Microcosm and Mediator*, 100.
9. Dionysius, *De div. nom.* PG 3, 585–984.

as a theophany. In showing how human knowledge unfolds in this world, Maximus makes use of the earlier philosophical tradition. Like Aristotle, he views existing things as particulars. Through knowledge of them, we move toward universals.[10] This is the process by which human beings become able to see the one Logos beyond the logoi of creation.

THE DICHOTOMY OF THE SENSIBLE AND INTELLIGIBLE REALMS

The dichotomy of the sensible and intelligible realms; the manner in which human knowledge progresses from sense perception, through discursive reason and the logoi, to the mind's higher intellectual vision; and the relationship between soul and body are questions that had already been explored by Plato, Aristotle, Evagrius, and Nemesius. Furthermore, these topics constitute aspects of Maximus's psychology and anthropology that Hans Urs von Balthasar, Lars Thunberg, and Jean-Claude Larchet have addressed in the secondary literature.. The basic dichotomy between the intelligible and sensible realms that the Church Fathers collectively inherited from antiquity can also be seen in Maximus's writings. Yet, it is clear that the new formulations which we find in his works look at the same issues from a different angle.

Dichotomy and the Relationship of Body and Soul

The fact that human beings belong to two realms is decisive for their intermediary role, which involves overcoming the differentiation between the sensible and intelligible spheres through the wholeness and unity of their being. Their task as mediating entities is to unify the five divisions that exist between created and uncreated nature, the sensible and intelligible realms, heaven and earth, paradise and the inhabited earth, and male and female entities.[11] Since human beings are both rational and sensible, they stand in the middle ($\mu\acute{\epsilon}\sigma o\nu$) between universal opposites and must discriminate between them.

---

10. See Steel, "A Commentary on Ambigua ad Iohannem," 246.

11. *Amb. Io.* (41) PG 91 1304D–1305C; *Q. Thal.* (48) PG 90 436AB. Laga-Steel, CCSG, 333.

In Questions to Thalassius, Maximus makes the following connections: According to scripture, the division is between spirit and letter; in the case of creation, it is between inner principles (λόγοι) and outward appearances; and with human beings, it is between the mind and the senses (αἴσθησις). Thus, the senses are linked to sensible, bodily natures, and the mind is associated with intelligible, incorporeal elements. Moreover, in the Ambigua, Maximus says that sense perception ascends to the realm of the mind by means of reason, and thereby unites all of the components of being in one gradual, successive process.

This anthropocentric conception is also part of Maximus's Christocentric philosophy. Given their state of existence, human beings must mediate between the extremes of being, and the paradigm for this is the Logos himself. Yet, more importantly perhaps, this mediating position enables human beings to move toward unification. According to Aristotle, motion and the ability to sense are the main characteristics of the soul.[12] Like Dionysius, Maximus concurs that the soul has three motions: "That of the mind is simple and direct; the motion of reason is analytical since it deals with the logoi of things; and the motion of the senses is synthetic and complex, as it gains insight into the logoi in the form of symbols that refer to reason."[13]

Thus, dichotomy is a precondition of the natural movements of the soul's primary components. Nevertheless, the correlation between the soul's different aspects—relative to their dichotomized state—is so far from splitting it into separate entities that the soul fosters the unifying movement of the whole. Of this dynamic, Maximus says: "For [by] virtue of dichotomy, the sensible part of the soul is in fact not only sensible but also intellectual. And the rational part is not only immanent but also transcendent, and the mind knows of dichotomy, since it is not only intellectual but also passible."[14] "And thus," in Thunberg's words, "the soul's motion is conditioned by a dichotomy in each of its parts, which not only safeguards their individual characteristics but also serves the on-going motion from lower to higher."[15]

It is important to examine Maximus's postulates in the context of his work. Although he largely appropriates Nemesius's views, he moves beyond

12. Aristotle, *DeAn.* 2.
13. See *Amb. Io.* (10) PG 91 1112D–1116D.
14. *Amb. Io.* (10) PG 91 1116A.
15. Thunberg, *Microcosm and Mediator*, 183.

the Platonic standpoints of Dionysius and Origen. The Confessor quotes ad litteram from passages in which Paul speaks of body, soul, and spirit (πνεῦμα) and Nemesius of Emesa and Plotinus discuss the trichotomy of the sensible, rational, and intelligible realms. Maximus calls the mind (νοῦς) "the thinking subject" or "the inner man," which, according to Lars Thunberg and Vladimir Lossky, is equal to the "person."

Maximus does not consider these divisions to exist in an ontological sense or metaphysically. For him, the key factor is the distinction between the sensible and intelligible spheres, which is overcome by the mediating role that human beings play between the two. This approach contrasts sharply with the ontological ladder of Dionysius, who describes the whole process of attaining knowledge in ontological terms. According to the Areopagite's system, every higher level must reject the lower stages in order for the highest state of purity to be achieved in the end. In Maximus's estimation, every level of the quest for perfection is dependent on both the lower and higher stages; thus, each level necessarily incorporates the preceding one and mediates towards its completion. This theory reflects Maximus's conviction that the divisions between the soul's faculties should lead to unity.[16] Although all of the components of the human soul share the state of dichotomy, its task is to unite the divided hypostasis of existence. Maximus develops this theme in Ambigua 10:

> For having received from God a soul that has intellect and reason and perception that [includes] besides the intelligible perception also this sensible, just as reason includes besides its inward disposition (ἐνδιάθετον) also its expressed form (κἄτα προφοράν), and intellect includes besides the intelligible [intellect] the passive [intellect], they reasonably thought that the activities of these [...] were needed, not so as to apply them to themselves, but to God—because from him and to him are due all things.... Those having soul are given with its mind, reason and senses; together with the intelligible they possess the sensible, reason—for the inner and outer expressed word or logos; mind for the intelligible and passible. The last one is called imagination applicable to the living thing ... the wise men say that because of this, the sense perception has been created [as] the tool for perceiving the imaginable.[17] The

---

16. Some authorities on Maximus see Chalcedonian postulates in this theory, but I am more interested in its philosophical significance than in the theological aspects of the Councils' decisions. See Törönen, *Union and Distinction in the Thought of St Maximus the Confessor* (2007).

17. *Amb. Io.* (10) PG 91 1116B, trans. Steel.

wise men referred to here undoubtedly include Nemesius of Emesa (and through him, Aristotle), whose views Maximus uses to describe the role that the imagination plays in the relationship between the senses and reason.[18] Nemesius locates reason in the front part of the brain, while Dionysius says that the rational element is in the head and what he calls the "irascible feature" is in the heart. In the Aristotelian tradition, the imagination is thought to be a faculty that retains "sensible species"—that is, impressions received from the external senses. In this regard, Steel notes that in Neoplatonic psychology, "phantasia is the passive intellect, ... [while] perception functions as the faculty that makes us aware of what we have retained in our imagination."[19]

All three motions of the soul are gathered into a single endeavor; ennobled by reason, sense perception thinks, imagines, and has the task of revealing the logoi that are present in created beings. Thus, the external senses are the means by which the mind "perceives" the logoi of human creatures. Within every human being, all psychological functions and acts come together to seek and find the God who is beyond existence. Sensations are turned into perceptions, so to speak. Thus, from one vantage point, the intellect and the sensory faculties are ontologically unified. Since they are both actualized in the Spirit by the spiritual qualities of matter, they have a common material basis. As a result, an action by a sensory faculty invariably incites the intellect to act.

The faculties must be viewed in terms of their activities, and the fact that they are united ontologically points to their epistemological unification. Thus, Maximus unites the trichotomy of the sensible, rational, and intelligible domains with the three ontological modes of existence that he identifies as being, well-being, and eternal being. Being and eternal being are solely dependent on grace, while well-being depends entirely on the disposition of the will (gnomi) and motion.[20] This pairing invites several conclusions regarding Maximus's understandings of knowledge, which are related to the middle position that human beings occupy between the sensible and intelligible realms and to their dispositions to seek goodness or its opposite.

---

18. See Aristotle, DeAn. 3.5.

19. Steel, "A Commentary on Ambigua ad Iohannem," 242.

20. *Amb. Io.* (10) PG 91 1113A, trans. Steel. See also trans. by Maximos Constas, On Difficulties, 163.

Cognitive Faculties and Types of Knowledge

Maximus presents his clearest sketch of the soul's functions in a section of the Mystagogia that is devoted to the characteristics of its practical and theoretical parts. The soul's endeavors eventually lead to Goodness by virtue of the activity of reason (λόγος) and to truth through the activity of the mind (νοῦς). Evil (ignorance) results from a misuse of the human will that impacts the principles of (or divine will for) all beings. These logoi are not Platonic ideas; rather, they represent the divine intention for every created being to acquire its proper place by relating nature to energy, or logos to tropos, to use Maximus's terms. The Confessor's originality is evident when he relates the logoi to the Logos. Indeed, the actualization of the logoi within the Logos constitutes the foundation of his theory of knowledge. He even describes sense perception as the faculty that has revealed the logoi ever since ignorance became part of human existence and prohibited contemplation of the divine logoi. Thus, all of the soul's motions are seen through the dialectics of pleasure and pain.

In his longest Ambigua, Maximus says that "every forbidden pleasure has come to be through passion aroused through the senses by some object of sense. For pleasure is nothing else than a kind of feeling formed in the sense, or a form of sensible energy constituted by an irrational desire."[21] For Maximus, the main point is not where pleasure is experienced, but what object produces pleasure. This conception reflects the Epicurean emphasis on the joy of the mind and the pleasure of the body, as well as the views of pleasure that Nemesius formulated. In other words, he is primarily concerned with what causes reason to be distracted from direct contemplation and what eventually leads it to embrace sense perception and discursive reasoning. Misuse of the soul's faculties is the source of apostasy from direct contemplation. That is why Maximus perceives that all of the soul's faculties are grounded in "logicized" meaning, both in the case of reason and with regard to the logoi of creation.

I will now present three definitions of the senses that appear in Maximus's work: 1) In the introduction to Questions to Thalassius and its scholia,[22] Maximus explains the nature of sense perception by making use of Gregory of Nazianzus's well-known reference to Plato's allegory of the sun.[23] Maximus says that when reason prevails, the senses no longer

---

21. *Amb. Io.* (10) PG 91 112C. See also trans. by Maximos Constas, On Difficulties, 161.

22. Although the authorship of the scholia is unclear, I will refer to them as I attempt to clarify some of Maximus's insights.

23. Gregory of Nazianzus uses this allegory in 2830 69A, but it originally appeared

survive because their power is invariably connected to sin in some way, tempting the soul to passion by virtue of the hypostasis of flesh and sensual pleasure that they share.[24] The scholia include a discussion of the path to enlightenment. Reason may be corrupted by the senses, but when virtue is strong and resilient, it leads the soul away from the flesh and close to God. The soul is said to become akin to the flesh in one of two ways; either, soul and flesh form one substance, or when the soul does not obey reason, it becomes involved with the flesh through the senses. In another scholium, virtue is identified as divine enlightenment, which is often portrayed as playing the same role for reason that light plays for the eyes by teaching the soul about virtue and about rejecting the desires of the flesh. Yet, body and soul form an unbreakable union, one hypostasis, and one individual; they are called to be connected to one another in a single hypostasis.

2) Another scholium says that sense perception (αἴσθησις) is the bridge of the soul when it is alienated from sensory things, insofar as the soul ascends to reason before proceeding from reason to the mind and from the mind to God. Maximus then explains that the evil inclinations of the thinking soul originate in the forgetfulness of natural goodness that results from the soul's passionate attachment to the world of flesh. It is reason's task to elevate the soul to a higher level of knowledge. Otherwise, it will remain in the realm where "the law of sin rules" as Maximus writes, referring to Romans 8:2.[25] Obviously, this law is opposed to the "natural law" that Maximus presents in the Ambigua when he reflects on difficult passages in the writings of Gregory of Nazianzus and Dionysius the Areopagite. In this context, he expounds on the passage where Gregory maintains that we deduce the existence of God and of the creative, teleological logoi of everything that exists from our eyesight and natural law.[26] Eyesight directs us to beautifully configured, visible things that are simultaneously in motion and motionless, while natural law leads us from visible and well-ordered beings to their creator.

According to Maximus, eyesight (ὄψις) is the link between the sense organ and sensible beings, while natural law (φυσικὸς νόμος) is composed of natural energies and activities of the soul that have their beginning in the sensory realm, but are directed toward reason and the mind. He says that

---

in Plat. R. VI.500c.

24. *Q. Thal.* (Introd.) PG 90 244A. Laga-Steel, CCSG, 17.

25. Ibid.

26. *Amb. Io.* (15) PG 91 1216D; Gregory of Nyssa, 28.6 32C.

"eyesight is the simple, rather than a determined, direction of the senses toward sensible things, ... and natural law is the natural motion from lower to higher, from [the] senses to reason and [the] mind."[27] Like a growing sensual sun, the body, as a whole, rises in the same way. God, the intelligible sun of truth, grows in the mind, as long as he is present in creation through his energies, desiring the revelation of the true logoi (λόγοι) of every intelligible and sensible being.... Without light, the eyes cannot perceive the sensible realm and without knowledge of God, the mind cannot achieve spiritual contemplation. As light gives the eyes the ability to see the visible, knowledge of God gives the mind knowledge of the intelligible.

In Ambigua 10, Maximus describes the three motions of the soul in terms of the mind, reason, and the senses, and concludes that they ultimately give rise to one motion.

> The first of these, where the soul moves around God without knowing him in any way, is simple and inexplicable. In the second case, reason takes the lead, as the soul is moved by nature and gets to know the natural *logoi* of things, which have been formed according to knowledge (κατ᾽ επιστήμην) and by its movements (ἐνεργείας).[28] The third motion is complex, as the soul relates to visible things and imprints their logoi as if they were symbols. Here, the Confessor explicates the relationship between these three movements and their inclination to join the one motion that leads to knowledge. He says that sense perception not only deals with the visible realm, but also with the intelligible sphere. Likewise, reason (λόγος) involves both the inner and the outer powers of the soul, and the mind is not only intellective, but also passionate (as is the imagination.)[29]

Another text attributed to Maximus, which is entitled "On the Soul," maintains that the term "sense perception" (αἴσθησις) refers to the first sighting of a visible object. Yet, sense perception is also identified as direct contemplation and the highest form of knowledge. This is the reason for the close connection that Maximus makes between the world of visible, sensory things and the intelligible realm. Dionysian Neoplatonism is

---

27. *Amb. Io.* (15) PG 91 1216D. Ὄψιν οὖν ἐκάλεσε τήν ἁπλῶς, ἀλλ᾽ οὐ τήν πῶς, πρός τά αἰσθητά τῆς αἰσθήσεως προσβολήν (οὐ γάρ αἰσθήσεως ἁπλῶς τό ἔκ τινος ἕτερόν τι συλλογίζεσθαι καθέστηκεν ἴδιον), νόμον δέ φυσικόν τήν διά τῆς αἰσθήσεως γινομένην κατά νοῦν καί λόγον φυσικήν ἐνέργειαν.

28. *Amb. Io.* (10) PG 91 1112D, trans. Steel.

29. Aristotle, DeAn. 3.3 428b30, 56.

overcome by this link between all of the stages of knowledge and through the mutual dependence and interrelation of every step of the process of acquiring knowledge.

3) The senses are images of the soul's potencies.[30] In this respect, Maximus makes a connection between the four elements and the four Gospels.[31] Likewise, he postulates a link between the five senses and the five capacities of nature that he specifies.[32] Along with its particular organ, every sense naturally—and in a mystical way—corresponds to a power of the soul. He maintains that the mind's ability to think is related to sight; rational activity and reason, to hearing; passion (thymos), to olfaction; desire, to taste; and vitality, to touch. In particular in Ambigua 21, he calls "sight . . . an image of the mind."[33] According to Maximus, the bodily senses are not evil in themselves. Only their misuse, which is caused by ignorance, leads human beings down the path of evil. This perception leads the Confessor to propose that knowledge coincides with the "proper use of the senses"—which leads to an awareness of the logoi (divine principles) of every existing being that are hidden from human eyes in the postlapsarian age.[34] Thus, the operation of the senses is governed by the law of nature, which is the designation that Maximus gives to the deeper operations of reason and the mind.[35] Consequently, reason must gather all of the logoi of existing beings into the one Logos. This conclusion is related to Maximus's overarching emphases on human beings' mediatory position and their task to overcome the five universal divisions between created and uncreated nature, the sensible and intelligible realms, heaven and earth, paradise and the inhabited earth, and male and female entities.

In Mystagogia 5, Maximus delineates the practical and theoretical aspects of the soul's various powers and its functions during the process of acquiring knowledge. The soul's practical component consists of the operation of reason and leads to Goodness, and its contemplative component encompasses the activity of the mind and leads to Truth. The actualization of the virtues—which is part of reason's purview since it reflects the Logos's

---

30. *Amb. Io.* (21), trans. Ponsoye, who writes: 'des icôns à l'image des puissances de l'âme' (252).

31. Steel, "Elementatio evangelica," 219–43.

32. *Amb.Io.* (21) PG 91 1248A.

33. *Amb. Io.* (21) PG 91 1248C.

34. *Amb. Io.* (21) PG 91 1248C.

35. See the previous comments regarding Gregory of Nazianzus.

increasing presence in human beings—is associated with the activity of the senses. As Maximus explains in the Ambigua, the soul's practical and theoretical capabilities are linked to human beings' abilities to see, hear, smell, taste, and touch. Ultimately, all of these operations lead to an aretology devoted to practicing the good and to pure contemplation wherein truth prevails and all of the soul's activities cease.

The differentiation between the various activities of the soul-body unity has a special place in Maximus's views of knowledge, which may aptly be understood in terms of the gradated movement of the whole human composite toward the central point where communion with the divine creator takes place. This process includes the external senses; the soul's internal capacities to reason and think; and ultimately, pure prayer and mystical union with God in ekstasis. "The biblical notion of the heart is the locus of communion with God".[36] In the Platonic and Aristotelian traditions, the faculty through which God is apprehended is the nous, while the heart is more prominent in Stoicism. The heart also plays an important and multifaceted role in the Bible, and many patristic authors follow its lead. This is particularly true in the case of the Fifty Spiritual Homilies that are traditionally attributed to Saint Macarius the Egyptian, who has a vivid sense of the profundity of the heart and of its capacities for good and evil.[37]

This line of thought plays an important role in Maximus's holistic view of knowledge. The entire process consists of a constant logicization of the unity of the human soul and body. This method is designed to disclose the divine presence in human beings by means of discursive thought and to reveal the divine intentions or principles (logoi) that are hidden in creation. Yet, this schema also reflects Maximus's understanding of the will and of human beings' intelectual capacities to become godlike by overcoming the divided state of the logoi within the unity of the one Logos. In the end, the separation of the sensible and intelligible spheres is not a true dichotomy for Maximus in an ontological or gnoseological sense. In fact, he defines perception as "symbolic contemplation" since it occurs through the symbolic images of intelligible things conveyed by sight in its function as an image of the mind.[38]

---

36. Athanasius, quoted by Khaled Anatolios, *Athanasius* (The Early Church Fathers), 46.

37. Bradshaw, *Aristotle East and West*, 187.

38. See *Myst.* (5) PG 90 495-506.

SENSE PERCEPTION AS THE FIRST STEP TOWARD GNOSIS

The possibility of acquiring any type of knowledge lies beyond human capabilities. Thus, knowledge begins with a realization of the self-limitations that exist within and come from our shell of existence. Human beings are persecuted in the web of space and time, but they bear this cross by virtue of transcendent grace and their own gnoseological efforts. Sense perception is a crucial part of the process of attaining knowledge even when it is viewed from the perspective of the purportedly superior stages of rational and noetic knowing. The subordination of sense perception to the mind does not diminish its importance in the process whereby human beings grow in knowledge. Thus, Maximus asserts that

> the person who courageously closes his senses by means of deliberate and all-embracing practice of self-control and patience, and prevents sensory forms from entering the intellect through the soul's faculties, easily frustrates the wicked schemes of the devil and turns him back, abased, along the way by which he came. The way by which the devil comes consists of material things which seem to be needed for sustaining the body.[39]

The next paragraph of this text says that "the intellect reaps true knowledge from natural contemplation when, in a way that conforms to nature, it unites the senses to itself by means of the intelligence." Maximus then maintains that

> the knowledge of sensible things is not entirely disconnected [from] the noetic faculty, nor does it depend altogether on the activity of the senses. On the contrary, it is . . . the intermediary between the intellect and the senses . . . and brings about the union of the two with each other. So far as the senses are concerned, it impresses on them the forms of sensible things, each according to its own kind; so far as the intellect is concerned, it transmutes these impressions into the inner essences of the forms. It is therefore fitting that the knowledge of visible things should be described as a river flowing through the middle of the city, for it occupies the middle ground between the intellect and the senses.[40]

In Chapters on Theology 1.22, Maximus says:

---

39. *Th. Oec.* 2. 79 in *Philokalia*, 204.
40. *Th. Oec* 2.80 (S), 81 (M), in *Philokalia*, 204.

Cognitive Faculties and Types of Knowledge

> there are ... two forms of sense perception. The first is a habitual state and persists even when we are asleep. It does not grasp any particular object and it serves no purpose because it is not directed towards an action. The second is the active sense-perception through which we apprehend sensible objects. Similarly there are two forms of knowledge. First there is academic knowledge, which is theoretical information, gathered merely from habit, about the inner principles of created beings, and which serves no purpose because it is not directed towards the practical execution of the commandments. Secondly, there is actively effective knowledge which confers a true experiential apprehension of created beings.[41] This statement corresponds to a passage in the Mystagogia where Maximus quotes James 2:17 and 2:26, where it is said that "faith without works is dead."[42] Every essence exists through its activities and energies; thus, knowledge without praxis and faith without reason do not realize their potential power and serve no purpose. As the virtues are actualized through experience and practice, dialogue with the Logos becomes possible through natural contemplation that finally leads to divine-human communion.

According to Maximus, the sensible and visible forms of things are like the garments of the logoi that constitute their inner content.[43] These sensible and intelligible essences are mediators between God and human beings, while the human mind, which is moving toward God, appears to be above them. In its spiritual activity, the mind does not fall under the influence of the sensible essences, and in contemplation, it is not under the power of the intelligible essences.[44] In Maximus's estimation, the gap between the sensible and intelligible realms is bridged by a mediatory "microcosm" that unites the divided universal hypostasis. The second person of the triune God embodies both full divinity and perfect humanity; thus, he unlocks the way to knowledge of self and God. Only through Christ is the multiplicity of existence overcome by the unity of the Logos. Participation in the divine-human unity, in the Eucharist, and in Christ bestows knowledge of God's revelation, to the extent that this is possible for human beings.

---

41. CT 1.22, in *Philokalia*, translated by G.E.H. Palmer with Philip Sherrard and Kallistos Ware, 114-163.

42. See *Myst.* (5) PG 90 678B.

43. Q. *Thal.* (51) PG 90 476C. Laga-Steel, CCSG, 395.

44. Q. *Thal.* (51, Scholia) PG 90 485D. Laga-Steel, CCSG, 409.

Human Knowledge According to Saint Maximus

The strands that link creation—which is divided according to the hierarchy of the existing world—are the logoi. Human beings can reach these divine principles of, and intentions for, all existing entities by the grace of God. The revelation of the Logos to humankind takes place beyond the realm of sight in the logoi that provide the starting point for, and subsequent direction of, human knowing. Knowledge of the logoi that constitute creation naturally leads to knowledge of the Logos, insofar as the world's polarities are overcome in and by the hypostasis of the Son.

It thus appears that the distinctive themes of ontology, gnoseology, and Christology are interwoven in Maximus's work, even though he clearly distinguishes three modes of interaction between created and uncreated nature in his hermeneutics. Knowledge of the many logoi leads to knowledge of the one Logos, wherein these divine principles find their consummation and the knower reaches a state of perfection and beatitude. The Christocentric perspective and the focus on human efforts on behalf of existence—not for their own sake, but for and in God—plays a central role in Maximus's philosophical writings. The hierarchy of existence is anchored in the logoi, where the relationship between creator and creation is to be found. God knows the logoi before their creation, the way they were in God "who is the truth of all things."[45]

As the focal point of Maximus's system, Christology poses basic questions and provides answers regarding a whole range of problematic points in his theology. In its postlapsarian tropos, human knowledge begins with sense perception. The precondition and guarantee of our knowledge lies in the incarnate Logos. It is Christ's hypostasis that provides a paradigm for the knowing human being to become a person, or rather, as a hypostasis. The human being is created with the potential to be a person.[46] Therefore, knowing persons are individuals who—by bearing the image of God—realize the logos of their nature in the course of reaching their divine likeness; that is, in the tropos of existence. The coexistence of divine and human natures in the hypostasis of Christ makes the act of knowing possible for human beings; facilitates the coexistence of, and interaction between, body

---

45. *Amb. Io.* (7) PG 91 1081D.

46. Arch. Sophrony Sakharov, *We Shall See Him as He Is*. He calls this knowledge "a being with" (the author's translation of "so-bitie"), insofar as "God answers the question 'what is Being?' with the words, 'I am Being (Life)'" (150). This Someone enters into communion with us in lively ways and is known to us in communion. The act of knowledge is no longer a distant, isolated act relegated to a subject-object relationship.

and soul in the human hypostasis; and enables the event of be-in-g being-in-God, to be realized. In the words of Yankiev,

> God is not a being or an idea that we can somehow, *a mondo sublimiori,* "achieve;" rather, God is an event—an encounter—that we may summon. . . . God reveals himself, from himself to us in "our place," where he finds us so that he can transform us and make us for himself.[47] Thus, the act of knowing opens the door to personal growth and to a return to the beginning and source of everything that exists. The course of knowledge, which is the tropos that leads to God, perfects our nature, and in the end, knowledge perceived as existence through God signifies existence in God. Perichoretic unity is not mentioned purposelessly in this context. Constant pulsations between a permanently consummated essence and its permanent acts of striving toward—or falling away from—well-being in God are characteristic features of Maximus's thought. Indeed, these motions are manifest in every aspect of existence; we find them in the christological mystery and in the perichoresis of body and soul. The anthropological significance of this pattern is discussed elsewhere.[48] The emphasis here is on the movements of the soul and on the role of the body and the senses in the course of the process of acquiring knowledge.

Maximus defines sense perception as an "instrument of the soul, [an] ability . . . to perceive the outer world."[49] He also says that the senses are devoid of reason (ἄλογος αἴσθησις) and adds that such perceptions are an inadequate means of understanding things. What is captured by perception provides insufficient knowledge of existing things unless we allow ourselves to be misled by them. The senses are able to give us a true picture of things, of beauty and nature, and of the character of the visible part of earthly creatures only when they are led by reason. The sense organs must be properly orientated toward the telos that is reached through the workings of reason and the mind if the Logos to be the center of all of the movements of the knowing soul. It is only when human capabilities are focused in a way which is right and healthy that the divine quintessence enters into communion with us in the dialogue of theosis.

---

47. Yanakiev, Богът на опита, 15 (author's trans.).
48. Dimitrova, От образа към подобието, 37.
49. This quotation is taken from a text that is attributed to Maximus: "On the Soul" in its Bulgarian translation by Kapriev, G. in *Архив за средновековна философия и култура,* 1–15.

Therefore, it is essential for sense perception to be engaged in individual experiences in the context of the fall. As the imperfect first stage of human beings' return to God, sense perception bears the mark of the fall; it is characterized by estrangement from the riches of creation in a world lacking in vision. In the world of space and time, human beings have lost the God-given eternity in which they had dwelt in Goodness and attained the Truth. In the postlapsarian tropos of being, human knowledge starts from a position characterized by limitations where self-defining boundaries must be embraced according to our status within these parameters. Knowledge no longer means being in Goodness and abiding in Truth; now, it is a process of ascending, of striving toward life in Goodness and well-being. The transformation of Origen's schema of spiritual growth which focuses on apocatastasis—the ultimate restoration of, and return to, the original state of being—is to be found here.[50] This return to God initiates a permanent process of seeking perfection that overcomes the space-time continuum and re-creates humankind's fallen nature.

The visible world and its sensory phenomena direct us to their inner meaning, to a structure that is based on the logos, which known by human beings before the fall, but which now requires effort and ability in order to be "read." The sphere of sense perception and the domain of intelligible essences become part of the schema of knowledge only when sense perception (αἴσθησις) and the mind (νοῦς) are differentiated. The human ability to recognize the logoi of sensual things is followed by contemplation of their appearance (τά φαινόμενα), which is contingent on the self's ability to turn the senses away from a hedonistic inclination (ἕξις) toward sensual things so that they can be brought to a higher plane where they belong to the mind. This leads to a "disciplining" of the senses themselves.[51] The human task is not to reject the inferior faculties, but to bring about a unity of the diverse elements that we call human.[52] Sensory phenomena make it possible for us to perceive things, but their real tour de force begins when they

---

50. See Daley, "Apokatastasis and 'Honorable Silence,'" 309–39.

51. Some thinkers contend that such motions by the soul could lead to a "radical neglect of the senses." Yet, negation of the sensible may be beyond what this statement suggests. Although it is a problematic aspect of the process of acquiring knowledge, "subordinating" the senses does not have a negative slant in Maximus's writings. "Disciplining the senses," which is the term that Thunberg uses in *Microcosm and Mediator*, is probably a better phrase.

52. For more discussion of this possibility, see Blowers, "The Dialectics and Therapeutics of Desire," 435–51.

turn toward the logoi and the second stage of knowledge, which involves the ability to think and understand. In this regard, Maximus observes that "reason is what differentiates between things and knows them in the right way; . . . [thus], if it is possible for [such things] to be understood, there must be a greater power that follows from them than the senses."[53]

According to Maximus, "αἴσθησις" signifies the instrument of sense perception and the activity of the senses. It is part of the triad of αἴσθησις, λόγος, and νοῦς, which the Confessor inherited from Aristotle and the Stoics. In Plato, κόσμος αἴσθησις is opposed to κόσμος νοητός, but it would be a mistake to see the same opposition in Maximus's thought. In the Mystagogia, θεωρία συμβολική corresponds to θεωρία πνευματική in such a way that the world of visible things and the realm of intelligible entities are parallel. Maximus declares:

> The whole spiritual world seems mystically imprinted on the whole sensible world in symbolic forms, for those who are capable of seeing this, and conversely the whole sensible world is spiritually explained in the mind in the principles which it contains. In the spiritual world, it is in principles; in the sensible world, it is in figures. And their function was like a wheel within a wheel, as says the marvelous seer of extraordinary things, Ezekiel, in speaking, I think, of the two worlds.[54] The ascent from the visible (phenomenal) world toward its logoi represents a "return" to the same existence. However, it is no longer experienced as a phenomenal occurrence; rather, it manifests itself in its deep, spiritual essence. Thus, we may close the circle of knowledge with the image of a wheel within a wheel.[55] The intelligible sphere beyond the arcane symbols and forms of the sensual world may be seen by those who are able to unite the visible world and the world beyond in their mind. Insofar as αἴσθησις is knowledge of that which is perceptible

---

53. "On the Soul," 18–20/ PG 91 354–62.

54. See *Myst.* (2) PG 90 668C–672A. The biblical imagery mentioned here is found in Ezekiel 1:15.

55. Sidorov, Творения, note to *Myst.* "With the phrase σχέσιν αλώβητου, Saint Maximus first discloses the 'purity' and 'innocence' of the interrelationship of everything that exists. This can be attained by the mind only in spiritual contemplation. In the earthly (phenomenal) world, this connection is 'darkened.'" Elsewhere, it is said that "it should not be forgotten that the ultimate principles of being are the logoi. . . . Neoplatonic motifs and the gnostic disdain for the flesh and the material realm are absent in Maximus's thought. For him, the 'sensible world' is not an ephemeral ghost, nor is it a dissolution or diminution of being; rather, it belongs to the fullness and wholeness of existence." (author's trans.)

by the senses, τά φαινόμενα is an essential component of human knowing.

Ontologically speaking, the division of the created world into intelligible and sensible spheres—and noetic and phenomenal worlds—necessitates this link, which unites divided realms and leads to the one principle which is beyond the multitude of things; that is, to God, the creator of all things visible and invisible. The paradigm of such a movement is provided by the second hypostasis of God, which reveals the Logos in human beings. Thus, people who have been created in the image of God gain the ability to know the divine. In the Ambigua, Maximus uses the word "motion" to describe the soul's three faculties for knowing: sense perception, reason, and mind.[56] The soul is related to human beings' rational component, and according to Maximus, understands the logoi of the sensual world in the act of natural contemplation. In this motion, the material sphere is laid aside so that the logoi can be actualized within the Logos.

Knowledge of God includes different modes (τρόποι) of knowing the divine being because God reveals himself to creation through natural law, written law, and the law of grace. Yet, in each case, knowledge of God is related to revelation. God becomes knowable through his manifestation in this world. The act of creation is born of a longing for the existence of things—which is why human beings are given a way to return to the creator. The ability to read the syntax of the logoi of creation is the equivalent of understanding God's presence in the world, which is necessarily composed of God's energies and actions.

Within the framework of philosophical/theological scholarship, the manifestation of God's energies in human knowledge is naturally linked to the sacramental return to God that happens in the liturgy of the church, during theosis, or in union with the mysteries of God in Holy Communion. The theological foundation of the process of acquiring knowledge is the distinction between God's essence and his energies. The Church Fathers portray God's essence as transcending human intellectual categories and abilities; knowledge of God is possible only through an experience of unity with his energies. Knowledge means unity with God and the theosis of human beings. Knowledge is not just an intellectual activity because the whole person is engaged in this process and attains life in Christ by grace. Such knowledge is truly experiential insofar as it is reached by means of the soul's capacities for knowledge and through a particular mode of knowing.

56. In *Amb. Io.* (10) PG 91 1112D, Maximus writes: Πῶς καί πόσαι κινήσεις εἰσί ψυχῆς.

Cognitive Faculties and Types of Knowledge

As a motion of the soul, sense perception is complex and heterogeneous in comparison with the simplicity of the rational and noetic realm. With its help, the soul "tears [itself] apart from the outside world and—as if they were symbols—turns toward the logoi of visible things."[57] In some sense, visible things are agents of a natural motion toward knowledge that transcends time and space. The composition of body and soul confirms the relationship between creation and the transcendental creator and between the material and spiritual worlds. Human beings participate in both the sensible and intelligible worlds that constitute the two realms of creation. In light of this, human beings know and are known, and participate in existence either through sensible or intelligible elements, which is to say, either through matter or spirit.

The fact that human beings are corporeal (σωματικός) and carnal (σαρκικός) when they pursue life without God shows that the body is an integral part of the indivisible human nature. Yet, it simultaneously leads to an emphasis on bodily ascesis. This juxtaposition means that the fight against the passions, or more precisely, against the improper use of the soul's passionate component does not result in crucifying the body; rather, it leads to crucifying the flesh. Asceticism requires the participation of the entire human being, including the body. In this regard, Joshua Lollar writes:

> Being a mediator between created and uncreated nature, the human being's role is seen as the central point of managing the motions of [the] human soul [on] the ascending path of knowledge of God. The human mind can gain knowledge of the diversity of the world because of its diverse sense faculties, but this in no way threatens the unity of the human being, who is made in the image of the one God. In this way the human intellect becomes the place where the world is united in its intuition of the worlds through the senses.[58] The eschatological view which underlies Maximus's conviction that in nature, human beings remain entirely human in soul and body, and by divine grace, they also become entirely God in soul and body not only affirms the indivisible unity of soul and body in an ontological sense. It also makes it possible for the "creaturely" aspect of human nature to be overcome by grace and through participation in the life of the divine. Before the fall, human beings were theocentric and Christocentric creatures who lived naturally (κατὰ φύσιν) and wholesomely in close

---

57. *Amb. Io.* (10) PG 91 1113A.
58. Lollar, *To See Into the Life of Things*, vol. 2, 162.

relationship to, and communion with, God. Since the fall, sinful human beings have existed in a "paraphysical" state of being. In the ascetical context, this situation necessitates a return to true life and personal communion with God through the grace of the Holy Spirit.

It is important to distinguish natural (κατά φύσιν) from unnatural (παρά φύσιν) forms of human existence because by doing this, the opposition of virtue and passion and of good and evil becomes less a question of philosophical ethics and more a matter of the ontology of human existence.[59] Thus, the concern is not with solving the problem of duality; it involves finding a way to restore the natural mode of existing. In this sense, the paraphysical state is not the antithesis of kata physin; it is a deviation that should and can be overcome. Evil is understood similarly, as a privation of the good, rather than its total repudiation. Hence, life's objective is not the rejection or the annihilation of naturally given possibilities and capacities (including those of the body); instead, it involves seeking the edification and transformation required to turn wrongly directed passions toward the virtues that constitute their natural functioning.

Maximus relates living according to the virtues to the tropos of human existence—that is, to the realization of its logos. Existing things, which are understood by the human mind (νοῦς), are "outward" objects that are present in the mind through thoughts. Yet, the objectivity of the visible world, which is independent of the mind, demonstrates that νοῦς also belongs to the material realm. Mind and the senses are two faculties of knowing that are permanently intertwined insofar as they both lead to knowledge of the sensible and/or intelligible worlds.

It is possible for the mind's thoughts to recognize the relationship between these realms. Therefore, we know the sensory world through the sense organs, and for knowledge of the intelligible world, we have the soul's capacities or "senses," as Maximus calls them. Insofar as the senses are instruments of the soul, a split in the process of knowing cannot be found in the human composite of body and soul. All of their capacities for knowing the world elevate human beings to knowledge of God. Sense organs are one of the capacities that are essential for human beings to obtain perfection. Their use can be good or bad depending on the circumstances, telos, and disposition of the will. Thus, Maximus concludes:

---

59. Toutekov, Личност, Общност, Другост, 64–92.

Cognitive Faculties and Types of Knowledge

> If the soul could be used in a good way [by] the senses, through the respective powers, gathering the many logoi of being and if it could deliver wisely everything that it contemplates and in which God is hidden ... then it would create a better world in ... thought according to ... free choice.[60] Through such a good use of bodily senses, the soul is led to knowledge of the visible realm. Here, the phrase "good use" is a synonym for "natural" use, which reflects the objective of the senses' involvement in human activities of body and soul. The senses' deflection from their divine nature is a consequence of original sin. Yet, for Maximus, it is only through the senses that we know existing things.

Maximus maintains that sensible things contain within themselves. the logoi of their existence through which the soul and body are related. Therefore, the material world forms a synthesis with the spiritual realm and becomes an instrument of the soul's knowledge, which initially has to do with the divine spirit in matter and then involves the image of God that lies hidden in the logoi.[61] The soul is directed to knowledge of God by the senses. These reflections call to mind the relationship between the soul and the three motions of knowledge that are initiated by the senses, reason, and the mind. Their harmony and interdependence are apparent in this reiteration of Maximus's contention that every being is fashioned according to its logos—which is the reason behind, and source of, its energies. The soul begins to gain knowledge of God from the senses. Therefore, its movement toward knowledge cannot be viewed as something that is independent of human beings and of the harmonic unity of body and soul. The senses direct the soul to knowledge of the most perfect principles of existence; that is, the logoi of things.

Knowing God through the senses includes both making use of, and passing beyond, them. Sense perception, time, and space are categories that cannot be applied to God, which is why knowledge of God must transcend them. Yet, sense perception is not rejected by Maximus; on the contrary, body and the senses join the soul in pursuing the path to perfection. This means that sense perception is not reduced to the status of being a mere instrument that is applied and used to the limits of its inner capacities. Every existing thing, whether it be material, rational, or noetic, has its primary logos beyond its own occurrence as, for example, a human body. Human beings are complete not only by virtue of the aspect of their hypostasis that

---

60. *Amb.Io.* (21) PG 91 1248CA.
61. *Amb. Io.* (21) PG 91 1245B.

is comprised of the soul; they are reliant on the body as well. God embraces the body that is connected with the soul and, by analogy, makes these two components like himself.

In the introduction to Questions of Thalassius, which devotes a great deal of attention to the fall and the tree of knowledge, Maximus asserts that ignorance of God is the reason for sin. Evil is ignorance of the benevolent reason for the existence of things; by transforming the human mind and giving priority to the senses, ignorance has led human beings completely away from knowledge of God, and knowledge of sensible things has become mere sense perception.[62] Elsewhere, Maximus describes ignorance as a consequence of several interrelated factors, which he identifies in terms of self-love (φιλωτεια); seduction by sensible things that have features which charm the senses; and captivation by pleasure.[63]

The idea that resisting God's commandments prevents the direct contemplation of things is expressed several times. To contemplate the logoi, human beings need to be sufficiently mature, passionless, and unchanging, but they have been seduced by sensory phenomena and have let themselves be attracted by pleasure.[64] They have become incapable of seeing the logoi and are not flawless enough to know that God is both above them and present within them through their logoi.[65] Thus, instead of waiting to become mature enough to spiritually contemplate creation in a way that would relate them to God, human beings surrender themselves to sense perception and the kind of knowledge that results from ignorance of God and is connected with sensuality, rather than with spiritual pleasure.[66] Thus, "the passions may be expected to intensify."[67] Maximus expresses a similar view when he interprets the scene where Adam tastes the fruit of the tree of the knowledge of good and evil. He maintains that the reason for Adam's

---

62. See Q. Thal. (Introd.) PG 90 256A. Laga-Steel, CCSG, 35.

63. Regarding self-love, see Ep. (2), PG 91 396D; regarding the charming aspect of sensible things, see Ep. (2), PG 91 396D; and regarding pleasure, see Q. Thal. (Introd.) PG 90 257C. Laga-Steel, CCSG, 37.

64. Pleasure occupies a central place in Maximus's understanding of original sin. He puts even greater emphasis on the role of pleasure than characterized the work of Gregory of Nyssa, who was his main source regarding this topic.

65. Regarding the role of the fall in Maximus's thought, see Larchet, *La divinisation de l'homme*, 187–94.

66. Q. Thal. (Introd.) PG 90 253D. Laga-Steel, CCSG, 31. Also see Cap. Gnost. 2.39, 2. 27, 2.38.

67. Q. Thal. (Introd.) PG 90 253D. Laga-Steel, CCSG, 31.

digression is not his capacities for knowledge, but their use, or, as the case may be, their misuse.[68]

By describing these capabilities in detail, Maximus shows that the mind has turned away from God and has sunk into the morass of sensible things.[69] The motion of the mind should have its telos in the spiritual delight that comes from contemplating God, but it has changed its focus to the sensible sphere and the pleasures of the flesh.[70] This falling away takes place at the level of desire. More than once, Maximus observes that the first man turned away from his natural motion and shifted his desire from that which was permitted to that which was forbidden by God's commands.[71] Sin is a sign that Adam—in accordance with his inclination, or predisposition, to will (γνώμη)—turned away from his own logos and used his abilities against nature. Maximus writes that sin resulted from the human "disposition [to will] against the logos and [the] law of nature."[72] He also says that "in paying less attention to nature than to formless passions out of his ardor for them," Adam "has ignored the principle of nature."[73] Moreover, "the first man has neglected the motion of his natural abilities and their aim."[74]

Maximus also notes that "Adam freely rejected (I mean the birth by the Spirit leading to divinization), and for which he was condemned to bodily birth amid corruption."[75] He has exchanged true theosis for pseudo-theosis.[76] Adam's sin is that he understands the serpent's promise that "you will be like God" as auguring a change of status, as if becoming like God means becoming God in actuality. Likeness to God is a process of self-perfection, which is guided by love, but it is not self-love. Self-love is a self-centered motion that lacks a vision of the logos which bears the image of God. Likeness to God is promised to human beings, but opening the book of the logos—that is, understanding the divine intentions inside of us—is an extremely difficult task. Conversing with God is a way to enter into this

---

68. See the section on the knowledge of good and evil.
69. *Q. Thal.* (Introd.) PG 90 253 C, 257A. Laga-Steel, CCSG, 31, 35.
70. *Q. Thal.* (61) PG 90 628AB. Laga-Steel, CCSG, 85.
71. *Ep.* (2) PG 91 397A; also see *Amb. Io.* (7), PG 91 1092D.
72. *Th. Pol.* (16), PG 91 192A.
73. *Pater*, PG 90 905 A.
74. *Q. Thal.* (Introd.) PG 90 253C. Laga-Steel, CCSG, 33.
75. *Amb. Io.* (42) PG 91 1348C. Trans. by Maximos Constas.
76. Lollar, *To See Into the Life of Things*, vol. 2, 385.

understanding, but that is possible only when our eyes are turned toward God, rather than away from him.

Since the fall, knowledge has been focused on sensible things. Thus, it is complex and divided, differentiating between good and evil, which human beings are inclined to relate to pleasure and pain. Since they do not know God, people view things that can be known in terms of their sensory features and distinguish between them only in reference to the senses. This entire situation is a consequence of the sin of tasting the fruit of the tree of the knowledge of good and evil. The passions are a result of the allure of pleasure and of our efforts to avoid pain. Maximus maintains that all of these appetites are based on three universal primal passions: ignorance, self-love, and tyranny (despotic power over others). This triad constitutes a succession that begins with ignorance and progresses to self-love and tyranny. Being ignorant of God lies at the heart of the human passions, and self-love disrupts the natural activity of the human soul. Everything is focused on a longing for pleasure and a desire to avoid pain, instead of on turning our gaze toward God, who is the source of everything that exists.[77]

When the mind dominates the passions, it makes the senses instruments of virtue. Conversely, when the passions dominate the mind, they cause the senses to conform to sin. Thus, in *Various Chapters*, Maximus says that

> the relationship between the intellective faculty and intelligible realities, and between the sensory faculties and sensible realities, is in each case extremely close. Since man is constituted of soul and sentient body, he is limited and defined and he himself imposes limits and makes definitions by virtue of the natural and distinctive reciprocity that exists between himself and these two aspects of creation.[78] Thus, human beings limit existing realities according to their faculties, but these faculties simultaneously define human beings, insofar as they belong to both the sensible and intelligible realms. A little later, Maximus defines sensual pleasure as "the mode of sensitive activity when this is set in motion by desire that is contrary to the intelligence.... The saints recognize that the soul assumes an earthly form when, contrary to nature, it is impelled towards material things by means of the flesh."[79]

---

77. For more discussion of this issue, see Larchet, *La divinisation de l'homme*, 203.
78. *Th. Oec.* 5.71 in *Philokalia*, 277.
79. *Th. Oec.* 5.72 in *Philokalia*, 277.

Maximus uses various metaphors to describe the senses. For instance, he speaks of "a river flowing through the middle of the city."[80] Moreover, in one of the scholia, Maximus says that the sensory faculty is "a bridge of the soul that has separated itself from the things that are perceived by the senses. Together with it, the soul ascends toward reason; from reason, to the mind; and from the mind, to God."[81] Here, Maximus's view differs from the traditional understanding of sense perception because he considers the senses—and even the flesh—to be means of transition and mediation. Sense perception is not viewed negatively; instead, its ambiguity is disclosed. On the basis of Maximus's works, his translator, Eriugena, introduces the idea of an inner and an outer sense because the Confessor describes the senses as constituting the beginning of knowledge, while simultaneously placing perception and the whole spectrum of experiential knowledge beyond the scope of philosophical discourse.

At first glance, there may appear to be a connection between Maximus's view and Kant's conclusion that knowledge does not have to do with the essence of a particular object, but with that object's appearance. Yet, Maximus's conception of the knowledge of the logoi that underlie everything is different than Kant's understanding insofar as such knowledge is not only a posteriori, experiential, and sensible, but is also transcendental. Apparently, knowledge that is based on experience and temporal occurrences cannot be reduced or restricted to intuitive, transcendental knowledge because the soul reaches the second type of knowledge by means of the first. The ascent from the first level of knowledge to the higher stage of the soul's motion takes place because human beings belong to the intelligible sphere. This state of being makes the higher type of knowledge independent of experience. In fact, knowledge of the essence of created things is not the final goal of the act of knowing in Christian thought. The objective is knowledge of God through knowledge of the created world.[82]

Maximus uses the word "αἴσθησις" to refer to knowledge that is not reduced or limited to the activity of the senses and surpasses the boundaries of the first stage of the act of knowing. As noted previously, αἴσθησις is used analogically in Questions to Thalassius to describe knowledge that only the human mind (νοῦς) is able to reach. Gregory the Theologian does not place the mind and the senses in the traditional dualistic framework.

---

80. Q. Thal. (49) PG 90 455B. Laga-Steel, CCSG, 363.
81. Ibid.
82. Karayiannis, *Essence et énergies*, 285.

The boundaries of both capacities are strictly defined. They are opposites and do not mix their activities, but it seems that they also do not work one against each other. "That is why we belong completely to the visible creation, but only partially to the invisible, intellective realm that lies beyond the visible sphere. [Thus, we are] placed between mightiness and nothingness."[83] Gregory the Theologian presents a balanced view of the capacities and limits of the human mind. The activity of the mind finds its raison d'être in obtaining knowledge of God, but contemplation of the divine essence includes a whole range of activities that represent a discursive route to theosis, in addition to the other type of knowledge—the mystical unity of silence—which is expounded extensively by the Cappadocian Fathers and Maximus.

It is difficult to differentiate between intellective senses and senses that connect us—the mediators between the sensible and intelligible spheres—to the external world. In Maximus's writings, and most explicitly in the Ambigua, the Incarnation becomes a paradigm for transforming ourselves into mediating beings. Just as Christ exists as two natures in one hypostasis, we similarly exist as a human composite of body and soul. Thus, one of the tasks facing human beings involves overcoming the differentiation between soul and body. The bodily mechanisms that enable us to achieve knowledge—the sense organs—must be "trained," to use Maximus's own word. Their function is to enable us to distinguish between sinking into pleasure and ascending to wisdom.

According to Maximus, discursive knowledge prepares the soul for the second stage of knowledge where mystical contemplation occurs. He uses the word "αἴσθησις" to delineate a type of knowledge that exceeds not only sense perception, but also the discursive mind. In his Commentary on the Our Father, Maximus uses the phrase "αἴσθησις νοηρά."[84] A more fundamental contrast between created and uncreated nature is evident in the tradition of the Church Fathers than in Platonic thought, which places sensible and intelligible realms (κόσμος νοητός and κόσμος αἰσθητός) in opposition to one another. According to Maximus's use of these terms, the mind (νοῦς) is considered to be part of uncreated nature. Thus, instead of being viewed as a paradoxical notion, αἴσθησις νοηρά entails regarding godly affairs as an analogy of the relationship between the senses and sensible things. Such unity can also be seen in the soul's motions. Although

---

83. *Orat.* 38.II, *Orat.* 39.II.

84. Madden, "Aistesis noera," 53–60.

its three faculties (sense perception, reason, and the mind) have their own activities, they are all penetrated by the light of God and seek the deity as their telos through the soul's unified motion toward knowledge and communion.

Maximus notes that sense perception was not created to provide experiences of pleasure and pain. Instead, God implanted a certain noetic capacity in it, through which human beings could enjoy him in an inexpressible way.[85] Maximus calls this capacity the "mind's natural longing for God."[86] Aristotle says that only animals are motivated to act in response to present or anticipated feelings of pleasure and pain. In human beings, there is a much more complex psychological process, which is based on rational decisions and is directed beyond the immediate moment.[87] In Maximus' words: "Although they have a common nature, it is not possible for the mind to leap [διαβῆναι] to the intelligible entities without contemplating the mediating sensible things, but it is also entirely impossible to contemplate anything without the senses (. . .) being related to the mind.[88] Maximus warns that because of this interrelationship, the mind could easily follow the senses, instead of moving in the opposite direction where the mind leads the senses to true knowledge. If, in this encounter with visible, sensory things, the mind does not follow the senses, but—freed from their outward form (σχήματα)—penetrates the structure of their logos, it attains life in Goodness and reaches Truth.

Questions to Thalassius 49 is another place where Maximus stresses the interrelationship between the soul's capacities for sense perception and the mind's involvement in natural contemplation. Apparently, knowing sensible things is neither completely separated from intellectual capacities, nor entirely governed by the activities of the senses. Instead, it consists of the movement of perceptions between the mind and the senses. Such knowledge embodies the mind's unifying potential; it "translates" the foundation of outward forms into the principles of the logoi.

Knowledge of visible things is rightfully called "a river flowing through the middle of the city" because it is positioned between the activities of the mind and the senses. The sensible world itself does not provide knowledge of existing things, rather, it orientates human beings toward essential

---

85. Pater as transl. in Philokalia, 243.
86. Q. Thal. (61) PG 90 628AB. Laga-Steel, CCSG, 85, 87.
87. Aristotle, Nicomachean Ethics, 1172a25.
88. See Q. Thal. (59) PG 90 609A. Laga-Steel, CCSG, 53.

principles that lie beyond the visible realm and enables the relationship between the creator and creation to be discovered in the logoi of things. Although it is part of the sensible sphere, the flesh is viewed positively. The rational human soul has the task of making the right judgements and choices, so that the inclinations of the flesh can be overcome. Then, the soul is able to move toward knowledge of God. Regarding this process it is concluded that "the energy for knowing, which is imprinted on human nature, has a direct cosmological and ontological correlative. Although it does not have the highest value, knowing truth is not a mere goal."[89]

Every created being thus becomes a revelation of the divine—which human beings may expand with the help of their capacities for knowledge. According to the degree to which they become like God, human beings themselves become a revelation of God. In this context, Maximus's affirmation that humans' likeness to God includes both soul and body is of key importance. This view is in concert with the Christian tradition that affirms the theosis of the whole person and with traditional understandings of the resurrection of the body and the sacrament of communion.[90] Communing with the body and blood of Christ during the liturgy sanctifies both soul and body. The human likeness to God is transformed into a source of saving grace from God. The relationship between the creator and creation that is confirmed in theosis is demonstrated by the paradigm of the Incarnation of God, the Son. The Incarnation reveals that "God and man are paradigms [of] each other; thus, inasmuch as God becomes human through his love for creation, man is deified through the love for God."[91]

Ambiguity characterizes attempts to translate "λόγος," which means both "immanent reason" and "expressed word."[92] Eriugena translates "λόγος" simply as "ratio."[93] Every cognitive capacity ultimately acquires its value as a result of the way it is used by human beings. Unlike Dionysius, Maximus contends that the cognitive abilities of the higher orders do not exclude or negate the lower levels. Sense perception leads to communion with God's energies and intentions. By contemplating these basic components of created nature, discerning human beings participate in the divine,

89. Hristov, Йерархията на битието, 35 (author's trans.)
90. See Cooper, *The Body*, 64.
91. *Amb. Io.* (10) PG 91 113B transl. by Louth.
92. See Nemesius, "On Immanent and Expressed Reason" 14. Nemesius was an important source of inspiration for Maximus.
93. See Sidorov, Творения (1993).

but that same faculty can also be misused when only the outer form of things is known and when human beings sink into the temporal order and do not search for their eternal logoi. The use of reason can similarly lead to well-being or to falling away from the good.

This focus on sense perception is not just an introductory step that initiates the next, more perfect level of knowledge, which is constituted by reason's activity. Maximus points in this direction when he writes: "Since it is natural for the sentient being to have the ability to compare the visible nature of existing things, he contrasts scripture, creation, and himself; he compares scripture to word and spirit; creation to the logos and its outer form; and himself to the mind and senses."[94] Nevertheless, the Confessor does not divide the soul's capacities; instead, he discloses their unified activity and the motion that enables knowing persons to attain perfection through theosis. This approach is evident in the passage where he writes:

> We are content to use the present life in such a way as not to refrain from sustaining it by bread alone or from keeping up its good physical health; as far as this permitted us, not in order to live but rather to live in God. We thus make of the body rendered spiritual by its virtues a messenger of the soul, and by its steadfastness in the good, we make the soul a herald of God.[95] Since the ultimate goal of human life is to live in God, the sensible world should serve our mission to be mediators between the sensible and intelligible worlds and should thereby lead us to God. In his Commentary on the Our Father, Maximus offers this credo, which also appears in the Ambigua: The Logos "united through himself heaven and earth, joined sensible to intelligible things, and showed the unity of created nature, internally coherent in its furthest parts, by virtue and exact knowledge of the first cause."[96]

In Chapters On Knowledge 1.13, Maximus says that the senses should be "sanctified . . . with uncontaminated images" in order to add likeness to a given image and to thereby synchronize the tropos of existence with the logos of nature. Likewise, in 1.14, Maximus emphasizes the necessity of "teach[ing] the senses to reflect honestly on the sensible world and whatever it contains so as to announce to the soul the magnificence of the principles of things."[97] If the Logos unites flesh and spirit, we need to search

---

94. Q. Thal. (32) PG 90 372C. Laga-Steel, CCSG, 225.
95. Pater as transl in Philokalia, 285.
96. Ibid.
97. Car. 1A.13, 1.14. Also see *Philokalia*, where these words are found: "teaches his

the logoi for the unity of the visible realm and the invisible sphere that Maximus describes as being without a body.[98] He perceives that the senses must lead us to this deeper meaning of things.

RATIONAL KNOWLEDGE
Introduction to Rational Knowledge
  Multiple Logoi and a Single Logos
  The Movement and Limit of the Cognitive Process

INTRODUCTION TO RATIONAL KNOWLEDGE

This section is devoted to activity of reason, but it also has several subtopics. It explores the nature of this movement of the soul by engaging in a detailed analysis of a section of Maximus's *Mystagogia* that clearly presents the structure of this type of cognitive activity. The focus of this consideration is the mind (logos) and its relationship to known things and to the soul's other cognitive capacities. The purpose of this part of the book is to present and interpret Maximus's conception the activity of reason. To this end, it offers a conceptual analysis and compares Maximus's understanding with that of the earlier philosophical tradition. It also examines the relationship between the single logos and the multiple logoi that underlies the mind's movement from multiplicity to unity. The objective is to demonstrate the manner in which Maximus transforms Neoplatonic views and to assess his position with regard to Dionysius and Origen's teachings.

Reason is an attribute of rational beings, which enables them to judge things and determine their reality. "Λόγος" signifies a collection of things and the logical order of their relationship to one another. This definition shows the influence of Greek thought on Maximus's terminology. In the biblical sense, which relates logos to revelation, it is a way for human beings to know God. In Greek thought, logos denotes the ability to order existing things that are perceived by the senses. However, these two aspects of logos

---

senses to form holy images of the visible world and all the things in it," 116.
  98. See *Car.* 1.90.

constitute a whole since human beings are linked to creation by the senses in the ancient philosophical definition, while logos refers to the transcendent dimension in the biblical sense. The position of reason (λόγος) and of the attributive properties by which human beings reach knowledge of the good (ἀγαθὸν) are systematized and described in the Mystagogia, which is one of Maximus's most remarkable works. There we find the following sequential schema: λόγος, φρόνησις, πρᾶξις, ἀρετή, πίστις, and ἀγαθὸν. Reason moves through prudence to action; through action to virtue, and through virtue to faith, which is a truly steadfast, unwavering, complete trust in the divinity.[99] Reason encompasses faith as a capacity (δύναμις) that makes reasoning possible and manifests that capacity in activity (ἐνέργεια) through acts of virtue wherein faith is disclosed by deeds.

It is through faith that the mind moves toward Goodness, which provides it with an end and a purpose by releasing its inherent energies in a way that illuminates its power (δύναμις), state (ἕξις), and reality (ἐνέργειας). Reason (λόγος) is usually considered in relation to the mind (νοῦς). Prudence is a power (δύναμις) of reason. Envisaged as a state of mind, hexis (ἕξις) is related to praxis, and its energy (ἐνέργειας) is virtue. The final stage of reason's movement is faith, which Maximus characterizes as truly steadfast, unshakeable, complete trust in the divinity. All of the mind's activity culminates in Goodness. Goodness is its end and goal. Once again, Maximus's writings show that the mind's different faculties and properties represent successive stages through which human beings strive for perfect knowledge of true being. However, this process should be seen, on the one hand, as a gradual extension of the cognitive dimension, and on the other hand, as reflecting the dynamic sort of progress that characterizes the cognitive path which leads human beings to God. Through each of its properties, the mind becomes aware of new aspects of the reality that is revealed.

Rational knowledge and natural contemplation are heterogeneous and complex, but they also provide the basis for a personal relationship between God and humankind. The process of knowing God focuses on seeking truth, whether that be dialogical communion between God and human beings or the discovery of the logoi—the principles of all existing things that lie beyond their manifestations in the visible world. Therefore, rational knowledge extends far beyond discursive understandings of the principles of created things to a supranatural experience of God. Even the

---

99. *Myst.* (5) PG 91 677C (paraphrase).

soul's practical component is involved in actualizing the virtues; thus, as Aristotle says, "we are inquiring not in order to know what virtue is, but in order to become good."[100] This means that practical knowledge should be viewed as part of the holistic experience of knowing God.

The experience of the divine—or more precisely, experiencing God by communing with his energies—is a topic of special significance. Such experience transcends the possibility of knowing the giver of this ability, insofar as some of Maximus's predecessors maintain that it is reason or the mind which constitutes the image of God in humankind. The experience of knowing God thus goes beyond discursive techniques and the mind's limits, while simultaneously confirming the importance of the whole process of cognition, which proceeds from the physical realm to the noetic sphere to the silencing of all mental capacities. It is in this experience that human beings' significance as the crown of creation is revealed. As a unity of body and soul, they have the freedom to refrain from surrendering to "sensory thinking," but to grasp the meaning that lies behind the veil of sensation and to thereby enter into contemplation of the presence of the divine in the world.

In addition to rational knowledge, the higher forms of experiential knowledge and face-to-face communion with God are presented at this point in an attempt to demonstrate the inadequacy of reason as a means of achieving knowledge of the creator of existence. All human cognitive abilities are discursive and carry out their activities by virtue of God's manifestation in his economy, wherein his energy presents itself in the world. Experience (πεῖρα) is a type of knowing (κατ' ἐνέργειαν) that follows rational knowledge; while perception, or sensation (αἴσθησις), pertains to what is known. Thus, this sort of knowledge also follows mentally attainable, noetic knowledge. Therefore, it appears that «theology» (θεολογία) is not just words about God; rather, it involves the overall movement of human beings through the mind, reason, and the senses to knowledge of God.

Knowledge attained through reason and the mind is relative; it is devoid of personal experience. Maximus uses the term "relative knowledge" (νῶσις σχτική) to refer to the basic knowledge that human beings have of earthly life. As discursive thought, relative knowledge does not reach the absolute, although it plays an important role in facilitating the unity of the corporeal world during its ascent to God. One of the fundamental disunities within the hypostasis of existing things, which separates the intelligible

---

100. Aristotle, *Nicomachean Ethics*, 1103b25–30.

and sensory realms, must be overcome by a type of human knowledge that is equal to angelic knowledge and is at such a level that it becomes a more sublime "cognitive science" (γνωστική ἐπιστήμη) regarding the logoi of existing things.

When—upon reaching truth as its limit and telos—knowledge itself is dialogical communion arising from a personal act of being open to and turning toward the Other who has revealed himself to us, it is necessary to have "sense" in order to understand. In everyday speech, there is an unquestioned tendency to use the words "sense" and "feeling" to refer to the very opposite of bodily perception—that is, to that which lies beyond sense perception—without considering the whole progression of cognitive stages that are involved in intellectual discourse. In this respect, discursive knowledge is said to be relative. Moreover, the intrinsic human properties of reason (λόγος) and mind (νοῦς) are not displaced by experiential knowledge, insofar as that entails surpassing what has been achieved by the two movements of the soul; rather than rejecting the properties themselves.

In this regard, Maximus maintains that although all of the soul's movements are ultimately reduced to one motion, all cognitive faculties are necessary stages of the soul's ascent to God. Yet, direct knowledge of the divine energies and a sense of being within them takes place beyond the scope of ideas and concepts—in communion with God who is turned toward us. Through its active presence and by actualizing the virtues of the soul, reason moves beyond the natural necessities of the existing beings whose logoi it knows and gathers within itself. The mind also surmounts its natural energy and arrives at knowledge of the primal cause of all existing things. Thus, rational concepts and principles (λόγοι) compose human knowledge of the cause of the created world, which goes beyond the categories that the mind can grasp.

The Logoi

The next part of this chapter will present Maximus's teachings about the *logoi*. It will examine the principles, or divine intentions, that constitute the core of existing things by analyzing the way in which Maximus develops his doctrine of the logos. His particular understanding of the idea of "logos" will be elucidated, and attention will be devoted to the foundation of his doctrine of knowledge, which outlines a process of achieving insight into the structure of the logos of things. This will lead to a consideration of the manner in which discerning the single Logos that lies beyond multiplicity may be discovered.

The word "principle" is used as the equivalent for "λόγος" which appears to be closest to its intended meaning. However, the logos of a thing is not simply an idea about that thing; nor is it the principle that underlies its existence. Maximus inherited the connotations that this term had in earlier philosophical traditions, and was involved in restoring Origen's repudiated teachings by relating those to Dionysius's views. These considerations led Maximus to put forth his own interpretation of the logos, which was based on the writings of Gregory the Theologian and viewed the logoi in terms of ontology, asceticism, and the divine economy. From an ontological perspective, the Logos is seen through the lens of the metaphysical problem of the One and the many. Origen resolves this question by means of the doctrine of the henads, which Proclus identifies as being intermediaries between the One and the world of multiplicity. Dionysius addresses this issue in terms of the natural processes and hierarchy of existing things. However, both Dionysius and Maximus follow the Neoplatonic model, which portrays all of the components of existence as flowing (emanating) from the One. To further clarify the metaphysical context, however, we must also mention the conception of the Logos as the image of God the Father that the Apostle Paul puts forth in Colossians 1:15–17 where he portrays the Word as existing with the Father and being responsible for creation.

The logoi are neither the divine Logos nor his essence, which exists eternally and is apophatically unattainable. Furthermore, the logoi are not present in existing things as the Logos, but they exist in every created being in an individual and personal way. Yet, thanks to this preexisting plan, God can be called Providence, not simply because he occupies the first rung on—or is even beyond—the ontological ladder, but also because he holds the logoi and timespan of all beings within himself. Unlike Dionysius, Maximus does not portray the transcendent aspect of divinity as being totally detached from the multiplicity of hierarchically placed things; the Logos carries the logoi of existing beings within itself without any mediation. Borrowing the Neoplatonic Dionysian formula of abiding, procession, and return (μονή, πρόοδος, επιστροφή), Maximus places the center of the enlightenment and invigoration of every being at the furthest extremity of a vertical schema. In contrast to the Neoplatonic notion of "divine ideas," Maximus does not depict the logoi as being emanations of the divine essence; they are the result of God's volition.

Cognitive Faculties and Types of Knowledge

In Ambigua 42, Maximus presumably upholds the unchangeableness of both soul and body because nothing created by God's will can be turned into—or returned to—nothingness.[101] Yet, the radical difference between the essence of God and his creation, which results from God's desire, obviates the necessity for God's essence to flow into the world as a natural emanation. Ultimately, the principle of creation ex nihilo is introduced, creating a new horizon. This is a distinctively Christian doctrine—-a real "novelty"—that is contrary to all Greek and heretical conceptions in which a continuous circulation of souls in an eternally-existing world takes away existing creatures' opportunity for personal independence. The concepts of "person" and "personality" are unviable and inapplicable in non-Christian contexts, which do not share the belief that since human beings have been created in the image of God, they have been formed as a unique composite of body and soul.

Maximus's explication of the theme of the logoi also includes a discussion of the relationship between these divine intentions for all things and God's creative energies. In addition to the concept of the Logos, which makes the relationship between the reator and creation clear, the conceptual framework that encompasses the three kinds of law should also be mentioned in considerations of the divine-human relationship. These include the natural and written laws that find their fulfilment and completion in the transcendent spiritual law of Christ. The divine Logos that governs everything with wisdom for the sake of humankind's salvation initially guides human beings out of the material realm in which they are unable to see the truth that lies beyond visible forms as a result of ignorance and alienation from the divine actions and energies that constitute its beginning. That is why, the Logos becomes embodied and recreates human beings through a cognitive relationship that is free of corporeality and is focused on praising divinity.

The concept of the kinds of three law gives Maximus yet another way to depict our presence in God by relating the divine economy to our communion with the Logos, which comes from actualizing the virtues. The ativity of reason is primarily tied to knowledge of the logoi and the practice of virtue. However, human beings became vain in their mode of "reasoning" (διαλογισμός), and their hearts, which thereby "lacked understanding," became darkened.[102] There is universal human ignorance of God; human

---

101. *Amb. Io.* (42) PG 91 1329C.
102. Lucas, "Distinct Portraits and Parallel Development of the Knowledge of God," 64.

beings are unable to know (οὐκ ἴσχυσαν εἰδέναι) the eternally existent One or to recognize (ἐπιγινώσκω) their maker. In Maximus's estimation, knowledge is both salvation and a covenant. Knowledge of God and everlasting salvation are identical; but if true seekers of knowledge were forced to choose between the two, they would unhesitatingly choose knowledge, preferring a dynamic progression to static possession, as Clement of Alexandria says.[103] Salvation is deification and the sort of union with God that is symbolized by Moses's experiences on Mount Sinai.

Human capacities can transcend bodily limitations and arrive at knowledge of God through reasoning and mystical experience. Rational/practical, knowledge is the next step in the process of knowing. In keeping with the Aristotelian term, this stage is also called φιλοσοφία πρακτική. A contradistinction between practice and theory is found in the works of Origen, Gregory of Nazianzus, and Gregory of Nyssa. Already in Philo's writings, "πρᾶξις" denotes a stage of spiritual life; thus, practice is subordinated to theory. Plato uses "πρακτικός" as a technical term for "handicraft," while in Aristotle's work, the term comes to mean "general activity." The Stoics broaden the definition to include the fields of politics and social endeavors. Finally, Gregory of Nazianzus applies "πρακτικός" to the active life of monks.[104]

RATIONAL KNOWLEDGE

As mentioned previously, Maximus speaks of "sensible thinking" and of the danger that the soul's thinking aspect will be misled by the "visible forms of things," or "the garments of *logoi*."[105] This is the reason human beings turn away from God and the crux of evil in a gnoseological sense. In *Chapters on Love*, Maximus says that evil is "the passion of the natural representation, which does not have to exist in our use of representations if the mind is watchful."[106] Passion is not an emotion; rather, it is ignorance or irrationality. Referring to Gregory of Nyssa and Evagrius, Maximus maintains

---

103. Clement of Alexandria, *Stromata* 4.136.5.

104. Evagre le Pontique, *Traite pratique ou Le moine*, 38–63.

105. *Q. Thal.* (27, Scholia), PG 90 360BC. Laga-Steel, CCSG, 201.

106. *Car.* 1.15. "Τί οὖν ἐστι τὸ κακόν; The Δῆλον ὅτι τὸ πάθος τοῦ κατὰ φύσιν νοήματος, ὅπερ δύναται μὴ εἶναι ἐν τῇ τῶν νοημάτων χρήσει, ἐὰν ὁ νοῦς γρηγορ." Maximus describes evil as the irrational motion of the natural energies toward something that is different than their telos also in Ambigua to John.

that initially, the passions were not part of human nature; they came into being after the fall in the lowest part of the rational nature being.[107] The passions of the flesh are deviations that result from a wrongly directed will. It is tempting to interpret these words in the dualistic tone that is used to describe ascetical theology. However, we should not regard the virtues as being opposed to the passions and the spirit as being contrary to the flesh. Such a stance would reintroduce the dualism between the fallen and natural (healthy) states of being human, between eternity and corruption, and between life and death.

In Chapters on Knowledge 1.75, Maximus says:

> When the mind shakes off the many distractions about things which are pressing on it, then the clear meaning of truth appears and gives it pledges of genuine knowledge after it has driven off the preoccupations bothering it of late as scales on its power of seeing, as with the great and holy apostle Paul. For notions about the mere letter of Scripture and considerations of visible things prejudicial to sense . . . hinder the passage to the pure meaning of truth.In 1:76, Maximus adds: "[A human being] is known only to a certain extent through his activities."[108] Thus, the passions must be transformed into the virtues, and reason (λόγος) must be guided by the ascent toward God. Maximus affirms the beneficial of necessity of such foci when he writes: "He who contemplates the logoi of the visible "figures" with his mind discerns the figures of the intelligible realities and learns that nothing in the visible realm is impure because everything that God has made is good."[109] Although the sensory components of thought and sensible aspect of thinking must be overcome, a direct correlation between sense perception and the mind is established. Perception involves proper use of the sense organs—which leads to knowledge of the logoi of things. The sensible realm should not impel people to sink into changeability and different modes of existence; sense perception is identified as being part of the divine. Thus, it becomes clear that the sensible sphere is not evil; rather, its misuse makes it evil.

Here, we arrive at the tasks of reason and the mind, which constitute the soul's higher faculties. Nevertheless, even in Aristotle's writings, it is unclear whether the mind is part of the soul. Thus, Maximus sometimes says

---

107. *Q. Thal.* (1) PG 90 268D–269D. Laga-Steel, CCSG, 47.

108. *Cap. Gnost.* 1.75, 1.76.

109. *Q. Thal.* (27, Scholia), PG 90 360B. Laga-Steel, CCSG, 201. The biblical allusion is from Genesis 1:31.

that the soul (ψυχή) includes the senses and reason, while the mind (νοῦς) is "the summit at which the soul is said to touch God and unite with him in a totally metaphysical and therefore ineffable way."[110] Elsewhere, Maximus places reason and sense perception counter to one another in a way that is comparable to the antinomy between the intelligible and sensible spheres—and between soul and body—-that Plato develops. In analyzing Maximus's work, Basil Tatakis says that "in this contrast . . . reason designates the intellectual and rational aspect of man, and sensation, the irrational and sensory part."[111]

In Questions to Thalassius 51, Maximus says that thanks to God's grace, sensible things that need intelligible realities, must necessarily be commingled with images of God's greatness that can lead the human mind to God.[112] Allegories and symbols of the relationship between the sensible and intelligible realms are found in Maximus's work. Human beings contemplate the divine by means of symbols and by a "progressive stripping away" of ensuing ideas and images in an apophatic manner in order to achieve the level of contemplation to which the angels are privy.[113] Subsequently, the saints' direct contemplation—which corresponds to angelic knowledge—will be achieved. Reaching the logoi of things is a task that lies before the human soul. Basil maintained that even the logoi of created things are inaccessible to human reason.[114] Of course, the aim is not to "obtain" them, nor to reach the goal of the soul's activity because the telos of rational knowledge—of the human drive for knowledge—is life in Christ.

Knowledge of God is not simply an aggregate of categories or syllogisms. Thus, Maximus declares that "every beginning, middle, and end does not totally exclude every category of relation. God, on the contrary, being infinitely infinite, well above every relationship, is obviously neither beginning nor middle nor end nor absolutely anything of what the category of relation can be seen to possess."[115] Yanakiev's reflections may bear repeating here:

> God does not stand "in front" of human beings throughout their life. He is not to be found in a being as an "object." . . . God is

110. Tatakis, *Byzantine Philosophy*, 57.
111. Ibid.
112. *Q. Thal.* (51) PG 90 476 C. Laga-Steel, CCSG, 395.
113. Gersh, *From Iamblichus to Eriugena*, 280.
114. See Kapriev, Византийската философия, 23.
115. *Cap. Gnost.* I.7.

Cognitive Faculties and Types of Knowledge

not a being or an idea that we can somehow, *a mondo sublimiori,* "achieve;" rather, God is an event—an encounter—that we may summon . . . God reveals himself, from himself to us in "our place," where he finds us, so that he can to transform us and make us for himself.[116] The act of knowing involves an interpersonal relationship; it is a dialogical transformation that occurs through an act of I-Thou communion in which the concept of virtue has the primary place.[117] In his Mystagogia, Maximus portrays reason (λόγος) and the mind (νοῦς) as constituting the soul's two movements toward God.[118] Reason's ultimate limit is the Good (ἀγαθὸν) and the mind's terminus is Truth (ἀλήθεια).[119] In Dionysius's works, Goodness and Truth are two of the virtues that function as divine names which point to the absolute limits of the degree of knowledge that is possible for human beings. Although God's essence is unknowable, these transcendent images provide us with a way of knowing the divine economy. Thus, it may be that Maximus declares: "Truth and Goodness . . . reveal God. Truth does this when the divine seems to be revealed in its essence, for truth is something simple, unique, one, identical, indivisible, immutable, impassible, all-seeing, and wholly eternal."[120]

The two horizons of knowledge consist of the limit of human capacities to reach the creator, on the one hand, and the mystery that lies beyond him, on the other. In Christian thought, a syllogistic sequence leads to the types of confirmation that are necessary for reason to comprehend its beginning and its end, while the One who stands beyond and makes all knowledge possible is inaccessible, inexpressible, and supranatural. Maximus calls to mind Plato's Phaedo when he describes reason as "the pure, rational part of the soul, which is directed toward examining existing beings and things previously deduced [from sense perceptions]."[121]

From the perspective of reason (λόγος), the other motion of the soul is directed toward knowledge of the unknowable. Of the three motions of the soul that Ambigua 10 describes as being condensed to one, it is the second motion that demarcates the unknowable. The soul's natural motion knows everything only in term of the principles that have been implanted in

---

116. Yanakiev, Богът на опита, 15–16 (author's trans.).
117. Karayiannis, *Essence et énergies*, 298.
118. *Amb. Io.*(10) PG 91 1112D.
119. See *Myst.* (5) PG 91 673AB.
120. *Myst.* (5) PG 91 673CD.
121. "On the Soul," PG 91.362.

creation. Knowledge of these natural logoi is revealed to the soul by means of its activities (ἐνεργείας).¹²² However, reason operates on a different plane; its task involves defining the unknown. It is aligned with the divine principles ((λόγοι) of things that are found in each existing being. Through knowledge of these divine intentions, reason (the logos) ascends toward the single Logos of God. Thus, "natural knowledge" unfolds through reason.

Maximus transforms the opposition between the practical and theoretical (πρακτικός and θεωρητικός) spheres that Plato and Aristotle introduced. According to Aristotle, the practical and theoretical minds have different goals: In contemplative reasoning, "the good state" is truth, whereas in practical reasoning, it is "truth in agreement with right desire."¹²³ This means that desire is decisive for—is at the very core of—practical knowledge. In Aristotle's assessment, ct, it differs from theoretical knowledge. Maximus also distinguishes these two realms, and even links practical reasoning to inclination and desire—despite the fact that he unites the soul's practical and theoretical activities in a unified process of moving toward knowledge of God.

Practical reasoning provides us with reasons to desire and choose. Therefore, it is significant that practical wisdom presupposes not only the ability to reason correctly, but also the capacity to reason correctly with a view to the right end. Thus, it presupposes the ability to truly envision the end. Desire spurs the soul's motion within the context of the telos. Thus, all practical activity exists within the framework of the general principle that is known as the Logos. As Paul Blowers asserts,

> the rational and conceptual knowledge of God in Maximus feeds desire (ἔφεσης), which in turn motivates the urge toward a higher, experiential and participative knowledge of God in deification. At this level, in concert with faith and hope, love (ἀγάπη), as the ultimate theological virtue, prepares the mind to become sublimely immovable in God's loving affection, affixing the mind's entire faculty of longing to the desire for God.¹²⁴The distinction between merely having knowledge and experiencing knowledge represents the difference between potentiality and actuality, or in other words, between having a capacity and exercising that capability. Thus, Aristotle's theory of practical and theoretical knowledge maintains

---

122. *Amb. Io.* (10) PG 91 1112D.

123. Aristotle, *Nicomachean Ethics*, 1139a30; also see Milo, *Aristotle on Practical Knowledge*.(1966).

124. Blowers, *The Dialectics and Therapeutics of Desire*, 434.

Cognitive Faculties and Types of Knowledge

that these modes of knowing are an acquired capability, or habit (hexis). Theoretical knowledge is the capacity to disclose truth, while practical knowledge is the capacity to act. Furthermore, for Aristotle, "philosophic wisdom" is a capacity for contemplation, and practical wisdom involves reasoning and acting according to whether something is good or evil.

Maximus defines true philosophy as "true discernment and activity concerning beings" and asserts that this true philosophy is "defined (. . .) by the exercise of the practical life. In other words, the saints' insight into the nature of reality and their activity with respect to this insight do not constitute a realm independent of *the practical life*. As such, when Gregory [the Theologian] defines philosophy in terms of reason (λόγος) and contemplation (θεωρία), Maximus takes this definition as including practical philosophy within it, for "praxis is always joined to rationality, and philosophical discernment comes as a result of contemplation. Practice and contemplation, which Maximus calls 'philosophical virtue . . . [Yet,] while the life of contemplation presupposes the practical life of virtue, it also goes beyond it and the life of practical virtue is lived in the service of contemplation and not as an end in itself, a clear rebuke to any of the ascetically minded who would have disparaged the pursuit of intellectual knowledge.[125] Mind (νοῦς) and reason (λόγος) are two different motions by which the soul moves toward knowledge, but they are connected insofar as reason is perceived to be the source of the mind's energy and activity.[126] Reason is the energy, actuality, and occurrence of the mind. Unlike irrational beings, creatures who are endowed with reason can consciously know and participate in God. Thus, knowledge of God leads rational creatures to experience conscious ekstasis in God, while irrational beings act instinctively. Moreover, reason is a characteristic by means of which rational creatures are able to assess and define existing things and the reality in which they exist. Reason (λόγος) signifies both the sum of things and the logical order of the relationship between them. This definition demonstrates the influence that the Greek tradition had on Maximus. In the biblical sense of revelation, logos is a way of knowing God. In Greek thought, the word "logos" is used to refer to the human capacity to order the things that the senses perceive. However, these two aspects of the Logos constitute a single unity since

---

125. Lollar, *To See Into the Life of Things*, vol. 2, 259, 260, 262.
126. *Myst.* (5) PG 91 680B.

human beings are connected to the whole of creation through the senses in the Greek understanding, while the Logos is related to the transcendent dimension in the biblical sense.

In the Mystagogia, the place of reason (λόγος) and of the associated attributes through which human beings reach knowledge of the good (ἀγαθὸν) are systematized and described in the following way: λόγος, φρόνησις, πρᾶξις, ἀρετή, πίστις, and ἀγαθὸν.[127] In conjunction with this matter, Maximus says that "through its rational reason belong reasoning, prudence, action, virtue, and faith, all directed to the good."[128] He then adds:

> For its part, the reason, which we called prudence, ends up at the good by means of faith in the active engagement of its body in virtue.... As for reason, it is analogously moved by prudence and arrives at action; through action it comes to virtue; through virtue it comes to faith, the genuinely solid and infallible certainty of divine realities. The reason possesses it at first in potency [δύναμις] by prudence, and later demonstrates it in act [ἐνέργεια] by virtue through its manifestation in works. Indeed, as the Scripture has it, "faith without works is dead" [James.2:17, 26].... But when by means of faith it arrives at the good which is its term, the reason ends its proper activities because its potency [δύναμις], habit [ἕξις], and act [ἐνέργειας] are now concluded.[129] Reason (λόγος) is usually considered in relation to the mind (νοῦς). Prudence is reason's potency (δύναμις). Reason's habit, or state (ἕξις), is praxis and action, and its energy is virtue.[130] The last stage of reason's movement is faith, which Maximus describes as "the inward and unchangeable concretization of prudence, action, and virtue (i.e., of potency, habit, and act).... Its final term is the good, where, ceasing its movement, the reason rests. It is God, precisely, who is the good at which ever potency of every reason is meant to end."[131]

Once again, this citation shows that reason's various qualities are successive stages through which human beings arrive at perfect knowledge of true being. This process should be regarded as a sequential expansion of the spectrum of that which can be known and as evidence of the dynamic progress that may characterize the

---

127. See *Myst.* (5) PG 91 628, 630.
128. *Myst.* (5) PG 91 673C.
129. *Myst.* (5) PG 91 673B, 191.
130. Maximus says that "virtue is act." *Myst.* (5) PG 91 673B.
131. Ibid.

path of knowledge which leads human beings toward God. Every quality introduces reason to new aspects of the revealed reality.

The various definitions given to some of these qualities could be viewed as categories of knowledge that are totally different from those that are conveyed by the art of speaking. In fact, in the case of knowledge of God, reason adds its own categories, which are expressed through the "φιλοθέος λόγος." As noted earlier, faith is "the genuinely solid and infallible certainty of divine realities."[132] This means that faith is a source of knowledge of the divine that is without error and is completely certain, even though faith discloses the logos of God's true nature and its manner (τρόπος) of existing without using logical categories. Φιλοθέος λόγος has faith in the potency that leads it to knowledge of divine things. By practicing the virtues, reason (λόγος) transforms its activities (ἐνέργεια) and faith. When faith is thus activated by virtue, the logos reaches its goal of acquiring knowledge of Goodness. Consequently, faith may be regarded as "rational"—since it is in the logos (λόγος) as potentiality and transforms reason's qualities of prudence (φρόνησις), activity (ἐνέργεια), and virtue (ἀρετή) into actuality.

Prudence simultaneously is the potentiality (φρόνησις) of reason and the potency (φρόνησις) of the logos. Furthermore, praxis (πρᾶξις) is reason's habit (ἕξις), insofar as hexis leads the logos to experiential knowledge. Maximus also notes that virtue is an activity of the logos:

> In fact, . . . prudence [φρόνησις] is the potency of reason and that reason is prudence in potency. Also that action is habit, that virtue is act, and that faith is the inward and unchangeable concretization of prudence, action, and virtue, (i.e., of potency, habit, and act). Its final term is the good where, ceasing its movement, the reason rests.[133]

This passage shows the relationship that exists between the logos and the qualities that belong to its nature insofar as "faith is [their] inward and unchangeable concretization." As a conveyor of the art of speech, the logos (λόγος) does not need these qualities because it is concerned with the pleasure of hearing and is not related to the soul's ascent. Yet, as reason and ratio, the inner logos (λόγος), which constitutes a mechanism for understanding and uniting the different images of divine Goodness, passes through all of

---

132. *Myst.* (5) PG 91 677C. τὴν δὲ πίστιν φρονήσεώς τε καὶ πράξεως καὶ ἀρετῆς, ἤγουν δυνάμεως ἕξεώς τε καὶ ἐνεργείας, ἐνδιάθετον πῆξιν καὶ ἀναλλοίωτον.

133. *Myst.*(5) PG 91 677B.

these qualities in order to lead the soul to a knowledge of Goodness where "ceasing its movement, the reason rests. It is God, precisely, who is the good at which every potency of every reason is meant to end."[134] This statement calls to mind the graceful silence that occurs, when, after having had an experience of God and Goodness, reason reaches a new stage where all motion ceases: potency (δυνάμει), habit (ἕξις), and activity (ἐνέργειας).[135] The life of the soul begins beyond the movements of discursive through in the experience of seeing God face to face.

The difference between the logos, its activities, and experience (ἐmpeiríaj) is described in Questions to Thalassius where these words are found:

> The wise men say that it is impossible for the experience of God and reasoning [λόγος] about him—or the perception [αἴσθησις of God and the thought of Him [τὴν περί αὐτοῦ νόησιν]—to coexist. I call reasoning [λόγος] about God the analogy that comes from the essence of noetic contemplation of God [τῆς περί αὐτὸν γνωστικῆς θεωρίας. I call perception the experience of being interrelated with the superexistent through communion with him. I call thought simple and unified knowledge of God by his creatures. And regarding every other thing, we may also discover that experience puts a stop to discursive knowledge of a certain thing; perception empties thoughts of it. And this is exactly what the great Apostle may teach us: as for prophecies, they will pass away; as for tongues, they will cease; as for knowledge, it will pass away [1 Corinthians 13:8].[136]Here, Maximus appears to be speaking of knowledge that finds its limit and its goal in the rational activity of thinking. The three motions of the soul that lead to knowledge of God—mind, reason, and sense perception—are also discussed in Ambigua 10. Here, the phrase "sense perception" (αἴσθησις) does not refer to a function of the body; instead, it connotes perception's transcendental role in disclosing the perfect state of knowledge that lies beyond the discursive activities of mind and reason. In the broadest sense of the term, "theology" (θεολογία) is thinking about God, but the knowledge that theology provides is limited

---

134. *Myst.* (5) PG 91 677C.

135. See *Myst* (5) PG 91 677A and 677B, where Maximus writes of the moment when "reason ends its proper activities because its potency, habit, and act are now concluded."

136. Q. *Thal.* (60), PG 90 621D. Laga-Steel, CCSG, 77.

because experiencing and participating in the mysteries of God is knowledge that is beyond all thought.[137]

Rational knowledge is akin to natural contemplation of God. The goal of knowledge is participation in divine realities, but this does not mean that the process of attaining knowledge involves a subject-object relationship. Natural knowledge and rational knowledge are heterogeneous and complex, but they also provide the basis for a personal relationship between God and human beings. Seeking knowledge of God is focused on knowing truth, regardless of whether that concerns dialogical communion between God and human beings or disclosure of the logoi, which constitute the principles of all existing things that lie beyond their occurrence in the visible world. Therefore, rational knowledge extends far beyond a discursive understanding of the principles (the logoi) of created things to a supranatural experience of God.

Experiencing the divine by participating in God's energies is extremely important. This experience exceeds the human capacity to know the Giver of this ability, insofar as some of Maximus's predecessors maintain that it is reason or the mind that constitutes the image of God in humankind. This conception also entails a transformation of the techniques of discursive thinking; it involves crossing a border. However, it simultaneously is the fulfilment of the whole process of knowledge, which proceeds from the sensible realm through the apprehensions of reason to the cessation of thinking at the end. This experience confirms human beings' significance as a crown of creation—as a unity of body and soul having the freedom to refrain from falling into the pattern of sensible thinking and the liberty to understand the meaning behind perceptible realities and to contemplate God's presence in the world.

The fact that rational knowledge is imperfect and ultimately does not satisfy human beings is revealed by the higher forms of knowledge, which include experiential knowledge and face-to-face communion with God. Thought is just "simple knowledge of God."[138] This definition is related to knowledge that is achieved through the mind. It is important to consider the relationship that exists between rational knowledge that is a synthesis of the images which the logos gathers from existing things—and knowledge that is achieved through the mind by means of thought (νόησις) that is simple and individual. Those two forms of knowing are inferior to the

---

137. See Riou, *Le monde et l'Église*, 98–101.
138. See, for example, Anselm who speaks about God in terms of the limit of thought.

types of experience (πεῖρα) and perception that occur when experiential knowledge goes beyond rational thought about something, and the perception (αἴσθησις) of transcendence takes away all thought of it.[139] The analogy provided by experiencing sensible things makes it clear that experience spells the cessation of rational activity. This means that these two types of knowledge cannot coexist. Therefore, a higher stage of knowledge is introduced by a notion of silence that does not signify a rejection of knowledge or ignorance; rather, this silence reflects amazement and supreme delight at the divine Goodness which the knower gets a taste of through experience. Reason is not able to reveal this experience. Thus, Paul's words find a perfect application:

> As for prophecies, they will pass away; as for tongues, they will cease; as for knowledge, it will pass away. For our knowledge is imperfect and our prophecy is imperfect, but when the perfect comes, the imperfect will pass away ... For now we see in a mirror dimly, but then face to face. Now I know in part; then I shall understand fully, even as I have been fully understood [1 Corinthians 13:8–10, 12].Experience (πεῖρα) is a type of knowledge (κατ' ἐνέργειαν) that succeeds rational knowledge, while (sense) perception (αἴσθησις) is participation in the known. Thus, participatory, experiential knowledge necessarily follows noetic knowledge. Therefore, theology can be regarded not only as words about God (θεολογία), but also as a holistic movement of the human mind, reason, and senses toward knowledge of God. Maximus calls the knowledge attained through reason and the mind relative knowledge (γνῶσις σχετική). Such discursive thought lacks personal experience and does not reach the Truth and Goodness that lie beyond the relative sphere—even though it is an important source of unity for created beings as they ascend toward God. One of the basic disunities of the hypostasis of existence that separates the intelligible and sensible worlds must be overcome by a type of human knowledge that is equal to angelic knowledge and represents a higher "cognitive science" (γνωστική ἐπιστήμη) regarding the logoi of existence.[140]

If knowledge that aspires to Truth as its limit and telos consists of a personal act of turning toward dialogical communion with the Other who thereby reveals himself to us, we need to acquire a sense of understanding. In everyday speech, there is an unquestioned tendency to use the words

---

139. See Q. Thal. (60) PG 90 620C. Laga-Steel, CCSG, 73.
140. Amb. Io. (41) PG 91 1305B.

"sense" and "feeling" to speak of "common sense" that lies beyond sense perception. Thus, we do not pass through the entire sequence of steps involved in the process of acquiring knowledge in everyday discourse; we say "you need to feel this," "you need to see that," "you have no heart for this," and so forth This pattern views perception as experience that lies beyond thought and beyond the senses. Surpassing all conceptualizations, this experiential knowledge comes after the cessation of thought. Insofar as it is based on images and representations, discursive knowledge is said to be relative, while experiential knowledge consists of participation in the divine energies that are the "object" of knowledge. Of course, as innate human attributes, reason (λόγος) and mind (νοῦς) do not cease to exist when experience begins; experience is beyond the limits of the soul's capacities and qualities.

A major characteristic of Maximus's thought—which Palamas also developed later on—is the contention that discursive and direct knowledge are not opposed to one another. Maximus contends that all of the soul's motions ultimately lead to one movement and all of its capacities for knowledge are necessary steps in the soul's ascent to God. Yet, direct knowledge of the divine energies and resting in these comes about through an experience of God that occurs beyond notions, images, and representations. As an ornament of the soul with an active presence that actualizes the virtues, reason goes far beyond the natural necessities of the existing things whose logoi it knows and gathers together. The mind also goes beyond its natural capacity and attains knowledge of the first cause of existence. Thus, the ideas and reasons (λόγοι) underlying temporal existence make up Reason's knowledge of the created world—which invariably goes beyond the categories of the intelligible realm. Such passing beyond the categories of intellectual understanding leads to human beings' participation in the divine and their deification by grace. The following excerpts from Maximus's writings offer a glimpse of this inexpressible occurrence:

> The divine melodies of the chants indicate the divine delight and enjoyment which comes about in the souls of all. By it they are mystically strengthened in forgetting their past labors for virtue and are renewed in the vigorous desire of the divine and wholesome benefits still to be attained.[141] If by reason and wisdom a person has come to understand that what exists was brought out of non-being into being by God, if he intelligently directs the

---

141. *Myst.* (24) PG 91 708A.

soul's imagination to the infinite differences and variety of things as they exist by nature and turns his questing with understanding towards the intelligible model [λόγος] according to which things have been made, would he not know that the one Logos is many logoi?[142]Logoi

The word "principle" is the equivalent of "λόγος" that is considered to be the closest to its intended meaning, but the logos of a thing is not just our idea of it or the component that leads to its beginning in God. David Bradshaw aptly says that "the logoi are 'inner essences' of things, the value and significance they have in the eyes of the Creator rather than our faulty human estimation." He goes on to say that

> the statement that the one Logos is many logoi" must therefore be understood as presupposing the divine decision to create. Given that decision, the logoi are the articulated content of the Logos, His manifestation within the created world; thus they are uncreated but have a content that is determined by God's creative intent.[143]Maximus inherits various connotations that had become associated with "logos," which he transforms and incorporates into his view of ontology, ascetics, and the divine economy. Ontologically, the question of the logos is looked at through the lens of the metaphysical problem of the One and the many. Origen resolves this question by means of the doctrine of the henads, which Proclus identifies as being mediators between the Absolute and the world of multiplicity. Dionysius addresses this matter using the concepts of natural emanations and the hierarchy of being. Both Dionysius and Maximus follow the Neoplatonic model, which portrays all of the components of existence as flowing (emanating) from the One. Using the Alexandrian language that is common in his writings, Maximus explains: "The multitude of logoi is to be found in the one indivisible Logos, divided by the difference between the created things, and [conversely], we see that in their [multiplicity], they are One in relation [ἀναφορά] to him."[144]

To clarify this statement, we must mention the biblical perception that the Logos coexists with God the Father, as Paul writes in the first chapter

---

142. *Amb. Io.* (7) PG 91 1077C, trans. Blowers-Wilken.

143. Bradshaw, "The Logoi of Beings," 9. In this paper, Bradshaw "identifies the philosophical sources" of the concept that underlies the Greek Fathers' teachings about the *logoi*. He also investigates how Maximus relates this issue to the body and the senses and how the "logicization" of the soul's capacities is designed to lead us to perfection.

144. *Amb. Io.* (7) PG 91 1077C.

of the Letter to the Colossians. In Ephesians, Paul similarly stresses that the very same Logos is present and multiplies in everything; this Logos, who is from God, exists in relationship to each thing and "unites everything in him" (Eph. 1:10). The Logos is the head by whose authority everything exists and from whom everything springs as it is, for the purpose for which it has been created—which is to move and participate in God. Thus, it may be that Dionysius says: "Let everything in its measure participate in God, as it is created by God or according to mind, or according to reason, or the senses, and or according to the life motion, or essence and suitableness [ἐπιτηδειότητα]."[145] In short, although Maximus uses the Alexandrian terms Logos and logoi, the heart of the passage from the Ambigua reflects the first chapter of Ephesians, which speaks of God's will and of the unity "of all things in heaven and on earth" in Christ (Eph. 1:5, 10). The logoi are neither the essence of the divine Logos, which exists eternally and is apophatically unattainable; nor are they existing things which manifest their realization in individualized, personal ways.

In Ambigua 7, Maximus describes the Logos that preexists in God as the beginning and source of everything.[146] This portrayal of preexistence is a reformulation of the allusions to "predetermination" that are found in Ephesians 1:4–5, 9, and 11. Yet, for Maximus, the logoi of created beings are not just archetypes that preexist in God; they are said to be "in the sight of God" (Prov 3.4). This affirmation of primordial preexistence is an appeal, a call for participation in the divine. God knows everything before its being by virtue of the logoi. If the logoi have been in, through, with, and within God from eternity—if they are in his knowledge—they carry their appointed time within them. They do not represent a mode of existing in God in a world that is out of time; they are God's eternal modus, economically, rather than metaphysically, speaking.

The supremacy of the logoi in relation to existing things is not grounded in the opposition between eternity and time; instead, it has to do with a type of preexistence that is characterized by grace and involves the preselection of the moment when the motion of the divine economy is actualized. This is because of the knowledge that preexists in divine providence, which is not only a result of God's supreme position above creation on the ontological ladder of existence, but is also due to his role as the keeper of the logoi and timespan of everything. Unlike Dionysius, Maximus does not

---

145. Dionysius, *On the Divine Names*.
146. *Amb. Io.* (7) PG 91 1085C.

portray the transcendent aspect of divinity as being entirely detached from the multiplicity of hierarchically placed existing things; the Logos carries the logoi of created beings within itself without any mediation. Borrowing the Neoplatonic Dionysian formula of abiding, procession, and return (μονή, πρόοδος, επιστροφή), Maximus places the center of the enlightenment and invigoration of every being at the furthest extremity of a vertical schema. In contrast to the Neoplatonic notion of "divine ideas," Maximus does not say that the logoi are emanations of the divine essence; rather, he perceives them to be the result of God's volition. Like Dionysius, Maximus describes the logoi as preexisting or divine intentions, undoubtedly in reference to the first chapter of the book of Ephesians.

It may bear repeating that according to Maximus, the logoi are the result of God's will, rather than emanations of the divine essence. As was noted previously, in Ambigua 42, Maximus presumably vouches for the unchangeability of both soul and body because nothing created by God's will can turn into nothingness.[147] Yet, the radical difference between God's essence and the creation that results from his will precludes the possibility of a necessary emanation of the divine essence flowing naturally into the world. Ultimately, this situation necessitates the principle of creation ex nihilo. This is a distinctively Christian doctrine regarding "novelty" that is contrary to pre-Christian Greek models in which a continuous rotation of souls in an unending world removes the possibility that existence can have personal worth. Thus, "person" is an idea that is inconceivable and inapplicable outside of Christian contexts, which do not share the belief that insofar as human beings have been created in the image of God, they are, like him, a unique unity of soul and body that is unrepeatable and indivisible.

Gregory of Nyssa writes that the body consists of incorporeal elements, which have been gathered together to form the flesh and which, at the time of the resurrection, will again be part of the "person" who is a unique unity of soul and body.[148] Since we are a unity of body and soul in one being and have been placed in the sensible world, we cannot see the logoi of existence very clearly. We cannot recognize the Logos who is within earthly things as if in a womb since the Logos who has put his principles and his words in them and is their source and foundation.[149]

147. *Amb. Io.* (42) PG 91 1329C.
148. Флоровски П., Восточные Отцы, 156.
149. Staniloae, "Commentaires," 383 (author's trans. of Larchet's rendering)

Cognitive Faculties and Types of Knowledge

According to Maximus, the divine logoi are the beginning and end of the whole created world. They should not be viewed as the logoi of intelligible things or sensible things; rather, they should be regarded as divine intentions and thoughts that call human beings to life in Christ, the Logos. In one of his scholia, Maximus criticizes the Platonic and Origenist understandings of the preexistence of the soul. Yet, he also notes that creation is eternally bound to its Creator, who is the reason, condition and aim of existence as these citations suggest: "He says that we received as a gift the faith in God, that is knowledge, direct and inwardly in God, knowledge that it is impossible to prove. Since 'faith is assurance of the things hoped for' [Heb 11:1], it cannot be grasped in the knowledge of existing things."[150] Elsewhere, Maximus adds: "And [the creator] knows the things, [so to speak], in conformity with [their logoi] before calling them into being because they exist in him and with him, the truth of each thing."[151] Thus, every created thing is known and willed by God from eternity.

The primary source of Maximus's dynamic concept of the "divine ideas" that represent God's intentions is Dionysius, whom he quotes at various points.[152] However, Maximus's doctrine of the logos is also influenced by the Stoics' modification of Plato's doctrine of ideas.[153] This evident when Maximus writes:

Thus if we exclude the highest and apophatic theology of the Word, according to which the Word is inexpressible, unthinkable, and is not related at all to the knowable ... and nothing in no way is not part of Him, then the many logoi are the One Logos, and the one, many.[154] Polycarp Sherwood criticizes Vladimir Lossky's interpretation, which regards the logoi as divine, uncreated energies because this would entail "translating" Maximus in terms of Dionysius and Palamas. Nevertheless, in *Ambigua* 22, Maximus himself calls the logoi "divine energies."[155] The unachievable, indivisible essence manifests itself in the divine activities and energies, which represent a special mode of existence.[156] The logoi are present as the proto-

---

150. *Q. Thal.* (51, Scholium 4) PG 90 485C. Laga-Steel, CCSG, 409.
151. *Amb. Io.* (7) PG 91 1081A; *Q. Thal.* (13) PG 90 293D–296A. Laga-Steel, CCSG, 95.
152. PG 3 824C and transl. Дионисий Ареопагит, За Божествените имена 5. 8, 90.
153. Völker, *Mesiter des Geistlichen Lebens*, 305.
154. *Amb. Io.* (7) PG 91 1081C.
155. *Amb. Io.* (22) PG 91 1257AB.
156. See Riou, *Le monde et l'Église*, where he gives detailed attention to Lossky's interpretation.

typical design of Providence and are gathered in the economy of the Logos, which is the meeting place of the creature and creator. Thus, the doctrine of the logoi enables Maximus to respond to Origen's "cosmic economy" and Dionysius's ontology.

Maximus places particular emphasis on his doctrine of the logoi when he discusses the aspect of knowing God that is called natural contemplation (φυσική θεωρία). This term could be defined as spiritual or mystical contemplation of the logoi of creation, which leads to knowledge of the divine Logos according to which the world has been created and which is the final aim of acquiring knowledge of the divine Trinity.[157] Natural contemplation should be differentiated from direct unity with God (μυστική θεολογία), but Maximus does not make a clear distinction between natural contemplation and a direct "vision" of God. For him, natural contemplation (φυσική θεωρία) is not just rational knowledge; it also leads to some sort of participation in God. He often uses the phrase natural spiritual contemplation (ή εν Πνεύματι φυσική φυσι κή θεωρία).[158]

According to Maximus, the locus of the logoi is the Logos—the second hypostasis of the Trinity, which is the place where the Creator and creature meet. We understand the divine ideas and intentions through God the Son, and Christ reveals the logoi to the knower who has the task to become aware of their unity with the Logos. In Questions to Thalassius, Maximus elucidates John 6:54, where the Logos bids us to eat the flesh and drink the blood but does not speak of his bones.[159] There, Maximus maintains that the flesh of the Logos may be understood allegorically as knowledge (επιστήμη) that is given by the logoi of visible things. The blood that we drink is the deeper knowledge (γνῶσις) that is given to human beings by the logoi of invisible things, and the bones are the "logoi around God" (περί θεότητος λόγου), which are "beyond understanding," "transcend thought," and are "infinitely far away from every created thing."[160] Here, Maximus emphasizes the transcendent aspect of divine nature, although later in the same work, he speaks of the theosis (deification) that is granted to cre-

---

157. *Amb. Io.* (10) PG 91 1128C, *Q. Thal.* PG 90 296B.

158. See Völker, *Mesiter des Geistlichen Lebens*, 308.

159. *Q. Thal.* (35) PG 90 377 C. Laga-Steel, CCSG, 239. Here, Maximus's organic synthesis of typological and anagogical interpretations of the liturgy is evident. In this case, Maximus employs the Eucharistic symbolism that is typical of Dionysius, but is largely preempted in Orthodoxy following the iconoclastic controversy. See Sidorov, Творения, 211.

160. *Q. Thal.* (35) PG 90 377CD. Laga-Steel, CCSG, 239.

ated beings by grace. He identifies the bones of the Logos as an "unknown power" by means of which we attain theosis, and he calls them an unspoken theology (ἡ ἀπόρρητος θεολογία) when he writes: "The flesh of the Word is true virtue; the blood, ineffable knowledge; and the bones, unspoken theology."[161]

Elsewhere, Maximus relates "creatures" of God that have no beginning in time to divine qualities, such as goodness, life, simplicity, unchangeability, and everything that is essentially visible around him (καὶ ὅσα περὶ αὐτὸν οὐσιωδῶς θεωρεῖται) in which those creatures participate by grace.[162] God's essence is beyond the creature's capacities for knowing and beyond the divine economy that leads human beings toward theosis. Maximus surpasses the Neoplatonic influence that was passed on by Origen and Dionysius. He transforms the inherited philosophical tradition in a way that speaks to the Christian context with the help of Alexandrian metaphysics. Eternal divine ideas, which are brought to fruition in creation's time-space continuum, give way to an eschatology, which, according to Riou, involves nostalgia—although not in the chronological sense of longing for something that is past or future. Rather, this eschatology yearns for the actualization of the divine economy that is revealed to humankind through the drama of the Incarnated Christ and is achieved by each created being through a synergistic relationship with the Spirit.

In addition to the doctrine of the logoi, which helps clarify the connection between the Creator and creation, it is necessary to recall that a key conceptual framework of the divine-human relationship consists of three types of law. These include natural law; written law and Christ's spiritual law—which represents the end and fulfillment of the other types of law.[163] Of this framework, Maximus says: "Just as it is impossible to have light without the sun, the law cannot exist without the vital presence of wisdom that is the reason for its existence [and] fills the perceptive eyes of the soul with the light of the mind."[164]

The conception of the three laws raises the question of how the law of grace transcends the other two types of law, while the conception of the three incarnations reveals the manner in which the historical Incarnation surpasses the deity's incarnations in creation and scripture. The divine

---

161. *Q. Thal.* (35) PG 90 377D and PG 90 380AB. Laga-Steel, CCSG, 241.
162. *Cap. Gnost.* PG 90 1100CD, 1101A.
163. *Q. Thal.* (39) PG 90 392BC. Laga-Steel, CCSG, 259.
164. Ibid.

economy is not the central point here.[165] According to the ontological schema in which the Incarnation and the three laws are viewed in light of the priority given to God's Word, the divine Logos—who governs everything with wisdom and a longing for human salvation—leads human beings to that which is beyond the visible dimension so that they can recognize the logoi of creation and find Truth. Then, the Logos becomes incarnate and transforms human beings in a relationship of knowing that is free of corporeality. The theory of the three incarnations enables Maximus to describe, in yet another way, God's presence in the divine economy that is characterized by participation in the Word through virtuous living.

Noetic Knowledge: The Mind and Knowledge of the Truth

The Mind and Knowledge of Truth

   Nous and Noetic Ability

   Hexis

   Truth as a Boundary

   Knowledge and Philosophy

Noetic Knowledge: Introduction

The activity of the mind plays a key role here. As the limit of the mind's operations, Truth has a regulatory function; it is a corrective of cognitive activity. The purpose of this section of the book is to examine specific features of the mind's intellective capacities and to explore the relationship that Maximus's conceptions have to ancient models, as well as to the western philosophical tradition.

When pure knowledge and an emphasis on divine simplicity are involved, the mind's properties epitomize simplicity and unity. Simplicity and the mode of the mind's activity are comparable to God's divine simplicity and omnipresence. However, when the mind is occupied with knowing created things, its movement is compound and complex. Thus, we may conclude that when it has attained knowledge of the single, uncompounded divinity, the mind recognizes these properties in itself and

---

165. For a detailed discussion of this matter, see, Blowers, *Exegesis and Spiritual Pedagogy*, 121.

becomes one and simple, insofar as like knows like, whereas, knowledge of corporeal things alters the mind in accordance with constitutive thoughts about such things. The mind retains the forms of things—and their modes of existence—within itself, but the ultimate goal of the mind's movement is Truth to the activity of the mind, while reason (λόγος) governs the practical aspect of the soul, and leads it to a knowledge of Goodness.

The determinative factor in the two types of movement by the soul that are related to the mind and reason is the starting point or precursory condition (ἕξις) underlying this process. Hexis is central to Maximus's portrayal of the cognitive process. Thus, an objective of this part of the book is to highlight the role that personal choice, disposition, and attitude plays in the cognitive process. Hexis's special position between the power and energy—or between the possibility and actuality—of cognitive activity accords it a central place in Maximus's gnoseology. Hexis has three key connotations that contribute to its philosophical meaning: 1) possession/property, which is opposed to the notion of deprivation/deficiency (στέρησις); 2) a state of stability, which is opposed to the concept of a passing attitude (σχέσις), and 3) personal habit(s) acquired through experience or by disposition.

Maximus's definition of hexis can most accurately be encapsulated in the phrase "an inner personal state," or, to use an Aristotelian term, "disposition." The mind has a "learned ignorance," which is aware of the unattainability of its cognitive pursuits. Truth is the limit that determines the ultimate goal of knowledge. Truth reveals God in his essence, while Goodness reveals him through his energies. When ascending toward Truth, the mind does not know Truth itself; rather, it is cognizant of qualities that Maximus mentions: simplicity, uniformity, uniqueness, identity, indivisibility, immutability, insusceptibility to influence, truthfulness, infallibility, and immeasurability.

Truth is the limit, telos, and principle of the mind's activity. Goodness and Truth demonstrate the difference between essence and energy, which, in turn, reveals the disparity between eastern and western theology. In reference to God, essence and existence are not identical concepts. Consequently, the return to the creator does not enable creation to know God in his essence. This essence remains inaccessible to the human mind. The quest to know the logoi finally ends with the cessation of the mind's activity, and human beings become God by grace. Their souls and bodies are transformed, and their tropos of existence changes from the human realm to a supranatural mode of being in communion with the divine.

Human Knowledge According to Saint Maximus

As the limit of the mind's activity, truth has a regulatory function within the cognitive process, but it cannot be attained by thought or encompassed by concepts. However at this point, the topic under consideration is the mind's activity as one of the three motions of the soul. The intent is to present Maximus's conception of the sphere of the mind's activity; to identify the specific nature of this supreme cognitive act; and to place it in the context of the Confessor's total system of thought. Knowledge that is acquired through the mind comes from the operation of quintessential noetic elements, which include mind, wisdom, contemplation, knowledge, enduring knowledge, and truth (νοῦς, σοφία, θεωρία, γνῶσις, γνῶσις ἄληστος, and ἀλήθεια). Mind and reason are two movements of the soul that entail more than achieving their specific final goals; their activities are interrelated, with each higher level of knowledge including—rather than rejecting—the previous one. This is a characteristic motif in Maximus's work—and a key to his perception of the personal nature of the use of natural spiritual capacities. This is why so much emphasis is placed on hexis and gnomi in Maximus's work and in this part of the book. Things in the created world are not bad in and of themselves; it is their misuse that makes them so. It is not sensory knowledge that is sinful; it is the improper use of physicality that is evil.

This is also the reason Maximus places such strong emphasis on the purifying role and ascending trajectory that distinguish knowledge. The beginning of any approach to God involves purification of the soul-body composite, even at preliminary stages. Facing the Creator requires focusing the efforts of the soul's various activities that are scattered by the world's multiplicity, which constantly entices human beings to sink into inattention and ignorance. Yet, in the process of moving beyond the Origenist doctrine of apocatastasis, Maximus stresses the ascending trajectory of knowledge; there is no determination or predetermination involved in the movement whereby the soul falls away from the oneness of the perfect state and then goes back to the place established before the fall. Thanks to God's boundless love for human beings—and owing to their own efforts—the noetic picture is painted and completed in a different way in everyone. However, the cognitive path is not simply a return to God for anyone; it is an ascent, a design, a direction, and an aspiration, which are all aimed toward perfection.

In a sense, this perfection is divine Goodness and Truth. In his Mystagogia, Maximus portrays the Good as the end of rational activity and Truth as the telos of intellective activity. Goodness said to reveal God through his energies, and Truth is purported to disclose God in his essence. God is the Truth around which the mind moves ceaselessly and unfailingly. This movement never stops.[166] Yet, Maximus asserts that this Truth cannot be attained by the mind. The God who is Truth and Goodness gathers within himself all of the soul's powers and energies, which are grouped into five pairs: "mind and reason, wisdom and rationality, contemplation and practice, knowledge and virtue, and enduring knowledge and faith."[167] Thus, Maximus, in effect, defines Truth as the beginning and limit which constitute the principle that enables all of the mind's cognitive activities. It is the horizon that simultaneously opens and closes the field of knowledge. This understanding is comparable to a view that we find in Anselm's Summa Theologia, where it is said that "Truth is rightness, perceptible by the mind alone."[168]

Viewed from a noetic perspective, Truth turns out to be a corrective, rather than something that one comes across in the course of the soul's movements. Truth is something that already exists for anyone who is setting out on the cognitive path, since it eternally defines the beginning and end, as well as the meaning and purpose, of knowledge. Thus, the preceding section has not only analyzed the role of the soul's intellective activity and its schematic representation; it has also explored Maximus's understanding of the nature of truth. Thus, a distinction has been drawn between divine wisdom, which is the sphere of the mind's activity, and philosophy, which is the context of reason's activity.

We have already encountered the three motions of the soul that are identified as the mind (νοῦς), reason (λόγος), and the senses (αἴσθησις) in the Ambigua, where Maximus says: "The (first) one is simple and inexplicable, according to which the soul, moved in an unknowable way close to God, knows Him in a transcendent way that has nothing to do with any of the things that exist."[169] Maximus describes the mind as an unmixed singularity that seeks pure knowledge of divine simplicity. Nevertheless, when the mind is engrossed in knowledge of the created world, its motion is mixed and complex. Thus, Maximus asserts:

> Every thought certainly expresses several or at least a duality of aspects, for it is an intermediary relationship between two extremes

166. See *Myst.* (5) PG 90 678A.
167. Ibid.
168. Anselm, *Summa Theologica*, 16,1.
169. *Amb. Io.* (10) PG 91 1112D–1113A.

which joins together the thinker and the object thought of. Neither of the two can completely retain simplicity. For the thinker is a subject who bears the power of thinking in himself. And what is thought of is a subject as such or dwells in a subject, having inherent in it the capacity of being thought of, or else the essence whose faculty it is which formerly existed.[170] The mind (νοῦς) may be characterized as a power, or potency, that connects human beings with existing things by means of intelligible realities. Between the mind that thinks and the object of thought is the noetic capacity that links the mind with the observed thing. Therefore, the one who thinks and that which is thought of are subordinate to the intellect, which is the faculty that enables the mind to know. That is why we differentiate between the realms of mind (νοῦς), intellect (νόησις), and thought (νοούμενον). Yet, the mind's motion has two aspects. When the mind is directed toward spiritual knowledge of God, the mind's movement is simple, but when it is focused on the created world, its knowledge is complex. Divinity's unity and simplicity determine the nature of the knowledge that characterizes the mind's motion toward them. The relation between mind, intellect, and thought reveals the complex nature of the mind's activity and confirms that the intellect/intelligence (νόησις) consists of least two components: the one who thinks and the object of thought. The composition of particular thoughts also determines the nature of the mind's movement toward them. The mind's status as a center of knowledge depends on the state of its thoughts. In this regard, Maximus writes:

> When the mind receives the representations of things, it of course patterns itself after each representation. In contemplating them spiritually it is variously conformed to each object contemplated. But when it comes to be in God, it becomes wholly without form and pattern, for in contemplating the one who is simple it becomes simple and entirely patterned in light.[171] Alterations in the mind's noetic state happen on two planes, in conjunction with simple and complex motion. Therefore, in the course of knowing the one simple divinity, the cognizant mind recognizes these qualities and becomes one and simple itself; conversely, knowledge of created things alters the mind according to their manner (tropos) of being. The mind keeps its thoughts of things—their forms and modes of being—within itself. In this respect, memory (μνήμη), which

---

170. *Cap. Theol.* 1. (82) PG 90 1116C–1117.
171. *Car.* 3.97, PG 90 1045D.

may be described as the mind's capacity to preserve its thoughts of things, plays an important role here. The mind perceives the forms of objects and stores them in its memory. This type of knowledge involves the structure of things whereby the mind attains experiential knowledge of the divine.

However, knowledge is not restricted to empirical investigations of the external world that result in a posteriori knowledge. The mind can make abstractions out of that which is observed and can form thoughts by means of a spiritual mode of thinking, rather than an abstract process. These thoughts are just as valuable as those that have to do with concrete things. Kant calls such knowledge "intuitive," which means that it is a priori, rather than a posteriori.[172] According to Maximus, as the mind turns itself toward the life around it, it has an objective distance from the objects of thought because "things exist outside of the mind." Therefore, knowledge of existing things is not identical with their nature, although the mind's thoughts (νοήματα) about things are "inside of the mind." The Confessor concludes: "Things exist outside the mind while thoughts about them are put together inside. Therefore on it depends either their proper or improper use, for the abuse of things follows on the mistaken use of thoughts."[173]

The mind's motion in the course of acquiring knowledge of God is very different from the process described above, but it is not opposed to it. The mind's adherence to God enables a ray of divine knowledge to materialize. It is likely that Maximus inherited the terms "ray" and "ecstasy" (ἔκστασης) from Dionysius. In Maximus's work, the word "ray" represents the divine-human relationship that comes about through the unity of divine and human energies that is reached when human activities cease; this is a perichoresis of divine and human elements through the experience (πεῖρα) of real life in Christ. Maximus's source for the idea of ekstasis (ἔκστασης) appears to be the Neoplatonists. The Church Fathers make use of the moral meaning of this term, while for the Neoplatonists, ekstasis involves leaving the material realm, which is a burden that should be rejected. The mind, or soul, should leave the world of matter and become unified with the universal Soul from whom they have emanated.

Ekstasis has different connotations for Dionysius and Maximus. It entails rising above the sensible and the intelligible spheres. However, it does not involve leaving behind the world of matter as if it is something bad;

---

172. See Kant, *Critique of Pure Reason*, 1998.
173. *Car.* 2.73 PG 90 1008A.

rather, it is a means of entering into communion with the divine energies that sanctify matter and soul and deify body and mind. Maximus perceives that nature (which includes matter, flesh, and other aspects of creation) is good; it has a positive value because it was created by God. The world is not the result of an emanation from God, like it is in Neoplatonism; nor is it the result of the fall of human souls, like it is in Origen's estimation. Creation is an act of divine free will that is in keeping with the logoi of existing things that are within God.

In short, the mind has two types of knowledge. One of these involves knowledge of the created world, and the other consists of knowledge of God's energies. For human beings, the link between the thinking subject and the object of thought is determined by their own constitution in which soul and body are one. This unity means that human beings simultaneously belong to the sensible and the intelligible worlds. These contexts give rise to natural types of knowledge that correspond to the specific structure of human creatures. As the mind overcomes its inclination toward sensible and intelligible things, it ascends toward God and gives this facet of its knowledge to the soul. This sort of knowledge is not the result of a simple succession of noetic processes. Although the mind reaches this plane at its final stage, the course by which human beings ascend to God is quite complex insofar as it includes the capacities of soul and body that make up the unitary human nature. In the Mystagogia, Maximus presents the following outline of the soul's capacities and functions:

> The soul in general consists of an intellectual and a vital faculty, the former moved freely according to its will, the latter remaining without choice in accordance with nature. And the contemplative ... power belongs to the intellectual faculty [τό inθεωρητικόν] and the active power [τό πρακτικόν] belongs to the vital faculty. He called the contemplative power mind [νοῦς], the active power, reason [λόγος]. The mind is the mover [κινητικὸν] of the intellectual faculty, whereas reason provides [προνοητικὸν] for the vital faculty. The former, that is, the mind, is and is called wisdom [σοφία], when it directs its proper movements altogether unswervingly toward God. In the same way the reason the reason is and is called prudence [φρόνησις], when in uniting to the mind the activities of the vital faculty wisely governed by it in [a] sensible direction, it shows that it is not different from it but bears the same divine image by virtue as does the mind. [. . .] By means of it the mind, which, as we have said, is also called wisdom [σοφία] increasing in the habit of contemplation in the ineffable silence and knowledge

is led to the truth by enduring and incomprehensible knowledge [ἀκαταλήκτου γνώσεως].[174]Hexis

The ultimate goal of the mind's motion is Truth. Thus, Maximus associates truth with the mind's activity, while reason (λόγος) operates in the practical part of the soul to inaugurate a knowledge of Goodness. The definitive moment in the soul's movement in relation to the mind and reason is defined by the initial disposition or status (ἕξις) that underlies this process. In other words, an essential feature of the soul's motions of mind and reason is the starting point or habit (ἕξις) that gives rise to their activity. Hexis has three basic meanings that contribute to its philosophical substance: 1) possession/property, which is opposed to the notion of deprivation (στέρησις); 2) a state of stability, which is opposed to the notion of a passing relation (σχέσις); and 3) a personal habit, or disposition, that is acquired through experience.[175]

Maximus's definition of hexis can best be translated by the phrase "an inward personal state." This may be viewed as being the antithesis of a proposition, or thesis (θέσις), which is one of the concepts that is related to nature. In accordance with the Logos of being, all created beings are placed in a single order (τάξις) that defines their propositions (θέσις) and their relation (σχέσις) to others. In the works of both Aristotle and Maximus, ἕξις does not refer to something that is opposed to nature; rather, it is a fulfillment of the potential that is inherent in a predisposition. Hexis plays a mediating role and has a demonstrable potency. This summary suggests that the meanings which ἕξις has in the writings of Aristotle, the Stoics, and the Neoplatonists have important ramifications for Maximus's understanding of this concept. Yet, these various interpretations should be viewed from the Christian perspective. Hexis occupies an especially vital position in the New Testament, where it is mainly used in reference to deification that comes from the Holy Spirit. The influence of Christian authors like Clement of Alexandria, Origen, Evagrius, the Cappadocians, Nemesius of Emesa, and Dionysius should be mentioned here.

The Cappadocians, who inherited the term ἕξις from Aristotle, retain hexis as a middle term (μεσότις) between two extremes of deprivation (στέρησις) and energy (ἐνεργεία). Maximus uses the word ἕξις in different ways. It is primarily employed in relation to theosis, and is closely linked to the term ἐνεργεία. In addition, it is continually used in the triad that

---

174. Myst. (5) PG 91 672D–673A.
175. Kapriev, Introduction to the *Ambigua*, forthcoming in Russian.

presents the dynamic structure of existence as consisting of being, well-being, and eternal well-being (εἶναι, εὖ εἶναι, and ἀεὶ εἶναι). Maximus views ἕξις as a "constitutive characteristic" (συστατική ιδιώτες).[176] The meaning of this phrase is clarified by the Confessor's understanding of will (θέλησις). In describing the transition from will perceived as a natural potency to a qualified will (βούλησης or ποιὰ θέλησις) that has been personally shaped, Maximus asserts that the concrete will (γνώμη [gnomi]) is related to decision (προαίρεσης) in the same way that hexis (ἕξις) is related to energy (ἐνεργεία). Both γνώμη and ἕξις are defined as an inner longing or predisposition (ορέξις ενδιάθετος).[177]

In the other triad of becoming, motion, and stasis (γένεσις, κίνησης, and στάσις), ἕξις is related to the sphere of motion, where it is differentiated from ενέργεια. Drawing upon Cyril of Alexandria, Maximus connects gnomi (γνώμη) to the tropos of existence, which means that it is not related to the logos of nature. Gnomi and hexis are not completely identical, so, for instance, Christ does not possess gnomi. However, there is ambiguity in both hexis and gnomi since human beings have a hexis of virtue and vice, as well as a gnomi for virtue or vice. Thus, the possibility of deviating from the Good always exists. Maximus uses the affinity between ἕξις and γνώμη to describe inner predispositions. Indeed, in his estimation, habit and will are the main factors necessary for self-determination. Hexis has a place among potency, power, energy, and activity; it is located between intention and realization, between theory and practice, and between the inner and outer aspects of human life. Nevertheless, in contributing a personal dimension to the natural energies, it remains at the level of potential, rather than act.

Hexis gives being a dynamic, specific, and completely concrete characterization; thus, it may be regarded as being essential to the realization of human freedom. Through the "filter" of hexis, even natural powers and energies achieve personal concretization and definition. Potencies and energies are natural, but they are concretized in personal ways that are hypostatically defined and determined by the filter of hexis. This understanding accounts for the varying intensities of the natural energies of different people and even of the same person at different times. This personalization of natural energies makes every human being responsible for his/her own tropos of existence.

176. *Pyrr.* PG 91 352A.
177. *Th, Pol.* (1) PG 91 17C.

Maximus emphasizes that a stable disposition (κατ' ἕξιν παγίαν) enables human beings to participate in the virtues; attain well-being; and live in God according to the original logos of eternal well-being.[178] In this regard, Maximus differentiates between practical, contemplative and mystical forms of ἕξις, while noting that they all manifest unchangeability, stability, and steadiness. The practical feature of hexis is related to purification; the contemplative aspect of hexis (θεωρητικὴ ἕξις) is opposed to the disposition to ignorance (ἕξις τῆς ἀγνοίας); and the practical dimension of ἕξις ensures access to its contemplative form. Insofar as the realm of practice and contemplation should be differentiated, but not divided, Maximus speaks of «a predisposition to do good and knowledge (ἕξις τῆς ἀρετῆς καὶ τῆς γνώσεως).»[179] The highest level of hexis, which is available only to those who are deified, is the mystical stage (ἕξις μυστική). Maximus also presents the disposition to have love for God (ἕξις φιλόθεος) as being the highest of virtues.[180]

If ἕξις is considered at the ontological level in terms of the different planes of being, well-being, and eternal well-being, it may be inferred that at the first level, both hexis and gnomi are a result of human practice and will. Thus, by means of his teachings about ἕξις, Maximus rejects the opposition between human being's moral actions and the nature of their being. In particular with regard to well-being, these teachings shed light on the way individual human beings are connected to the Holy Spirit and demonstrates the personal tropos of existence. Well-being and theosis may be reached through ἕξις and the power of grace.[181] The energy of the Holy Spirit perceives and preserves human predispositions. This perception leads Maximus to emphasize that spiritual gifts and a divine life are shared by everyone in their own respective ways; that is, according to each creature's individual capacity for theosis.

It is necessary to note that perceiving one's ἕξις in its underlying logoi represents a gift of grace that not only acquires development by means of human beings' natural powers (δύναμις); the energy of deified persons comes from a disposition (ἕξις) whose source is energies of the Holy Spirit through whom a new mode of human nature is achieved. Human beings can participate in and become Godlike, but by means of the capacities of

---

178. *Amb Io.* (7) PG 91 1081B–1084B.
179. *Amb. Io.* (30) PG 91 1273C; *Q. Thal.* (64) PG 90 696B. Laga-Steel, CCSG, 189.
180. *Amb. Io.* (21) PG 91 1249B.
181. κατὰ τὴν ἕξιν διὰ τῆς χάριτος. See *Q. Thal.* (6) PG 90 281AB. Laga-Steel, CCSG, 71.

their own human natures—which is to say, according to the measure of perfection that is imparted by the logos and the capacities of concrete individuals.[182] Thus, by aspects of being human.

The soul's contemplative part comes from a contemplative hexis, while its practical aspect issues from its practical habitus. As was noted earlier, reason, which Maximus also calls prudence, ends in a state of Goodness through the practical actualization of the virtues and with the help of faith. True knowledge (ἐπιστήμη) of divine and human things, which is formed by the activities of the mind and reason, is incontrovertible knowledge and the limit (πέρας) of the whole Christian philosophy of God. The mind is privy to a "learned ignorance," which represents a recognition of the unattainability of the motions of knowing. Truth is the limit that defines the final goal of knowledge. Truth reveals God's essence, while Goodness discloses him through his energies and the divine economy.

Of course, Maximus's words make it clear phrases like "according to the essence" and "in the essence" do not refer to the transcendent, divine essence that is absolutely unachievable for human beings:

> Once it is in God, it is inflamed with desire and seeks first of all the principles of his being but finds no satisfaction in what is proper to himself [ἐκ τῶν κατ' αὐτόν], for that is impossible and forbidden to every created nature alike. But it does receive encouragement from his attributes [ἐκ τῶν περὶ αὐτόν], that is from what concerns his eternity, infinity, and immensity, as well as from his goodness, wisdom, and power by which he creates, governs, and judges beings.[183]

A little further on, Maximus advises:

> When you intend to know God do not seek the reasons [logoi] about his being [τοὺς κατ' αὐτὸν λόγους], for the human mind and that of any other being after God cannot discover this. Rather, consider as you can the things [logoi] about him [τοὺς περὶ αὐτόν], for example his eternity, immensity, infinity, his goodness, wisdom, and power which creates, governs, and judges creatures. For that person among others is a great theologian if he searches out the principles of these things, however much or little.[184]

Thus, the objects of the mind's knowledge are theophanies that have an anagogic function:

---

182. *Amb. Io.* (7) PG 91 1073C.

183. *Car.* 1.100; *Amb. Io.* (34) PG 91 1288AB. Petrov, Максим Исповедник, note 376, 183.

184. *Car.* 2.27.

Cognitive Faculties and Types of Knowledge

There are two supreme states of pure prayer, one corresponding to those of the active life, the other to the contemplatives. The first arises in the soul from the fear of God and an upright hope, the second from divine desire and total purification. The marks of the first type are the drawing of one's mind away from all the world's considerations, and as God is present to one, as indeed he is, he makes his prayers without distraction or disturbance [συναγαγεῖν τὸν νοῦν]. The marks of the second type are that at the very onset of prayer the mind is taken hold of [ἁρπαγῆναι τὸν νοῦν] by the divine and infinite light and is conscious neither of itself nor of any other being whatever except of him who through love brings about such brightness in it. Then, when it is concerned with the properties of God it receives impressions of him which are clear and distinct.[185] As it ascends toward Truth, the mind does not know Truth itself; rather, it is aware of the properties that Maximus mentions: simplicity, uniqueness, indivisibility, unchangeability, and ineffability. These qualities are primarily portrayed apophatically because divine greatness and "infinity [are] without quantity or parts and completely without dimension."[186] It is noteworthy that Truth is juxtaposed to divine wisdom in Maximus's writings. Truth is the limit, telos, and principle of the mind's activity. Goodness and Truth demonstrate the difference between essence and energy, which, in turn, reveals the disparity between eastern and western conceptions of God's essence and existence. Consequently, ascending to the creator does not mean that we know his essence. That is inaccessible to human thought.

The impossibility of knowing and attaining the divine essence has shaped Maximus's position regarding the logoi's accessibility to the mind. There are known to be logoi associated with visible things, invisible creatures, and every being, whether it be universal or particular. The Logos is the principle of the existence of each and every thing, insofar as every created being is willed by God and participates in him. Nevertheless, the logoi are unknowable. They enable contemplation of divinity—which involves seeing through their plurality and envisioning the one Logos that lies behind that multiplicity. However, they remain inaccessible to human knowledge.

In the end, the quest to know the logoi results in the cessation of all of the mind's activities, and human beings become God by grace. Their souls

---

185. *Car.* 2.6.
186. *Myst.* (5) PG 90 676C–677A.

and bodies are transformed, and their tropos of existence changes from human to divine. This is a transition from knowledge about everything that exists to a revelation of divine Goodness. Human nature remains unchanged by the act of knowing; only the mode of being is changed. The real goal of knowledge is this transfiguration into God. Reason is responsible for the discursive way of knowing God by gazing beyond visible forms and looking into the logoi of divine essences. This mode of knowing ultimately gives way to knowledge of the one Logos. Ascending toward knowledge of the divine logoi, which constitute God's energies and his means of proceeding in the world, leads to the pinnacle of perfection that distinguishes a virtuous life in God.

In this regard, "Truth [manifests its otherness] when the divine seems to be revealed in its Essence [ἐκ τῆς οὐσίας] for truth is something simple, unique, one, identical, indivisible, immutable, impassible, all-seeing, and wholly eternal."[187] These qualities are epithets for transcendence that reveal the finitude of knowledge. As the limit of the mind's activity, Truth has a regulatory function in the cognitive process, but it cannot be attained by thought or comprehended by conceptualizations. That is why Maximus goes on to say that the highest stage of knowing, which he identifies as enduring knowledge,

> is the perpetual and unceasing movement toward the knowable which transcends knowledge whose term is truth, the ultimate knowable. And what is admirable is how the enduring reality finds its end once it is included or comes to its term in the truth, that is, in God. For God is the truth toward which the mind moves continuously and enduringly and it can never cease its movement since it does not find any discontinuity there.[188] Truth's position as that which is unattainable, transcendent, and beyond the limits of knowledge does not permit us to relegate it to a subject-object relationship; rather, it provides the telos of the mind's activities. The mind reaches God through *docta ignorantia*, while reason is turned toward created things and knows them through scientific knowledge, understood in the Platonic sense. The rational composition of creation leads reason to realize that God is the source of goodness in the world, and this first step of knowing is where the purification of the multiplex nature of the forms that are perceived

---

187. *Myst.* (5) PG 90 677AB.
188. *Myst.* (5) PG 90 673D.

by the senses takes place. Yet, insofar as the goal of knowledge involves finding the Logos—the meaning, telos and purpose of it.

The mind directs its thoughts toward the one God and his virtues and unknowingly perceives [ἀγνώστως ἐπιβάλλειν] the unexpressed glory of his beatitude. In this process, reason becomes the interpreter and praises . . . thought and rightly thinks about the tropoi which are unified with him. Meanwhile the senses, dignified by reason and reproducing in the imagination the different powers and energies of the universe, share . . . the logoi of everything that exists [with the soul].[189] Maximus transforms the triad of νοῦς, διάνοια, and αἴσθησις into νοῦς, λόγος, and αἴσθησις. This shift from dialectical reasoning to logos means that this faculty is no longer exclusively associated with discursive thinking. Instead, διάνοια is related to the practice of speech, while logos is linked to immanent reason and the expressed word.[190] Maximus thus concludes that the mind moves around the divinity as contemplation of the Logos becomes clear knowledge to the νοῦς that gives birth to it. This is because "the Logos reveals the possibility of existing in God through the essence of the Mind toward which the practice of contemplation enables the human mind that seeks identity with God to grow in grace. In contemplation, the mind is freed from the diversity and immeasurable quantity of existing things and is joined with the divine One in the simplicity of stable and continuous movement around God."[191]

The path of knowledge and philosophy leads to the mind's reunion with God. It proceeds from sense perception, purification of the passions, and actualization of the virtues by dint of the mind's operations, but the superior stage of knowledge does not entail a rejection of the "inferior" steps. Every stage of the path to knowledge is part of the integral process that eventuates in divine-human communion. At the highest stage, the mind does not know God in terms of the categories of discursive thought; instead, God is known through absolute unity with him. Along with divine grace, the senses, reason, and the mind enlighten the soul. The knowledge that is achieved by the mind is the oeurve of the categories of wisdom, contemplation, knowledge, enduring knowledge, and truth (νοῦς, σοφία, θεωρία, γνῶσις, γνῶσις ἄληστος, and ἀλήθεια).

189. Amb. Io. (10) PG 91 1113D–1116A.
190. See Nemesius of Emessa, *On the Nature of Man*, 123.
191. Q. Thal. (25) PG 90 332AC. Laga-Steel, CCSG, 161.

Human Knowledge According to Saint Maximus

A unique feature of Maximus's thought is the realization that the soul's twofold capacities of mind and reason are not identical with achieving their final goal. Insofar as their activities are interrelated, the higher stage includes—rather than rejecting—the previous ones. This insight provides a key to Maximus's understanding of the personal nature of the use of the soul's natural capacities, which, in turn, shows why the emphasis on hexis and gnomi is of such great importance. Created things are not bad or good in essence, but only by virtue of the way in which they use their capacities. This means that their noetic faculties can lead human beings to well-being or can result in their falling into ill-being. This is why knowledge's purifying and perfecting role is so important to Maximus. The beginning of every ascent toward God involves a purification of the body-mind composite, which also happens at all preliminary stages.

Standing before the Maker requires focusing the efforts of the soul's various activities, which have been dissipated by the plurality of worldly things that constantly tempts human beings to sink into carelessness and ignorance. Yet, in the process of moving beyond Origen's doctrine of apocatastasis, Maximus emphasizes the role that knowledge plays in opening a path to perfection on which no determination or predestination is operative in the motion of falling away from and re-ascending to the perfect state. Due to God's boundless love for human beings and by virtue of their own efforts, the picture of knowledge is drawn and completed differently in every instance. However, the common feature in all cases lies in the fact that the process of acquiring knowledge is not just a return to God; it is an ascent, a "campaign," and a rush to perfection.

In a sense, this perfection is composed of divine Goodness and Truth. In his Mystagogia, Maximus regards Goodness as the end—the cessation—of discursive reasoning, and Truth as the telos of the operations of the mind. Regarding Goodness (ἀγαθὸν), Maximus writes: "In the opinion of etymologists the word which derives from 'to be in abundance,' 'or to be settled,' or 'to run' signifies that it is a bestower of being, continuation, and movement to all beings."[192] Goodness mirrors God's presence in the world. By means of the analogy that he draws between the essence of the virtues and the Logos, Maximus provides us with a formula for achieving knowledge of the divine. This does not entail knowing God as he is; it does not involve attaining divine thoughts and logoi, However, the vision of these which arises from contemplation that goes beyond what the

---

192. *Myst.* (5) PG 90 673D.

Cognitive Faculties and Types of Knowledge

senses can perceive opens the door to recognizing and participating in the One who is the reason for all of the world's plurality and diversity. That is why, in his manifestation as Goodness, God is the immanently achievable transcendent condition of each and every being. Truth is a limit belonging to a different order; it is the limit of thinking. The mind finds its telos in "the truth toward which the mind moves continuously and enduringly, and it can never cease its movement since it does not find any discontinuity there."[193]

Mind (νοῦς) and reason (λόγος) are the soul's first potencies, and the first energies of mind and reason are wisdom and prudence respectively. The mind is linked to divine knowledge, while reason is occupied by discursive thought. Practical philosophy (πρακτική φιλοσοφία) is involved in the work of reason, and the mind's activity is directed toward wisdom (σοφία). The mind sets wisdom in motion, which is its power (δύναμις), even as contemplation is its hexis (ἕξις). This is why it is necessary to emphasize the basic role that hexis plays in the process of attaining knowledge. The mind's energy and activity constitute knowledge (γνῶσις). "That enduring knowledge (of wisdom, contemplation, and knowledge, i.e., of potency, habit, and act) is the perpetual and unceasing movement toward the knowable which transcends knowledge whose term is truth."[194]

God is the Truth around which the mind moves unceasingly without falling into forgetfulness. This movement never ceases.[195] Yet, Maximus maintains that this truth cannot be attained by the mind. The God who is Truth and Goodness includes all of the soul's powers and energies, which Maximus groups into five pairs: "mind and reason, wisdom and rationality, contemplation and practice, knowledge and virtue, and enduring knowledge and faith."[196] Maximus also says that from the vantage point of unity, energy is a manifestation of the soul; reason is an embodiment of mind; prudence, of wisdom; practice, of contemplation; virtue, of knowledge; and faith, of enduring knowledge. These components are points of turning toward Truth and Goodness—that is, toward God. This state of being is the heart of divine knowledge (Θεία ἐπιστήμη), true knowledge, love, and peace where—and through which—theosis is completed.

---

193. *Myst.* (5) PG 90 673D.
194. *Myst.* (5) PG 90 676CD.
195. See *Myst.* (5) PG 90 676D.
196. See Bingaman-Nassif, *The Philokalia: Exploring the Classic Text of Orthodox Spirituality*, 331.

Maximus describes the mind as rest because it constitutes peace and unites the beginning of human activity with Goodness. Every spiritual pursuit must originate in Goodness, and every contemplative act aims at knowledge on account of Truth. Thus, the soul that is beyond creation and thought is able to move toward God, the One who is good and true and is above all essences and thoughts.[197] This is knowledge (ἐπιστήμη) of the knowable God, the divine attributes, and the actualization of the virtues. Yet, it is also knowledge that is truly grounded in Truth; thus, it provides the soul with an experience of the divine.[198] Regarding this state of knowing, Maximus writes:

> Thus when the soul has become unified in this way and is centered on itself and on God there is no reason to divide it on purpose into numerous things because its head is crowned by the first and only and unique Word and God. It is in Him as the Creator and Maker of being that all the principles of things both are and subsist as one in an incomprehensible simplicity. Gazing with a simple understanding on Him who is not outside it but thoroughly in the whole of reality, it will itself understand the principles [λόγοι] of beings and the causes why it was distracted by divisive pursuits before being espoused to the Word of God. It is by them that it is logically brought safe and sound to Him who creates and embraces all principles and causes.[199] Reason is linked to the logoi, insofar as it examines divine intentions that lie beyond the visible parts of existence; yet, it is the mind, rather than reason, that has truth as its final aim. Using reason to know the logoi may result in imperfect knowledge; mistakes can occur. This mode of knowledge is called "philosophy," while knowledge that is independent of the material and sensory spheres is called "wisdom." and stands in opposition to philosophical gnosis. Reason is not able to know the truth of divine simplicity, unity, and similar attributes; this is why it can only arrive at truth in an apophatic way. Thus, Maximus concludes that "it is preferable to speak about God using the categories of privation and negation [τὰς στερήσεις τε καί τὰς ἀποφάσεις—to use a term from Aristotelean logic], entirely rejecting any settlement or affirmation."[200]

---

197. *Q. Thal.* (54) PG 90 512B. Laga-Steel, CCSG, 447.
198. See *Myst.* (5) PG 90 673D.
199. Ibid.
200. *Amb. Io.* (17) PG 91 1224C.

Cognitive Faculties and Types of Knowledge

Although human reason should search for the divine logos of Truth, this quest does not mean that perfect knowledge of the created world and the Logos will follow. Rather, reason enables human beings to become acquainted with the structures (logoi) of existence and to attain a vision of the Logos that lies beyond their multiplicity. Such knowledge unfolds by means of a "deepening" that moves from visible forms to the truth or "flesh of the Logos." As the limit of knowledge, truth can be reached, but it can never be defined by a concept. However, the mind's knowledge proceeds in a different way. It is free of all materiality, and through wisdom, it reaches the highest possible sort of human knowledge, which is the true, enduring knowledge of the mind.

In Ambigua 10, Maximus interprets an excerpt where Gregory of Nazianzus discusses the saints' passage beyond matter and the passions. The result of their ensuing alignment with divine light is deification. Thus, those who truly want to live a philosophical life must transcend the material dyad by means of the unity that the mind derives from the Trinity. This vantage point suggests two ways to define "philosophy:" It is love of wisdom (φιλοσοφία), but it is also love of God (φιλώτεια).[201] Christian philosophy is based on divine wisdom. Thus, as has already been noted, reasoning is also oriented toward philosophy and the mind's activity, which is to say, toward divine wisdom. That is why true philosophy is impossible apart from God. The divine Logos, which is also divine Truth, is above all discourse, insofar as it does not relate to anything. Truth sets the limits and possibilities of such discourse, but truth itself serves a regulatory role; this dynamic opens the horizon of true philosophy.

Insofar as Christian and other philosophies are linked to natural reason, some sorts of knowledge may be imperfect and even contrary to the truth. This is an intrinsic feature of philosophical work, where, truth is seen "in a mirror dimly" (1 Cor 13:12). Yet, divine philosophy is higher; it is not as easy to reach this philosophy as it is to practice the virtues by which we attain well-being in Christ. Such wisdom is more an experience of divine life than a product of working with images and representations. This way of knowing is above all of the powers and energies of the human mind. This knowledge is conveyed by natural energies of God that are supranatural for the mind. This type of philosophy is supreme wisdom, the highest knowledge, and the source of—and reason for—everything. Only from its

---

201. Amb. Io. (37) PG 91 1296B.

perspective is it possible to relate the thinking subject to its object in a fitting context, since, as Maximus writes,

> divinity is absolutely indivisible because it is entirely inquantitative; it is entirely inquantatitve because it is absolutely simple; it is absolutely simple because it lacks body, and it lacks body because of [its] boundlessness; it is entirely boundless because it does not move; it is [entirely immovable] because it is beginningless; it is without beginning because it is not born; it is not born because it is perfect and only one; it is only one because it is absolutely unrelated and therefore absolutely unknowable and the only limit for any knowledge [needed] for .. moving toward it in a beautiful way.[202]

In conclusion, nous lies at the core of the mind's activity. Its potency is wisdom, but that fact does not mean that they are identical. The mind triggers wisdom, and contemplation becomes a hexis of the mind. This hexis not only includes speculative activity that is directed toward God; it also involves the soul's ongoing occupancy of this habitus. It is a capacity that turns the mind toward constant contemplation of God. Knowledge constitutes the energy of the mind because enduring knowledge passes through all of the limits of time, space, quality, and quantity. Through it, the mind achieves the constant motion around the sort of truth that Maximus envisions in this way: "With the word 'truth' he points to the final limit of all knowing and of those who would know him as the beginning and end of all existence. [This limit] gathers all existing things together as the Truth, Beginning and End of existence; Truth victorious, bringing all creatures to grow toward the deity."[203] Moreover, in a related scholium, we read:

> They say that the telos of active virtue is Goodness, which is realization of the divine act. God leads the rational soul to this . . . And the telos of the contemplative part is Truth—which is indivisible knowledge of everything that is around God. The mind rises toward this Truth where all sensible thought ceases. In this knowledge, we are able to find true dignity "in the image."[204]

Maximus maintains that the end of the soul's practical aspect is pure goodness, and that wisdom, which he identifies as pure truth, is the telos of the motion of the soul's capacity for knowing[205] Purified

---

202. *Amb. Io.* (17) PG 91 1232B.
203. *Q. Thal.* (54) PG 90 513A. Laga-Steel, CCSG, 451.
204. Ibid.
205. Ibid.

of sensory images, the mind leads reason—which compasses the soul's essential beginning—to God. The conjunction of mind and reason in goodness and truth reveals the glory that is evident "in likeness." For Maximus, achieving the likeness of the image is a unified process of ascent that involves the interaction of reason and mind. In one of the scholia, Maximus connects the image to gnosis and links the likeness to praxis.[206] However, in all cases, achieving true knowledge is associated with the activities and efforts of the entire human constitution, which is made up of a unified composite of soul and body.

As a power of the soul, the mind is different than reason, but it is not isolated from the other faculties of knowing. The mind is not the only "true" part of human beings who find themselves in the sensible realm and try to turn back to their rightful home and the state of human wholeness wherein they are called to utilize their own unity to restore the unity of the created world that has been split asunder by sin. Thus, Maximus defines truth as the beginning and limit/telos/end. It is the principle that makes all of the mind's knowledge possible, and the horizon that simultaneously opens and closes the field of knowledge. Maximus's view is shared by Anselm of Canterbury who defines truth as "rightness perceptible by the mind alone [rectitudo mente sola perceptibilis]."[207]

Considered in relation to knowledge, truth may also be viewed in terms of Plato's observation that truth is not just the final goal of knowledge; it is also the precondition of all knowing. In other words, truth is not just knowledge; it is the transcendent necessity for the possibility of knowledge. It is at the end and at the beginning of the process of knowledge.[208] In Maximus's estimation, truth belongs to the world, insofar as it guides the knower and demarcates the path to knowledge. It exists beyond creation and is of another order.[209] In this sense, it is the "other" that provides the limits of cognitive activity. Truth becomes a corrective of knowledge, rather than something we discover through knowledge. Truth already exists in revealed and written forms; thus, it eternally defines the beginning, end, and meaning of our knowledge.

---

206. *Q. Thal.* (1) PG 90 270A. Laga-Steel, CCSG, 47.

207. Anselm, *Summa Theologiae*, Part 1, Question 16, Article 1 Objection 3. Anselm of Canterbury, *De Veritate*, 29.

208. See Boiadjiev, Кръговрат на духа, 1998.

209. *Amb. Io.* (10) PG 91 1165C.

4

Levels of Knowledge

Practical Philosophy: Introductory Observations
   The Virtues
   Will and Knowledge: *Gnomic Will*

PRACTICAL PHILOSOPHY: INTRODUCTORY OBSERVATIONS

This chapter provides an analysis of the levels of knowledge that constitute the trichotomic cognitive structure which Maximus inherited from Evagrius and reformulated. The topic under consideration is the different spheres of activity that typify the soul's capacities. One of the goals of this discussion is to demonstrate the way in which these three motions become a single movement on the path of knowing, but, the main objective is to strictly demarcate the various cognitive steps whose common pursuit intersects on the path that leads to knowledge of God.

Praxis, which Maximus calls "practical philosophy" and, on occasion, "ethical philosophy", constitutes the first level of spiritual life. It is perceived to involve keeping the commandments and engaging in ascetic training. Such discipline does not necessarily entail only bodily abstinence; it may also involve any other activity by which human beings overcome the passions and purify the mind, body and soul by practicing the virtues. Since, according to Maximus, keeping the virtues is the ultimate goal, living virtuously may be viewed as being the main component—the very essence—of praxis. Maximus also maintains that attaining virtue is not a one-time process that ends in a blissful life in divine Goodness. Overcoming the passions and practicing the virtues is an ongoing pursuit that requires constant effort on the part of human beings. Achieving a virtuous life and continuing in goodness involves achieving a sustainable hexis and a specific gnomic aptitude for goodness.

This part of the book also presents an explication of Maximus's understanding of gnomic will. In the Confessor's work, gnomi (γνώμη) is a central concept that adds a personal dimension to cognitive activity, but it is a term that is extremely difficult to translate. The word "gnomi" is associated with free will, opinion, and individual positions, and Maximus maintains that such will is an innate feature of human (and divine) nature. It is a distinctive constitutive element of any rational, contemplative being. "Gnomi" refers to a hypostatic use of the will, to a personal aptitude or disposition for using this naturally given ability.

Yet another theme in this section of the book involves faith. The question of the relationship between rational activity and faith is resolved by praxis. Faith somehow envelops cognitive aspirations, thus imparting the beginning of reason's activity, or so Augustine seems to suggest when he declares: "I believe in order to understand."[1] Faith thereby carries out the cognitive activity associated with praxis by exercising its own activity through the Logos, as it emanates from the divinity and returns us to God—who is with us throughout this process. If the Logos bestows faith, our faith is designed to return us to the Logos, as we acquire knowledge of the logoi and practice the virtues that constitute the Word. Thus, it is through the virtues that faith links the seeking creation to its beginning and to the Goodness that is present in the world through the logoi. Therefore, faith cannot be thought of apart from the spheres of practice and contemplation. Maximus notes that in the structure of the spiritual gifts, faith and enduring knowledge form one of the five pairs of the energies of the soul that lead it to the one and only dyad, which consists of Goodness and Truth. When humankind falls away from faith, the entire cognitive edifice collapses. Thus, due to its central place in the life of the knower, Maximus puts faith at the end of the cognitive process of reasoning. By practicing the virtues, human beings find their logos, which is in God, or within the logos of well-being. This final step of the soul's practical activity corresponds to the attainment of a blissful life. Here, a distinctive feature of Christian philosophy is evident in the paradoxical dynamic where faith is both beginning and end.

1. Augustine, *Sermo* 43, 7, 9:PL 38, 257–58.

With this framework in mind, let us turn to the proposed consideration of practical activity, where askesis (practicing the virtues), faith, and reason operate in unity.

PRACTICAL PHILOSOPHY AS PRAXIS

The Logos hidden in the Ten Commandments "incarnates" itself in us, descending in practice [πρᾶξις] and re-ascending with us in knowledge [γνῶσις].

—*Quaestiones et Dubia* 61

The term "praxis" (πρᾶξις, πρακτική) is used extensively by Maximus and often forms a pair with "*theoria*" or "contemplation" (θεωρία). This expression is reconciled with the early Christian perspective of Origen and Evagrius. In eastern Christian spirituality, praxis is understood to be the first stage of spiritual life, while theology (θεολογία) is the third stage. Taken together, praxis, theoria, and theologia are steps of human spiritual development that constitute the ladder of knowledge and facilitate the development of self-unity during the pursuit of divine-human communion.[2]

As noted above, Maximus portrays the first stage of spiritual life as including the practices of observing the commandments and of engaging in ascetic discipline. Such discipline not only entails a privation of the flesh; it also includes all of the activities by which we fight the passions; purify the mind, soul, and body; and actualize the virtues. Since, according to Maximus, this sort of actualization is the ultimate goal of human life, living virtuously may be regarded as the key element—the essence—of praxis. For Maximus, praxis is not merely a preparatory stage in the process of acquiring the knowledge that is needed to reach the contemplative level.

Praxis has its own independent value and meaning, which have an important role to play until the highest point of spiritual life is reached. Praxis is not just the soul's preparation for a spiritual life, even though, as Maximus emphasizes, such a life is impossible unless a passionless, virtuous life has been attained.[3] Praxis is also an obligatory aspect of the continuous fulfillment of acts of contemplation. The fact that Maximus often links praxis

---

2. My preference of the term "divine-human communion," instead of "deification," is based on the work of Papanikolaou, *Mystical as Political*, 4.

3. Regarding a virtuous life see, Q. Thal. (55) PG 90 548BC. Laga-Steel, CCSG, 501. Concerning a passionless life, see Q. Thal. (50) PG 90 468D. Laga-Steel, CCSG, 383. Q. Thal. (54) PG 90 524BC. Laga-Steel, CCSG, 463.

and contemplation reveals that for him, they constitute an indivisible pair and are fundamentally one in nature. It is likely that this pair is said to be one because of the unity of human nature; yet, it also has two components because human nature is divided between the active practice of the virtuous life and the pursuit of contemplation. Nevertheless, Maximus declares that making them one by the Spirit, the Word calls them one man.[4]

Thus, one activity ceaselessly conditions and confirms the other. Praxis that does not develop into contemplation remains incomplete, and conversely, every attempt at contemplation that does not adhere to praxis is destined to fail because, as Maximus says, "the one who looks for God through contemplation without praxis does not find him. . . . Honest and pure is the person who achieves πρᾶξις through knowledge and contemplation that is not lacking in practice."[5] Elsewhere, he asserts that the mystery of salvation shows that praxis is one with active contemplation. Furthermore, the Confessor maintains that contemplation is a mysterious, mystagogical πρᾶξις and that "practice itself is contemplative, and not without a share in the grace of reason"[6]

Gregory the Theologian, who is one of Maximus's sources, says that the practical efforts of the faithful constitute one of the paths of devotion which enable human beings to ascend to God.[7] Maximus similarly writes: "The faithful should search for divine knowledge and its decoration of virtue . . . it is immeasurable to restrain from evil and ignorance and that is related to the successful end of knowledge and virtue. . . . Together they radiate the incomparable glory of God"[8] Therefore, it is not surprising that Maximus acknowledges that πρᾶξις plays a crucial role in the ascent to knowledge. He also looks at the purification of the passions from a gnoseological perspective, which focuses on acquiring virtue and entering into communion with the second hypostasis of the Trinity, the divine Logos. Virtue is where God and human beings meet, where we see the tantum-quantum principle of God descending and human beings ascending in divine-human communion. "The soul's task is to assimilate the body to God, making it rational

---

4. *Q. Thal.* (3) PG 90 273CD. Laga-Steel, CCSG, 57.

5. *Q. Thal.* (48) PG 90 440A. Laga-Steel, CCSG, 341.

6. *Amb. Io.* (30) PG 91 1273B. (Trans. by Maximos Constas).

7. Gregory of Nazianzus, Пет Богословски слова [Five Theological Orations], note to Oration 27, 140.

8. *Q. Thal.* (34) PG 90 376D–377. Laga-Steel, CCSG, 235. *Q. Thal.* (54) PG 90 512B. Laga-Steel, CCSG, 447.

through the exercise of the virtues, even 'mediating through itself the creator as an inhabitant of the body.'"[9]

The image of a paradise of virtues has its roots in the Alexandrian tradition. Philo is the thinker who interprets the passage from Genesis that gives rise to this idea in an allegorical way and calls paradise a "symbol of virtue."[10] Origen and Gregory of Nyssa carry this line of interpretation and typological explanation of the text even further. In Gregory's writings, there are particularly clear examples of the allegorical interpretation that conveys the idea of a paradise of virtues. The trees in paradise are the virtues; four rivers represent the four cardinal virtues, and so forth. Maximus offers his own interpretation of this matter. In contrast to the ethereal picture outlined above, he portrays a paradise that is on earth and is related to the idea of human virtue. Maximus regards this earthly paradise as an achievement of human beings in their capacity as mediators who unify earth and heaven (which, as we have seen, is one of the five divisions that characterize the hypostasis of existence.) Since human beings could not carry out this task, God descended to the human realm to reveal a paradigm for accomplishing the work of uniting heaven and earth by means of virtuous living. The way to paradise is revealed by Christ, who overcomes the division within the universal hypostasis.[11]

Maximus considers this reconnection of paradise and the moral aspect of the rest of inhabited earth to be a prefiguration of the beatitude that has been promised after our resurrection. The paradise of virtue is not an allergory of paradise. In a moral and gnoseological sense, it is a manifestation of the oneness of the Logos and the logoi of the whole of creation. Thus, Maximus interprets a passage from Gregory the Theologian that says: "If you are crucified together with [Christ] as the thief, know God as a wise man."[12] Maximus views the thief as a man who is subjugated to sensible reality, but also as someone who endures pain following this choice. Thus,

---

9. *Amb. Io.* (7) PG 91 1092B 12–15, trans. Lollar.

10. Phil. Allegor. Lib. I, 33.

11. *Amb. Io.* (41) PG 91 1309A: Ἐν γὰρ Χριστῷ Ἰησοῦ, φησίν ὁ θεῖος Ἀπόστολος, οὔτε ἄρρεν οὔτε θῆλυ. Εἶτα τήν καθ' ἡμᾶς ἁγίασας οἰκουμένην διά τῆς οἰκείας ἀνθρωποπρεποῦς ἀναστροφῆς μετά θάνατον εἰς τόν παράδεισον ἀπαραποδίστως χωρεῖ, καθώς τῷ λῃστῇ ἀψευδῶς ἐπηγγείλατο, Σήμερον, φήσας, ἔσῃ μετ' ἐμοῦ ἐν τῷ παραδείσῳ.

12. *Amb. Io.* (53) PG 91 1372C. ("If as a thief you should be crucified with Him, then as one who is grateful you should acknowledge God" in trans. by Maximos Constas. At the time of writing the book the translation of Ambigua by Fr. Maximos was not yet available and that is why alternative translations are present.)

the thief knows the Logos that exists in the logoi of the world and suffers by virtue of the Incarnation. His suffering is thereby transformed by the passive and active actualities of vita practica, and the thief enters the land—the paradise—of real knowledge with the Logos whereby he knows the reason for being. Maximus writes:

> The wise or prudent thief, crucified with Christ—this is every human being that suffers [πάσχων κακῶς] for his sins, as a guilty one that suffers together with the innocently suffering for Him Word and bearing his own state with gratitude knowing that with him is the Word. . . . This happens with him, suffering for sins . . . transformed from prudently gratitude in self chosen virtue through which he, together with Word enters the land of knowledge, i.e., in paradise.[13] In contrast, because of his iniquitous γνώμη, the imprudent thief is not able to know the Logos of righteousness who suffers for him out of love for human beings (φιλανθρωπία):

> The imprudent thief, being hostile . . . does not know the right Word, that suffers for Him for His love of humans, but he rejects the pondered judgment. Since he did not know the Word . . . and he did not ask for mercy for his sins, he stays estranged for the Kingdom of God, without having the promise of ever reaching it.[14] In the same passage, Maximus offers another interpretation of the Theologian's words. Each of us has a dual nature composed of soul and body. Thus, we are crucified according to the law of the flesh, like the imprudent thief, who resists the virtues, and the law of the spirit, like the prudent thief, who accepts the salvific Logos with whom he enters the banquet hall, where he experiences an outpouring of knowledge and is entirely liberated from the carnality (κατά σάρκα) of thoughts.[15] Like the imprudent thief,

---

13. *Amb. Io.* (53) PG 91 1372D. Trans. by Maximos Constas: "A grateful thief crucified together with Christ is every man who, in suffering ill treatment because of sins for which he is to blame, suffers ill-tratment together with the Word [...], and endures this with gratitude. [...] This is how the mortification of body's members, brought about by circumstances, comes full circle for someone suffering through sin: through grateful thanksgiving it is transformed into voluntary virtue, absolving him of his many debts incurred by sin, so that he lawfully enters with the Word into the realm of knowledge, by which I mean paradise..."

14. Ibid.

15. *Amb. Io.* (53) PG 91 1373B. Trans. by Maximos Constas "The ungrateful thief is one who, suffering ill treatment because of sin, for which he is to blame, fails to recognize because of his contentious frame of mind, the Word of righteousness, who in His love for mankind is blamelessly suffering together with him.[...] And because he failed to

the law of flesh is opposed to the logos of virtue, while the law of the spirit is viewed as being like the prudent thief and the saving Logos whose practical modes of being (tropoi) enable them to enter into the realm of full knowledge. In short, viewed in terms of praxis, life may be portrayed as manifesting such ways of being according to the logos of individual human beings and the role of the Logos who, as a consequence of his Incarnation through the virtues, countenances complete unity between creation and creator in paradise.[16]

Evagrius and his successors are the main source of Maximus's threefold gnoseological structure. In Evagrius's work, the process whereby human beings attain perfection involves three steps, which begin with practice (πρακτική). Classical philosophers associate this term with the soul's active life and contrast it with theory (θεωρητική), which signifies the soul's contemplative capacity. In Evagrius's estimation, practical activity is a way of cutting off the passions, which is characterized by efforts to follow the commandments, renounce the passions, and practice the virtues.[17] For his part, Maximus emphasizes the preparatory nature of this spiritual stage. Like Evagrius and the broader tradition concerning the operation and development of practical life, Maximus regards this step as constituting preparation for true knowledge. For him, it also (and primarily) entails a victory over the passions.

Through praxis, human beings rise above sensual flesh, as true knowledge transports them beyond the created world. Regarding this ascent, Maximus declares: "This mind is to be found above all visible creatures, since it is immediately carried above in a state of supreme beatitude and leaves behind all of the intermediate objects beyond which it had grown."[18] These words suggest that actualizing the virtues entails overcoming the passions, which is an act that corresponds to purifying wrong thoughts that impinge on the soul's contemplative activities. The Confessor contin-

---

recognize the Word [....] and because he did not ask forgiveness for his faults, he is sent away estranged from the kingdom... "

16. Maximus's fourth interpretation of this theme does not add to the analyses presented above. It develops the idea that the prudent thief disciplines the passions and accomplishes virtuous activity by means of reason and knowledge. It also stresses that it is possible to enter paradise—both here and in the world beyond—only through the Logos.

17. Louth, *Maximus the Confessor*, 35. In Maximus's writings, the practical part of the soul is not only related to ascesis. It is involved in the preparatory stage of knowing the logoi and is called "practical philosophy."

18. Q. *Thal.* (51) PG 90 481D. Laga-Steel, CCSG, 405.

ues: "And then with God's permission, disgraceful passions immediately turn against praxis, violating the pure until they are torn apart, and lying thoughts enter into the contemplation of things, obscuring the process of knowledge." Completing the circuit, Maximus adds: "When a mind that loves God . . . rejects all antagonistic powers with the help of virtue and knowledge which have been acquired through practical and contemplative devotion, it is crowned with absolute power against the spirits of evil wiles."[19]

Unlike Evagrius and his other predecessors, Maximus does not restrict his teachings regarding the practical life to overcoming the passions, nor to efforts to establish a type of inner balance in the soul. For Maximus, practical activity always has a positive side, which is dedicated to the actualization of virtues that actively manifest the two aspects of the "new covenant" alluded to in John 15:13. Thus, the many actions and functions of the practical life are viewed as an incarnation of the divine Logos. This is why the first stage of the spiritual life does not allow itself to be reduced to a mere moment of preparation or a destructive act of freeing the soul from the passions. Its significance lies in the act of establishing the foundations of real knowledge, and it includes both a rejection of the passions and a process of discipline and growth. As noted previously, even if the sensory dimension is not evil in and of itself, misusing it causes human beings to fall from their original status and tropos of being. Seeing through the logos of the sensible realm means re-visioning our own logos where a way to turn back to God is hidden.

For Maximus, the purification and "repair" of the human hypostasis takes place in the present moment—and in this world—thanks to "practical philosophy," as he calls it. The mind ascends toward God by means of contemplative insight.[20] Thus, in Chapters on Knowledge, Maximus necessarily concludes that persons who take up the practical life receive an incarnation of the Logos through the virtues. However, this type of incarnation is limited to the sensible world; it is contemplation and spirituality that help it reach the Father. Regarding this quest, Maximus says:

> For those who search according to the flesh after the meaning of God, the Lord does not ascend to the Father; but for those who seek him out in a spiritual way through lofty contemplations he does ascend to the Father. Let us, then, not always hold him here

19. Q. Thal. (52) PG 90 493BC. Laga-Steel, CCSG, 419.
20. Q. Thal. (3) PG 90 273A. Laga-Steel, CCSG, 57.

below though he came down here out of love to be with us. Rather, let us go up to the Father along with him, leaving behind the earth and what is earthly. . . . For without the Word, it is impossible to come to the Father of the Word.[21]

Here, Maximus is influenced by Evagrius, but he expands the practical realm by means of a specification, which, to some extent, can also be found in Evagrius's writings. He maintains that the practical way of existing includes the proper use of the rational faculty. Unlike his predecessors, Maximus points out that a virtuous life not only demonstrates a victory over the passions and reveals the docility of the soul's passionate aspect; it also involves human beings' rational nature as such. The activities of the practical soul are related to the functioning of the rational component (λόγος), while contemplative acts are dependent on the operation of the mind (νοῦς). In noting that praxis leads to prudence (φρόνησις) and contemplation gives rise to the wisdom (σοφία), Maximus uses the conventional division of the soul's capacities, so that its various capabilities, powers, and potencies can be understood. He emphasizes that the practical part of the unified soul encompasses a rich range of activities, which not only includes reason, but also incorporates prudence (reasoning), praxis, virtue, and faith. Furthermore, he observes that the contemplative part of the soul includes mind, wisdom, contemplation, knowledge, and enduring knowledge.[22]

In this context, Maximus introduces the image of "motion" as a way of speaking of the soul's activities.[23] The telos of the soul's first motion is Goodness; the aim of the second motion is Truth; and together, they reveal God. Thus, the spheres of vita practica and vita contemplativa are interrelated and cannot be separated—insofar as both of them ultimately lead to divine qualities and identify human creatures as rational beings. Maximus's vision of the fundamental interrelationship that exists between the soul's practical and theoretical activities is a key aspect of his work. His paradigm of the process of knowing is based on the interaction that goes on between body and soul in the course of the latter's (re)turn to and envisioning of God. Yet, it also is grounded in the relationship that links human virtues and qualities to divine attributes. Maximus emphatically emphasizes the strong connections that exist between reason and the mind, prudence (reasoning) and wisdom, contemplation and practice, knowledge and virtue,

21. *Cap.Gnost.* 2.47, PG 90 1145B.
22. See *Myst.* (5) PG 91 673B.
23. See *Amb. Io.* PG 91 1112D–1113A.

and enduring knowledge and faith, relating these to the divine attributes that reveal God in the energies of Goodness and the essence of Truth.[24]

This important feature of Maximus's thought is the reason scholars who interpret his writings often stress the division that leads to unity. The issue of unity within division, which characterizes the process of descending from and re-ascending to God, is not just a beautiful intellectual construct. Regarding this matter, Thunberg maintains that it is impossible to find Evagrius's division of the soul's "higher" and "lower" parts in Maximus's work.[25] Vita practica and vita contemplativa are separate and dissimilar activities of the soul, but they are interrelated by and in the common act of knowing. In other words, praxis and contemplation are two aspects of the path that leads to unity through knowledge. The activities of vita practica and vita contemplativa are features of human nature, and the defining moment for both is communion with the divine Logos. In Questions to Thalassius, Maximus describes the relationship that these two stages of spiritual life evince in the course of their transition from vita practica to contemplation and on to mystical union.[26] The following passage demonstrates that knowledge and virtues are unalterably united in the life of the discerning seeker:

> True knowledge is identified as being active because it is based on, and associated with, good action—that is, with the achievement of virtue—in contrast to incomplete, "partial" knowledge that is without action [erga] and with insufficient ascetical preparation. Furthermore, it is described this way because it involves a true perception of the divine illuminations that are experienced by monks in a spiritual manner that contrasts with a theoretical, superficial knowledge of words that is without a deep, heartfelt relationship to its content and without a real sense of the infinitely graceful power of heavenly illuminations and the pleasure of communion with God. The latter represents an understanding and a continuation of the former. Real knowledge is possible only for a virtuous contemplator.[27] Once again, this quotation reveals that unity is above diversity; our eyes should learn to see this unity before distinguishing between things. In other words, although

---

24. See *Myst.* (5) PG 91 676A.

25. See Thunberg, *Microcosm and Mediator*, (1965); Törönen, *Union and Distinction*, (2007).

26. *Q. Thal.* (Introd.) PG 90 245C. Laga-Steel, CCSG, 19.

27. *Q. Thal.* (Introd.) PG 90 248D. Laga-Steel, CCSG, 25. (author's trans.).

praxis and theoria are said to be independent ways of achieving the same goal, Maximus presents the two types of wisdom—that is, practical philosophy and divine wisdom—in such a way that they are united in the ontological unity of human existence. It is this manifestation of ontological unity that characterizes gnosis. Even if this process of perfection begins with faith and practice, as it does in the Alexandrian tradition, and continuous through contemplation which is connected with the divine wisdom that leads to "comm-union" with God, it is beyond all knowledge and beyond anything that human capacities can achieve.

In Maximus's works, we read that the Logos is formed in us as it descends with us into praxis.[28] This "incarnation" is followed by an ascent through knowledge that culminates in deification. In the second century of Chapters on Knowledge, Maximus poetically says: "In the active person the Word grows fat by the practice of the virtues and becomes flesh. In the contemplative it grows lean by spiritual understandings and becomes as it was in the beginning, God the Word."[29] As Clement of Alexandria noted before Maximus, contemplation is also a practice, but this praxis goes on within the spirit. This is why pseudo-ascetical spiritualism is completely alien to Orthodox theologians. For them, the passionless state that is a necessary precondition of contemplation is not nirvana; instead, it is an elevated work of the spirit that leads to transformed being and a new stage of growing in knowledge.[30]

In *Questions to Thalassius*, Maximus once again stresses the interrelationship between the activities of the soul that involve knowledge and virtue when he writes, "through knowledge, the mind reaches God directly, and as spiritual work, virtue leads it away from the changeability of the existing things."[31] Likewise, the *Commentary on the Our Father* says: "We thus make of the body rendered spiritual by its virtues a messenger of the soul, and by its steadfastness in the good we make the soul a herald of God."[32] Thus, we human beings should learn to use our reason in practice, so that

---

28. See *Qu. D.* (142) CCSG 10, 101.13–21.

29. *Th. Ec.* (2.37) PG 90 1141C.

30. See *Q. Thal.* (Introd.) PG 90 249C. Laga-Steel, CCSG, 25.; Творения, 321. Papanikolaou and Hamalis also identify love as acquired virtue and an act of faith and reason in "Toward a Godly Mode of Being," 277.

31. *Q. Thal.* (45) PG 90 417D. Laga-Steel, CCSG, 305.

32. *Pater* PG 90 877A.

we may not only be united with the angels through virtue, but may also become reconciled with God through knowledge.

In the Mystagogia, Maximus affirms that the mind, reaching the final limit of its efforts—that is, Truth itself—is not able to grasp it in thought or image; nor does the mind cease its movement "since it does not find any discontinuity there."[33] The movement toward divine-human communion requires the effort of the entire soul. Wisdom, contemplation, and knowledge are directed toward the realization of Truth. Prudence (reasoning), practice, virtue, and faith all end in Goodness. Both Truth and Goodness empower the soul's νοῦς and λόγος, which are regarded as theory (Θεωρητικῶν) and practice (πρακτικῶν), respectively. These potencies are directed toward the place where God, who is both Truth and Goodness, is revealed. Maximus maintains that realizing the virtues is not a single, one-time process that eventuates in the beatitude of life in Goodness. Overcoming the passions and attaining Truth is a dynamic process, not an acquired state. Therefore, it requires constant effort, according to one's own will to abide in beauty and Goodness. Attaining a virtuous life and keeping that life anchored in goodness requires acquiring a stable hexis and manifesting a "gnomic disposition" toward goodness.

GNOMI

"Gnomi" (γνώμη) is one of the terms in Maximus's writings that is difficult to translate. It is associated with free will, opinion, and individual positions. According to Maximus, the will is a natural feature of human *and* divine nature; it is a distinctive, constitutive element of every rational, contemplative being. In Hellenistic philosophy, there are discussions of the will, especially in the Aristotelean and Stoic traditions, but the term "will" does not yet have concrete ontological and anthropological content in the pertinent texts. In the fifth century, a statement by Diadochus of Photiki about the new context in which Christian thought ponders the question of will concludes that "self-determination [αυτεξούσιος] is the rational wish of a soul that strives [toward] everything . . . she wishes for."[34] Maximus bases his own perception that self-determination is the ontologically unifying principle within human beings on this sentence from Diadochus's *Gnostic*

---

33. *Myst.* (5) PG 91 678CD.
34. Diadochus of Photiki, *Gnostic Chapters*, 5.

Chapters, which he repeats almost verbatim.³⁵ However, the concept of will receives its most profound ontological content in the context of Maximus's christological and anthropological reflections.³⁶ The will is the ontological unity of the self, or in the words of the Church Fathers, the image that must acquire its eschatological fulfilment in its likeness to God.

Maximus identifies will with the natural motion that unites all of the other natural attributes in the course of the human ascent. He maintains that rational beings possess a type of self-motion (αυτεξούσιος κίνησις) or self-determination, which he calls will. The actions of those who have will are not dictated by the senses or the flesh. To use Diadochus's wording, these persons are guided solely by a rational self-determination or self-authority that enables them to manifest their freedom. Maximus stresses that the will is affiliated with nature because it is a natural attribute. All natural powers and attributes, as well as nature itself, are invariably disclosed by their mode of existence. Thus, according to the Church Fathers, the will is always a hypostasized nature.

The special position occupied by gnomic will is related to this differentiation between the logos of nature and the tropos of existence.³⁷ Natural will (θέλημα φυσικῶν) is the attribute through which nature exhibits its own dynamics and relates the gnomic will (θέλημα γνωμικῶν) to the elements of difference and otherness, as well as to the mode by which the personal will and its energies may be used. Gnomic will involves the personal (hypostatic) use and manifestation of natural will; therefore, it is related to the hypostasis, which is to say, to the individual person. As Maximus says in The Disputation with Pyrrhus, "the gnomi is nothing [other] than an act of willing in a particular way, in relation to some real or assumed good."³⁸ The gnomic will enables the free, self-determined realization of the logos of the natural will, and provides the personal (hypostatic) dimension of the existential motion of the logos of nature with its eschatological goal, which entails attaining life in Christ—or life in the likeness of God.³⁹

This passage picks up on these themes:

---

35. See Toutekov, Личност, Общност, Другост, 34–35.

36. See Bathrellos, *Nature, and Will* (2004). According to Nikolaos Loudovikos, Maximus is the first to use will ontologically.

37. Zizioulas, *Communion and Otherness*, 63–68.

38. Disput. Pyrr. transl. Farrell, 30.

39. Toutekov, Личност, Общност, Другост, 41.

Not only those who have examined the nature [of things] with their reason, and thus who have surpassed the multitude, but the usage of the uneducated hath also affirmed that what is natural is not taught. So if natural things be not acquired through teaching, then we have will without having acquired it or being taught it, for no one hath ever had a will which was acquired by teaching. Consequently, man hath the faculty of will by nature. And again, if man by nature possesseth the faculty of reason, and if rational nature be also self-determining, and if self—determination be, according to the Fathers, the will, then man possesseth the will by nature...

And again, if man was made after the image of the blessed and super-essential Godhead, and if the divine nature be self-determined, then he is by nature endowed with free will. For it hath been stated already that the Fathers defined the will as self-determination.[40] It thus appears that we may conclude that "the gnomic will is for Maximus a function of hypostasis, and it is for him characteristic not only of sinful, fallen humanity, but, seemingly, of all human existence on this side of the eschaton."[41]

An existentialist would see freedom as constituting an essential feature of the person, but nature—or essence—is bound to necessity.[42] Thus, the person must pass from the objective impersonality of nature and enter into the ekstasis of freedom. The opposite understanding holds true in Byzantine thought where freedom is an internal component of rational beings and of God. Thus, Maximus declares that "the natural actions of rational beings ... are not subject [to] compulsion."[43] God, angels, and human beings are free in their natures and not by virtue of their self-definition.[44] Self-determination is related to the Neoplatonic triad of remaining, procession, and reversion.[45] In the Ambigua, Maximus returns to Origen's schema regarding the motions of creation, which holds that no creature is an end or an exemplar of perfection in itself; yet, if every activity of a created being is

---

40. Disput. Pyrr PG 91 304CD, transl. Farrell, 24–25.

41. McFarland, "Naturally and by Grace," 429.

42. In Maximus's works, nature (φύσις) and essence (οὐσία) are used as synonyms. See *Th. Pol.* (14) PG 91 149BC and a text attributed to "Maximus the Confessor, 'Various Definitions'" in Archiv für mittelalterliche Philosophie und Kultur.

43. *Pyrr.* PG 91 293C.

44. See Törönen, *Union and Distinction*, 105.

45. See Gersh, Interpreting Proclus, 99–101.

directed toward an end, that end must be God who, since there is nothing prior to Him, is his own end.[46]

In one of the scholia in Questions to Thalassius, Maximus concludes that

> the end of the active part of [the] soul... is pure goodness [ἀγαθὸν]. And wisdom is the end of the mystical visions of the knowing part of the soul, and this end is the simple truth. The mind, purified of sensible images, leads reason toward it, subordinating the vital part of the soul.[47] This statement does not refer to the limit of the soul's capacities, but to perseverance at the boundary that Maximus beautifully describes when he writes. "Further, of the things made by God, whether intellectual or sensible, coming into being precedes movement. It is impossible to have movement before something has come into being."[48] With this assertion, Maximus challenges the Origenic triad of rest, motion, and creation (στάσις, κίνησης, γένεσις). Resolving the issue represented by these words in a Neoplatonic way, Origen considers the beginning of the material order to be characterized by a state of rest in which the intelligibles—by virtue of their own satiety (κόρος) with the contemplated divinity—turn to motion that is followed by the creator's act. Maximus rejects the prospect of primal rest because the notion of perfect rest is applicable only to God, who is totally unchangeable. In contrast, motion is typical for changeable creatures. Since motion always exists in a state of potentiality, it necessarily comes after the ideal essence. That is why, as Maximus eloquently contends in the following citations, motion is possible only after creation:

> Nothing that came into being is perfect in itself and complete. If complete it would have the power of action, but because it has its being from what is not, it does not have power of action. That which is perfect in itself is uncaused. [Nor is] anything that has

---

46. Gersh, *From Iamblichus to Eriugena*, 183.

47. *Q. Thal.* (54) PG 90 528B. Laga-Steel, CCSG, 469. Τὴν μὲν νίκην, τῶν κατὰ τό πρακτικόν τῆς ψυχῆς θείων ἀγώνων πέρας εἶναί φησιν· ὅπέρ ἐστι τό ἀμιγές ἀγαθόν. Τὴν δέ σοφίαν, τῶν κατὰ τό γνωστικόν τῆς ψυχῆς μυστικῶν ὑπάρχειν τέλος ἀποφαίνεται θεαμάτων· ὅπερ ἐστίν ἡ ἁπλῆ ἀλήθεια, πρός ἅπερ νοῦς τε, γενόμενος τῆς κατ' αἴσθησιν καθαρός φαντασίας, ἄγει καί λόγος, ὑποζεύξας ἑαυτῷ τό τῆς ψυχῆς ζωτικόν, ὧν, νίκης τέ φησι καί σοφίας, ἤγουν ἀγαθότητος καί ἀληθείας ἡ σύνοδος, μίαν δείκνυσιν, οἷς ἄν ἐγγένηται, δόξαν τοῦ καθ' ὁμοίωσιν ἀκραιφνοῦς ἀπαστράπτουσαν.

48. *Amb. Io.* (7) PG 91 1072A, trans. Blowers-Wilken.

come into being free of passions. Only what is unique, infinite and uncircumscribed is free of passions....

No created thing then is at rest until it has attained the first and only cause (from which what exists was brought into being) or has possessed the ultimately desirable.... It belongs to God alone to be the end and the completion and the impassible. It belongs to creatures to be moved toward that end which is without beginning and to come to rest in the perfect end that is without end, and to experience that which is without definition, but not to be such or to become such in essence.[49] Thought is an example of the capacity for movement which is associated with everything that exists. The soul, which is the intellectual (οὐσία νοερά) and rational (λογική ὑπάρχουσα) essence, thinks and concludes—by means of its noetic capacity and according to the movement of thinking and the activity of thought.

Although [thought] is the limit of thinking and of the one that thinks and the thing thought as far as limiting the relation of the opposed essences, ... when we learn the essential nature of living things, in what respect, how, and out of what they exist, we will not be driven by desire to know more.[50] These reflections invite the conclusion that rest belongs to a category of relationship that is not connected to the beginning; rather, it is related to motion, which constitutes its opposite. Rest means the end of motion.

In Maximus's estimation, rest manifests the divine component of divine-human communion. God, who is immobile, is the stasis and therefore, the telos of human motion.[51] Rest is one of the logoi of divinity and consequently, one of the logoi of human motion, specifically, the logos of eternal well-being. Rest is not perceived to be one of the energies associated with the logoi, which thereby obtains a place around the divine essence. Rest is the divine energy that descends toward human beings. Thus, rest represents the divine logos, and attaining that logos is the goal of humankind.

However, the word "eternal" has two meanings. When used in relation to achieving eternal well-being, "eternal" points to the created aspect of motion because the motion of creation consists of a power that is given by God. Therefore, creation must move constantly and eternally because the

---

49. *Amb. Io.* (7) PG 91 1072C, (7) PG 91 1073B, trans. Blowers-Wilken.

50. *Amb. Io.* (7) PG 91 1077B, trans. Blowers-Wilken.

51. Gregory of Nazianzus, *Orat.* 29.2; See Redovics, *Maximus the Confessor's Ambigua*, 250–57.

desire for the Creator and the longing to "return" to him never ceases. To take motion away from a creature means to deprive it of all of its natural powers and potencies, which essentially is the same as depriving it of being. Yet, the term "eternal" also refers to the divine aspect of motion and its endless movement around God. The creature moves eternally because of the endlessness of the "space" around God. Motion is a characteristic of the rational nature, a quality that is inseparable from its essence because "God in his supernal goodness creates each soul in his own image and brings it into being endowed with self-determination" [αὐτοκίνητον].[52] Moreover, "every act [energy], circumscribed naturally by its own principle, is the end of essential movement logically preceding it."[53] Furthermore, as noted above, the mind has its limit in the Truth around which it moves unceasingly, while the soul achieves stability through goodness and a "constant state by means of will."[54]

The relationship of the mind to Truth and of reason to the Good is discussed in the chapter devoted to the soul's various capacities. Here, the focus is on the relationship between the activities of practice and contemplation, as well as on the role that free choice plays in the process of attaining knowledge. Knowledge is inconceivable apart from free will and free choice. Maximus quotes Athanasius, who maintains that the mind is "either will, or desire, or motion according to something" and refers to Clement of Alexandria, who, in Stromata, book 6, defines the will as a mind desiring something and purpose as a rational desire or will directed toward some particular object.[55] In The Disputation with Pyrrhus, the issue of will is considered in terms of the relationship between nature and hypostasis, which is to say, between nature and person. Maximus follows his observation that in our postlapsarian, status, we have become possessors of gnomic will with this analysis: "Because of this, then, the gnomic will is fitly ascribed to us, being a mode of the employment [of the will] and not a principle [logos] of nature; otherwise nature [itself] would change innumerable times." Maximus goes on to add:

> It is thus not possible to say that Christ had a gnomic will. For the Same had being itself, subsisting divinely, and thus naturally hath an inclination to the good, and a drawing away from evil,

---

52. *Cap. Gnost.* PG 90 1088A.
53. *Cap. Gnost.* PG 90 1084B. Here, Berthold translates "energy" (ἐνέργεια) as "act."
54. See *Myst.* (5) PG 91 677A.
55. See *Disput. Pyrr. transl. Farrell*, 40.

just as Basil, the great eye of the church, said when explaining the interpretation of the forty-fourth Psalm: "By the same line of interpretation, Isaiah said the same thing: 'Before the child knew or advanced in evil, he chose the good,' because he also said 'before the child knows [to seek] good and to refuse evil, he chose the good.' For the word before 'indicates the he had by nature what is good, not inquiring and deliberating as we do, but because he subsisted divinely by virtue of his very being.'"[56] Maximus explains that in this case, the word "before" is used to indicate that divine knowledge of the Good is not like human knowledge of such, which is acquired "through examination and thinking."[57] For God, the Good is present naturally within the hypostasis that exists in a godly way. In this regard, human knowledge of good and evil is once again associated with sin and falling away from direct contemplation of the logoi that are in God.[58] Maximus maintains that "by nature we have an appetite simply for what by nature is good, but we gain experience of the goal in a particular way, through inquiry and counsel."[59] It is believed that this is why human beings have gnomic will. Although nature remains unmoved (and unmoving) its logos (λόγος), it has the capacity to act—and move—in different modes (τρόποι) of existence. These movements depend on a person's choice, which means that these modes of natural activity are defined by the human hypostasis in accordance with the disposition of the will (γνώμη) and its choices (προαίρεσης). As von Balthasar writes: The motion and realization are due to nature; the hypostasis is manifested first in the "how" of realization.[60]

Gnomi (γνώμη) and hexis (ἕξις) are not related to the logoi of nature; rather, they are associated with the way natural capacities are used (τρόπος χρήσης). Gnomi is not a direct act of willing; it is a state, or disposition (ἕξις), of the will, which provides the impetus for making a concrete choice (προαίρεσης) directed toward one thing or another. Gnomi (γνώμη) is not portrayed as being opposed to natural will; rather, as a differentiated manifestation of that will, its actuality is grounded in the status of nature

---

56. *Disput. Pyrr.* PG 91 308D.

57. See *Disput. Pyrr.* PG 91, where the Greek text reads as follows: καθ' ἡμᾶς ζητήσας καί βουλευσάμενος.

58. See the third section of the first chapter of this book, which is entitled "Knowledge of Good and Evil."

59. *Disput. Pyrr*, Farrell, 32.

60. See Von Balthasar, *Cosmic Liturgy*, 2003.

after the fall. The gnomi's concrete form depends on a human being's present mode of existence and especially, on the manner of being that characterizes the human hypostasis that makes the choice. This disposition of the will determines the choice of good or evil and the possibility of acquiring life in well-being by making good use of the rational element to attain the divine attributes of God's energies and "presencings" in this world. Choosing evil would represent a lack of sufficient good will to follow the path that leads to knowledge of God, which Maximus perceives to be a privation of good will.

With regard to choosing the good and knowing God as Goodness, The Disputation with Pyrrhus says:

Pyrrhus: Virtues, then are natural things?

Maximus: Yes, natural things.

Pyrrhus: If they be natural things, why do they not exist in all men equally, since all men have an identical nature?

Maximus: But they do exist equally in all men because of the identical nature!

Pyrrhus: Then why is there such a great disparity [of virtues] in us?

Maximus: Because we do not all practice what is natural to us to an equal degree; indeed, if we [all] practiced equally [the virtues] natural to us as we were created to do, then one would be able to perceive one virtue in us all, just as there is one nature [in all of us], and that "one virtue" would not admit of a "more" or "less."Maximus continues:

Asceticism, and the toils [that] go with it, was devised simply in order to ward off deception, which established itself through sensory perception. It is not [as if] the virtues have been newly introduced from outside, for they inhere in us from creation, as hath already been said. Therefore, when deception is completely expelled, the soul immediately exhibits the splendor of its natural virtue. For example, he that is not foolish is intelligent, he that is not cowardly is bold, he that is not intemperate is temperate, and he that is not unrighteousness is a righteous man. Reason, in a natural state, is prudence; the faculty of judgment, in a natural state, is justice; anger, is courage; desire, temperance. Consequently, with the removal of things that are contrary to nature only the things proper to nature are manifest. Just as when rust is removed the natural clarity and glint or iron [are manifest].⁶¹ In The Disputation with Pyrrhus, Maximus appears to reduce the connection between logos and tropos to simple naturalism, but he simultaneously differentiates these two concepts quite well. While the virtues are definitely characteristic of nature, they are not manifested in the same way by everyone because "we do not all practice or exercise the things that we all have by nature in the same way."⁶² Therefore, the individual human hypostases and the dispositions of will (gnomi) are responsible for the presence of evil in the world; yet, the key to human theosis also lies in the way these personal endowments are used. In the passage cited above, well-being depends on the individual human personality and its gnomic inclinations and desires. Maximus's entire line of reasoning is based on personal asceticism.

The difficulty here is that Maximus appears to relate will to the hypostasis—that is, to the person—rather than to nature.⁶³ This would mean that Maximus's argument affirms the Monothelites' belief that the will is a characteristic of the hypostasis. However, this is not true—Maximus himself rejects the Monothelites' position when he makes a clear distinction between nature and person. Here, the main focus is not on the important contribution that Maximus makes to Christian history with his teachings regarding Christ's two wills. Rather, the point of interest involves the Confessor's affirmation that even if Christ has a human nature and human will, he does not will the way human beings do because there is no gnomic will in Christ. Maximus thus succeeds in rewriting the prevailing theories of will and apocatastasis. He maintains that there are two natural wills in Christ that are responsible for his divine and human natures. Yet, he also holds that there is a mode of willing that is specific to each and every person. Therefore, for Maximus, there is no "will in principle" that can be abstracted from its hypostatic "application," or use.

This means that Maximus's understanding of apocatastasis is different than Origen's. For Maximus, the apocatastasis of human nature goes on within the context of the eternity and eternal well-being that characterize the general Resurrection, which Maximus describes in these terms.

> Resurrection is a rebirth of human nature that is realized above creation in paradise. Taken in a universal sense, it surpasses the

---

61. *Disput. Pyrr.* PG 91 308D.
62. See Plotinus, *Enn.* I 2, [19].
63. Maximus identifies the notions of hypostasis (ὑπόστασις) and person (πρόσωπον).

former, thanks to the]unchangeability of everything that participates in it. Yet, this superior mode of being is also realized in a particular sense, thanks to the inexpressible theosis that constitutes the grace of the saints.[64] Yet, this sort of resurrection establishes the parameters of human immortality, rather than reflecting the individual person's hypostatic state in this immortality—which could entail eternal well-being or be characterized by eternal ill-being. If it is true that "the Word of God, and God wills the mystery of his Incarnation to act always in everything" and that he "offers himself entirely, simply and with grace, because of his endless goodness to everything regardless of merits" nevertheless he gives "the permanency of the eternal being only as far as every man originates from Him."[65]

In this regard, we can read that "the difference between logos and tropos allows Maximus to stand against the Origenists."[66] because this differentiation enables Maximus to distinguish between Christ's human nature and that of human persons. The Monothelites' thesis that all created beings are determined is not entirely true for Maximus, insofar as it hearkens back to Origen, for whom creation is the result of necessity, rather than an act of free will. The Monothelites' principle is true insofar as it concerns an apocatastasis that is limited to nature alone. However, rejecting this statement means that it is no longer necessary to maintain that the will is hypostatic in order to have free will. By acknowledging the personal and natural aspects of the will, Maximus totally rejects the deterministic understanding of apocatastasis. Furthermore, he shows that he is a great theologian by balancing his attention to the division of person and nature between natural will and individual modes of willing or inclinations to will. The Confessor does not respond to the Monothelites with a one-dimensional (mono-lithic) statement regarding the two wills. The will is natural, but both it and nature have a hypostatic mode. The Disputation with Pyrrhus is an authentic record of the brilliant thought of this defender of truth. This work reveals the power of a spirit that is moved by faith. In fact, insofar

64. *Q. Thal.* (54, Scholium 22) PG 90 531D. Laga-Steel, CCSG (18), 475.

65. *Amb. Io.* (42) PG 91 1329AB. Trans. by Maximos Constas "To put it concisely, they move in accordance with their possession or privation of the potential they have naturally to participate in Him who is by nature absolutely imparticipable, and who offers Himself wholly and simply to all - worthy and unworthy - by grace through His infinite goodness, and who endows each with the permanence of eternal being, corresponding to the way that each disposes himself and is."

66. Riou, *Le monde et l'Église*, 82.

as Maximus places faith at the beginning, or more precisely, at the end, of rational activity, the spirit (or mind, according to his synonymous use of these terms) initiates, but also completes the one perfect person. The understanding of knowledge that Maximus sketches could be described as rational activity "grafted" onto faith, which allows thought to reach Truth.

Turning back to Maximus's words regarding the beginning of God's descent within the Logos in order to provide us with a way to return to knowledge, we once more see the link between the different practical and ensuing contemplative capacities that are united in the process of acquiring knowledge. In part 7 of the Ambigua to John, Maximus examines the relationship that exists between God and human beings as a result of the virtues. For human beings, virtue entails a hexis (ἕξις) toward the Good that is unvarying and free of passion. However, for God, the virtues are not a hexis. The Logos itself is virtue because

> here can be no doubt that the one Word of God is the substance of virtue in each person. For our Lord Jesus Christ himself is the substance of all the virtues, as it is written: This one God made our wisdom, our justice [and] sanctification and redemption" [I Cor 1:30]. These things are said about him absolutely, since he is wisdom and righteousness and sanctification itself. They are not, as in our case, simply attributed to him, as for example in the expression, a "wise man" or a "just man." It is evident that every person who participates in virtue unquestionably participates in God, the substance of the virtues. [1084A] Whoever by his choices cultivates the good natural seed shows the end to be the same as the beginning and the beginning to be the same as the end. Indeed the beginning and end are one. As a result, he is in genuine harmony with God, since the goal of everything is given in its beginning and the end of everything is given in its ultimate goal. As to the beginning, in addition to receiving being itself, one receives the natural good by participation; as to the end, one zealously traverses one's course toward the beginning and source without deviation by means of one's good will and choice. And through this course one becomes God, being made God by God. To the inherent goodness of the image is added the likeness [see Gen 1.26] acquired by the practice of virtue and the exercise of the will. The inclination to ascend and to see one's proper beginning was implanted in man by nature. In such a person the apostolic word is fulfilled: [1084B] In him we live and move and have our being [Acts 17:28].[67] If God

---

67. *Amb. Io.* (7) PG 91 1081D–1084B, trans. Blowers - Wilken, see also trans. by

is wisdom and judge, human beings can be wise and just only by participating in the creator. Thus, discerning human beings become part of the Virtue of the divine Logos by actualizing the virtues—which may be perceived as the divine energies and activities through which human individuals know God as they practice and participate in them. Wisdom, justice, holiness, and such do not reveal the divine essence; that is unknowable and inexpressible. The only "intelligible names of God," to use Dionysus's phrase, are provided by the archetypal forms (noütá). Foremost among these is the name that heralds God's Goodness because that is the only name which points to the boundless manifestations of divine providence that simultaneously include both supreme reason and its initiatory stages.[68] It is Goodness that reveals God through his energies.[69] By his descent and through his economy, he makes the creature part of himself by opening the door to participation.

This aspect of practical knowledge, which involves becoming like the Logos by practicing the virtues, is aptly described in Questions to Thalassius, where it is said that "the flesh of the Logos is true virtue; the blood, infallible knowledge; and the bones, unexpressed theology because like blood that changes its mode and becomes flesh, knowledge becomes virtue through act."[70] This emphasis on the manner in which knowledge manifests itself through virtue is another feature of the way Maximus depicts the relationship between practice and theory (or contemplation) and portrays the relationship between immanent and transcendent realities in the realm of knowledge, as well as on ontological and anthropological levels.

In this passage, Maximus likens the flesh of the Logos to "true virtue"—which means that those who practice the virtues are in communion with the flesh of the Logos. However, he then introduces a hierarchy of ascent toward participation in the Logos when he describes praxis as a preparatory stage in the process of knowing, which is followed by true knowledge. Regarding this process, Maximus writes: "The flesh is the locus of a full return to the self and of the restoration of the whole human being through the mediation of virtue and knowledge;" likewise, "the blood is theosis, which, by grace, unites this nature with ... eternal well-being."[71]

Maximos Constas, On Dificulties, 103.

68. See Dionysius, On *Divine Names*.
69. See chapter 5 in the *Mystagogia* for further discussion of this theme.
70. Q. *Thal.* (35) PG 90 380AB. Laga-Steel, CCSG, 239-241.
71. Q. *Thal.* (35) PG 90 380B. Laga-Steel, CCSG, 241.

Levels of Knowledge

In this interpretation of the significance of the flesh of the Logos, Maximus connects the activities of the self's practical and theoretical capacities, and the whole process culminates in a theosis given by grace—which is beyond our capacities of discernment.

In Letter 19, which is addressed to Pyrrhus, Maximus writes: "According to the generous disposition of your heart, practice and contemplation [act] like a breast feeding the Word, making it grow through your pious thoughts and modes of existence [tropoi] and by its own growth towards the theosis of the mind of the one that feeds it."[72] The Logos is the place where the human and the divine meet in his creative energies and by means of his relationship to the created world and to human beings who strive toward and participate in the Word. Thus, insofar as the virtues manifest Virtue, their essence is the Logos that binds together the logoi of existing things and causes them to participate in God. This kind of knowledge surpasses the simple moral level and leads to a transcendent sort of knowing that is beyond the created world in the realm where knowledge of divine things can be reached. We describe God in absolute terms, while human beings are defined by participation in God.

The virtues play an important role in Maximus's teachings, and as a power of the soul, virtue has an important place in the operation of rational knowledge. In fact, virtue figures prominently in the sequence of key attributes of the soul—which includes reason, prudence, action, virtue, faith, and goodness (λόγος, φρόνησις, πρᾶξις, ἀρετή, πίστις, ἀγαθὸν). Along with contemplation, virtue constitutes the foundation of Maximus's doctrine of knowledge. He emphasizes the relationship between the virtue associated with vita practica and the knowledge that distinguishes vita contemplativa. Evil may be associated with both practical and contemplative parts of the soul.[73] If the mind has been corrupted in some way, this development is reflected in instances of praxis and contemplation.[74] Thus, victory over the passions is interwoven with wisdom, virtue, knowledge, goodness, and truth in the same way that praxis and contemplation are.[75]

In Chapters on Knowledge, Maximus joins Evagrius in emphasizing the contrast between activities that lead to knowing. For example, the Confessor says that "anyone who glorifies God in himself through the

---

72. *Ep.* (19) PG 91 592AB.
73. See Q. *Thal.* (Introd.) PG 90 248D–249. Laga-Steel, CCSG, 23.
74. See Q. *Thal.* (52) PG 90 497A. Laga-Steel, CCSG, 425.
75. See Q. *Thal.* (43) PG 90 412D. Laga-Steel, CCSG, 295.

sufferings of ascetical practice performed for virtue is himself glorified in God through the tranquil illumination of divine gifts in contemplation."[76] Elsewhere, he analogically maintains that the reward for virtuous practice is knowledge (γνῶσις) that is freed from the passions. Nevertheless, Thunberg identifies a key difference between Maximus and Evagrius in this penetrating passage:

> If one compares the theological systems of Evagrius and Maximus, one is struck by a difference that concerns precisely this question of the position of charity. To Evagrius charity represents the culmination and end of the vita practica, but he gives a more elevated position to advancement in knowledge (gnosis), i.e., to the vita contemplativa. For Maximus, no virtue is higher than charity. In a wider sense, charity itself implies a preference [for] the gnosis of God over all other forms of knowledge, and it leads man through his intellectual activity all the way to the final communion with God.[77] The differentiation between gnosis and virtue has its roots in Philo of Alexandria and is developed by Origen before Evagrius takes up this theme.[78] However, it does not exclude the interrelation between the two that Maximus stresses at other points where he speaks of the mutual glorification of God and human beings in ways that modify the tradition handed down by Origen and Evagrius.[79] For Maximus, the interrelation between the two motions of knowledge is obvious because divine grace is necessary—even for natural contemplation—but most especially for a virtuous life. His views are shaped more by a quest for synergy than by the division that Evagrius emphasizes. Maximus's entire system of thought affirms the unity that the procedures of acquiring knowledge manifest as they purse their common and only goal; yet, it simultaneously differentiates and underscores the specificity of each of these methodologies.

The rational activity that underlies the soul's practical endeavors enables human beings to become participants in the goodness of God's creative energies in the world. The mind's contemplative function leads to the perimeter of thinking. Truth and participation in it are solely contingent on practicing the right way of thinking. When sense perception is properly oriented toward attaining knowledge of God and does not fall into sensible

---

76. *Cap. Gnost.* (2.72) PG 90 1157A.
77. Thunberg, *Man and the Cosmos*, 97–98.
78. See Von Balthasar, *Kosmische Liturgie*, 517.
79. For further consideration of this matter, see Florovsky, *The Byzantine Fathers*, 572.

modes of thinking, both it and rational activity—which focuses on the representations and logoi of things that are known through the senses—reach the third stage of knowledge. At this juncture, the mind, which has been freed of flesh and image, sinks into the state of eternal enjoyment that comes from contemplating the divinity. As was noted previously, this contemplation is characterized by an endless movement around Truth, which is the limit and the foundation of any act of knowing.

MORAL AND TRANSCENDENT KNOWLEDGE

Knowledge of God is related to the virtues' purifying capacity, which, in turn, is the necessary condition for knowing God. Maximus hints at this relationship when he writes of "the way [the] body commits sin and bodily virtues teach it to keep chastity." This perception leads the Confessor to conclude that "the mind [νοῦς] thus commits sin through passionate thoughts."[80] In other words, practicing the virtues is the sine qua non for achieving union with God at the end of the process of attaining knowledge. This purification of body and mind is also perceived to be a moral transformation that leads the flesh to be released from all of the passions and the mind to be liberated from all "passionate thoughts."[81] Through the process of purification, the mind gains the ability to see the presence of the divine in the world and to contemplate God "face to face" because only a purified mind has been "[transformed] in order to be a place of God."[82]

The mind provides the soul with knowledge through thoughts whose basis consists of reason's didactic function, which is concerned with the actualization of the virtues. Thus, mind and reason both contribute to a step that is absolutely necessary if purified knowledge that is freed from the passion is to be achieved.[83] Rational knowledge goes through the steps that have already been presented: Reason is set in motion by prudence, which, since it is already in action, proceeds to virtue; by means of virtue; it reaches

---

80. *Cap. Theol.* PG 90 1005A.
81. *Cap. Theol.* PG 90 1004A.
82. *Q. Thal.* (31) PG 90 369D. Laga-Steel, CCSG, 223.
83. Larchet interprets the actualization of the virtues as being more than a necessity stage on the path to knowledge. He maintains that reducing rational knowledge to the status of being a precondition for "true" knowledge is an incorrect understanding of Maximus's view of knowledge. Larchet points out that the soul's practical aspect has an important place in the process of acquiring knowledge of God, even if all of its motions are unified in one divine-human communion (*La divinisation de l'homme*, 1996).

faith, and in the end, attains knowledge of goodness—which is the final goal of the soul's rational movements. This outline confirms that the virtues have an extremely important place in Maximus's thought, although he does not present a clear classification, or develop a detailed structure, of vices and virtues, like the one that Evagrius puts forth. Indeed, it is noteworthy that in the course of the ascent toward God, rational activity and the pursuit of virtue leads to faith (πίστις). In other words, virtue is (pre-)positioned before faith.

As Paul says in Hebrews 11:1, "faith is the assurance of things hoped for, the conviction of things not seen," and according to Maximus, it involves the realization of expectations and trust in the invisible. "It is not outside, but inside of us: faith, which is set in motion by divine commands, becomes the kingdom of God that is known by those that have it. . . . Faith is the power—or the actualizing link—that binds us together with God."[84] These words suggest that faith is a mediating power in the activity of acquiring knowledge; thanks to faith, the divisions within existence are overcome. The sensible and intelligible worlds—and body and soul—must be reunited in order for human beings to achieve beatitude and real life in God.[85] This task lies before human beings who take up the path of knowledge. Maximus's whole ontology, anthropology, and eschatology are based on this premise. Because it is impossible for human beings to overcome the divided state of existence and to traverse the boundary between the created and uncreated realms by themselves, God descends in his infinite mercy, sending his Logos to teach humankind how world has been transformed by him.

One of Maximus's most beautiful texts—the interpretation of Oration 39 by Gregory the Theologian that is found in Ambigua 42—is devoted to the same theme. There, he declares: "Nature is renewed, and God [has become] man."[86] As the wreath of creation, human beings are the last of the creatures made by God. Because they are the center of created existence and the natural bond (σύνδεσμος) between all creatures, human beings have been fashioned to communicate between the different components of their own nature. That is why they have been renewed in Christ and

---

84. Q. *Thal.* (33) PG 90 374BC. Laga-Steel, CCSG, 229.

85. See *Amb. Io.* (42) PG 91 1329CD.

86. Καινοτομοῦνται φύσεις, καί Θεός ἄνθρωπος γίνεται. A study of this part of Maximus's interpretation of Gregory of Nazianzus and Dionysius the Areopagite is presented by Petrov in Максим Исповедник, (2007).

called to overcome the divisions in the hypostasis of existence by arriving at unity with the totality of existence. Discerning human beings are those who fulfil the divine commandments and desire their own return to God; their ascent shifts from being willed by God to being a state of existence with God that has been willed by the rational soul.[87] As the substratum that overcomes existential divisions and unites the rational soul with God, the bond between discerning persons and faith makes this cognizant attitude the foundation and fulfilment of all of the soul's rational activities. Thus, in the following passage, Maximus speaks of a "knowing faith" (ἡ γνωστικὴ πίστις): "Every mind ... receives rational power ... from [such faith]; cultivating the knowing faith in accordance with which the mind wordlessly learns about the eternally existing God."[88]

NATURAL CONTEMPLATION: INTRODUCTORY REMARKS

The next subtopic to be discussed in this chapter is natural contemplation. This discussion is a consideration of what Maximus means by this phrase, before turning to the scope—and the consequences—of the activities that go on at this higher level of knowing. This section analyzes the significance of natural contemplation and to simultaneously show its place in the larger cognitive framework.

In reexamining the three stage process of spiritual growth that leads to knowledge, Maximus once again emphasizes the important role that sense perception plays as the mind returns to its preexistent state. Yet, he also postulates a type of symbolic natural contemplation that reflects Dionysius's point of view. Maximus maintains that natural contemplation has a symbolic function that leads the mind to a knowledge of divine things, which paradoxically means that human beings must reexamine their weakness, not only as a consequence of their sinfulness, but also because human nature is dependent on—and different from—divine nature. The idea that symbolic natural contemplation is a "test" of nearly all of the symbolic reflections of divine realities and that it leads to an apophatic understanding of the human ability to know God is influenced by Dionysius and appears to be yet another rejection of Evagrius's Origenism.

---

87. See Q. Thal. (6) PG 90 280D–281AB. Laga-Steel, CCSG, 69.
88. Q. Thal. (49) PG 90 449BC. Laga-Steel, CCSG, 355.

The theoria (θεωρία), which Maximus, Gregory of Nazianzus, and Evagrius call natural contemplation (φυσικὴ θεωρία), holds an important place in the second stage of the process of knowing. Drawing on Evagrius, Maximus sometimes calls this practical stage gnosis (γνῶσις).[89] However, he more frequently uses the terms "natural contemplation" or "natural philosophy" (φυσικὴ φιλοσοφία). The notion of natural contemplation, which involves contemplating things by pondering their logoi, can be traced to Clement of Alexandria, who uses the expression θεωρία φυσική. Moreover, Origen, Evagrius, and Gregory of Nazianzus develop the idea of contemplation in different ways. For instance, Gregory identifies two spheres of contemplation; the existing realm, which presupposes a created world, and the noetic domain. The origin of such an interpretation can probably be traced to Plato. However, Maximus makes a unique contribution when he introduces three modes of contemplation (θεωρίας τρόποι) through which human beings know heaven, earth, and the cosmic realm lying between them.

NATURAL CONTEMPLATION

This part of the book seeks to show that the gradual movement from knowledge of visible things to knowledge of invisible essences which characterizes the stages of practice and contemplation does not require that previous stages be excluded from higher and more perfect modes of knowing. On the contrary, these various stages make up a complete picture of the ascent to God. In fact, insofar as they are interdependent and mutually determining, these steps reveal that their dissimilar cognitive activities reflect a common act of striving toward God wherein unity is given priority over difference. Thus, the Neoplatonic emphasis on casting away the lower dimensions is supplanted by unity—in the name of the One from whom the light of knowledge comes.

Regarding the natural contemplation of creation, Maximus establishes three modes of contemplation (θεωρίας τρόποι) through which heaven, earth, and creation are known. He perceives that creation understands and philosophizes about moral, natural, and theological matters by the power of the Logos (λόγος). Then, considering creation from the perspective of difference (διαφορά) and consequently discerning the essence of the two realms of heaven leads Maximus to conclude that there are two types of

---

89. Q. Thal. (55) PG 90 537BC. Laga-Steel, CCSG, 493.

knowledge: wisdom and philosophy (σοφία καί φιλοσοφία). Wisdom encompasses all of the pious features of knowledge and all of the enigmatic and natural logoi. The components known as disposition (ἔθος) and will (γνώμη), praxis (πρᾶξις) and contemplation (θεωρία), and virtue (ἀρετή) and gnosis (γνῶσις) belong to the field of philosophy; these features of thought are intimately related (οἰκείοτης σχετική) to wisdom—which constitutes their source.[90] This discussion should help clarify the place that philosophy holds in Maximus's work and may also disclose its relationship to other forms of knowledge.

In keeping with his emphasis on natural contemplation, Maximus uses the analogy of the four natural powers of water, earth, air, and fire to account for the fact that there are four Gospels. He maintains that the four Gospels should be regarded as a symbol of the interconnection that exists between faith, practical and natural philosophy, and theology. In this analogy, faith is related to earth and theology is associated with fire.[91] Although it is possible to talk about an inner hierarchy of natural powers, it is important to bear in mind that they are established as cosmic powers only by virtue of their undivided unity and interrelationship, thus, the absence or deficiency of any of them takes away from nature's meaning, sense, and purpose. This analogy relates faith, practical and natural knowledge, and theology to one another in the same way. Otherwise, according to Maximus, knowledge—and as a consequence, human existence—would turn into absurdity both on an individual level and in a universal sense.

In *Chapters on Love*, Maximus characterizes contemplation as being part of the mind's ascent to knowledge when he writes: "The virtues separate the mind from the passions; spiritual contemplations separate it from simple representations; then pure prayer sets it before God Himself."[92] The telos of contemplative work is knowledge of God, but how does the mind engage in contemplation? In this regard, Maximus is influenced by Dionysius's hierarchy of being. Thus, the Confessor maintains that in its lowest forms, the contemplation of visible things may not only include reflections on their natural logoi, but may also involve a consideration of what they symbolize or even their source (cause).

Moreover, Maximus says that when the mind passes on to the contemplation of invisible things—that is to say, the angels—not only their natural

---

90. *Amb. Io.* (10) PG 91 1136CD.
91. *Amb. Io.* (21) PG 91 1245D–1248A.
92. *Car.* 3.44.

logoi are pondered. The mind also reflects on that which is knowable and on the providence and judgment that are related to that. This means that natural contemplation not only involves the logoi of created things, which serve as signs of God's intentions for each being and relate all creatures to the Logos who is the Cause that sustains their unity. Natural contemplation also includes viewing the logoi of existing beings in terms of their symbolic relationship within the hierarchy that is directed toward God and is closely related to his providence and judgment. Maximus applies these two attributes to the contemplation of invisible things, which he identifies as angels. Here, the Confessor's approach is unlike that of Evagrius, who places providence and judgment at the lowest levels of contemplation. Thus, a hierarchical structure of existence—in which the unity and corresponding differentiation intended by God is seen on every level—is obvious in Maximus's work, although it cannot be found in Evagrius's writings.

According to Maximus, it is through such contemplative discernment that the mind succeeds in ascending to knowledge of the sole divine Cause. Along with the mind, which is devoted to natural contemplation of the Spirit, which is a "sensibility" that helps human beings learn the nature of sensible, visible things and their movement toward the divine logoi is also part of the process of acquiring knowledge. Maximus also stresses that in its function as creator, the Logos is known through such contemplation, although the highest part of the Logos is the divine nous toward which the Logos strives to lead the mind by providing intelligible images of divine things as the contemplation of existing things (θεωρία τῶν ὄντων) takes place.[93] The Logos contains the logoi of creation through which the nature of things is always disclosed. Historically, the incarnation of God's Logos is an act of immanent revelation, but this does not mean that God can be attained in either his divinity or his humanity—which are the two natures that exist in his one hypostasis. Yet, the Incarnation makes all human knowledge possible, insofar as it enables participation in the divine and allows creation's likeness to the Creator to be realized.

Maximus says that the Logos endows everyone with particular virtues in accordance with their abilities and dignity. In other words, the Logos "divides himself indivisibly" and "is shared out to those who participate [in him]."[94] In Ambigua 7, Maximus affirms that "the one Logos is the many

---

93. Q. Thal. (25) PG 90 332AC. Laga-Steel, CCSG, 161.
94. Amb. Io. (10) PG 91 1108C.

logoi and the many logoi are One."⁹⁵ The one Logos does not divide itself by means of an actual division; nor, as Proclus taught, by taking the form of a monad that becomes plurality; rather, the division takes place as the Logos directs his own logoi to embody his intentions toward the many existing things by engaging in acts of will. Thus, he divides himself through his creative activities toward the manifold things, while simultaneously remaining within himself as the subject who fulfills the acts of will. This is the paradoxical existence of the Logos of whom Maximus speaks. The fact that the Logos is present in accordance with each creature's specific level of existence and dignity means that the Logos manifests himself according to the trichotomic structure of the ascent to knowledge which includes practice, contemplation, and theology. As the transcendent principle of existence, the Logos is unattainable; however, he becomes immanent within his creatures through his creative acts of will.

Knowledge that leads to participation in divine existence is channeled through reason, mind, and the senses, which comprise the human capacity to participate in the essence of being (ἡ οὐσιώδης ἐπιτηδειότης) and to act according to hexis (ἡ εκτική ἐπιτηδειότης). Participation in this essence involves sharing in the divine activity that manifests existence in the created realm by perceiving the divine energies in a natural, cosmological way that is in keeping with the logos of the essence. However, participation that takes place according to hexis is grounded in creation's capacity to know the divine energies through the logos of well-being and eternal well-being. Such participation occurs when creatures are properly oriented toward knowledge of divinity and do not fall from the way that has been given to them so that the economy of salvation can be realized. The interrelationship between the Logos' Incarnation and the human ascent to knowledge of, and participation in, God—which corresponds to the process of repairing human beings' postlapsarian state—may be portrayed by means of Maximus's compelling vision which perceives that God and human beings are paradigms of one another. God becomes human out of his love for humanity to the same degree that human beings are deified by devout participation in the natural activities of the divine nature. If this really is the case, it could be said that the Incarnation is a precondition of participation.

The question of how God is connected to the plurality of the created world through his logoi and activities is addressed in Ambigua 22, where Maximus says that the creatures are many, and as a multitude, they differ

---

95. *Amb. Io.* (7) PG 91 1081C.

according to the nature that they were given by God through their logoi.⁹⁶ If creatures differ from one another, the logoi according to which their essences are dissimilar also differ from one another. Thus, there are many different logoi. This observation leads Maximus to bring up a problem: The senses have a natural ability to portray visible sensory realities as manifesting many different states. Likewise, when the mind (νοῦς) apprehends the logoi of existing things, it makes them many and infinite. The difficulty is that the mind does not have the power to obtain accurate knowledge of reality because it cannot fathom how God is related to the multiple world. Discerning human beings receive many impressions through the senses. Thus, they grasp the many essences by contemplating creation, and through rational activity, they reach the many logoi that are enwrapped in the essence of the visible, sensible world. Yet, how is it possible to grasp and apprehend this plurality by relating it to God's simplicity and unity? How is it possible for God to simultaneously be present in and beyond all human capacities to grasp the Cause of existence?

At this point, it is necessary to note that we frequently speak of God's relation to world using the words "beginning" and "cause," which are terms that refer to God's economy and do not have anything to do with his essence or his existence as the transcendent guarantor of our lives. Yet, with regard to God's "attainability," we may add that the difference between Thomism and the practice of the fathers of the Eastern Church is explicit and extensive. According to Thomas, God is transcendent (superesse) because, as Gilson writes, he is the existent one in a superior sense, he is the pure and simple Esse in its whole infinity and perfection.⁹⁷ In its perfection, the Esse is absolutely simple; yet, the absolutely simple cannot manifest itself as transcending our ability to know because that is a capacity which deals with that which is complex and composed of multiplicity. In other words, according to Thomism, created beings are like God ontologically (in a single "line" with, and on the same level as, him), while simultaneously being unlike him and powerless to know him. God is not transcendent ontologically; he is transcendent gnoseologically. Even if God is on the same level as the creature, that place of oneness is located far beyond the point that can be reached by human capacities for seeing and thinking.

In contrast, according to Dionysius, God is superesse (superexistent) because he has not yet manifested himself as esse in his highest proceedings.

---

96. See *Amb. Io.* (22) PG 91 1256D.
97. Gilson, *L'introduction à la philosophie de Saint Thomas d'Aquin*, 147.

Levels of Knowledge

Dionysius articulates this insight succinctly when he writes: "God in his superessential being surpasses the mind and being, and this is why [God] is not knowable nor existing."[98] Other Eastern Orthodox thinkers in addition to Dionysius develop this idea, which also appears in Maximus's Chapters on Knowledge:

> God is not essence [οὐσία], understood as either general or particular, even if he is principle; nor is the potency [δύναμις] understood as either general or particular, even if he is means; he is not act, understood as either general or particular, even if he is end of essential movement discerned in potency. But he is a principle of being who is creative of essence and beyond essence, a ground who is creative of power but beyond power, the active and eternal condition of every act, and to speak briefly, the Creator of every essence, power, and act.[99] Elsewhere, the Confessor similarly declares: "Since it is necessary that we correctly understand the difference between God and creatures, the affirmation of superbeing must be the negation of beings, and the affirmation of beings must be the negation of superbeing."[100]

God's economy is the sphere that we can attain. Thus, in a sense, we are able to discern God's essence as he manifests his energies, although what is known by us will not be identical with the creative energies, insofar as divine actions are not identical with created essences. Everything exists according to such action and energy, and without the energy of Being, nothing can be. The matter of concern here is not the profound debates that have gone on regarding the movement of knowledge within this kind of ontological relationship between the Creator and his creatures. Although Maximus himself continues this line of argument in the same part of the Ambigua, the important point here is the realization that God, who transcends his creatures in his actions, is always present in the same way.

The logoi determine the conditions under which the divine energies are manifested. In keeping with the double-faceted activities of the energies and the logoi, created beings are represented as distinctive, separate entities, each of which has its own specific features, but which are simultaneously united by the image that they carry within.[101] By contemplating the

---

98. See Dionysius, On the Divine Names.
99. *Cap. Gnost.* I .4.
100. *Myst.* (Intro.), col. 659.
101. Regarding Maximus's ontology, see Tollefsen, *The Christocentric Cosmology*, 64.

logoi of the created things (οἱ λόγοι τῶν γεγονότων) and by means of the simple ideas to which the logoi lead, the mind advances toward one simple, purified knowledge (γνῶσις) that is in harmony with the Logos. When the mind arrives at the end of knowledge, it will be united with the God who is beyond all images. Picking upon on this theme in Questions to Thalassius, Maximus asserts that we will see—as if in a mirror—the glory of God shining in the virtues and spiritual knowledge with whose help our union with God is realized by grace. Thus, the mind will awaken from ignorance and will cease to fall away.[102]

The intention of contemplation is to arrive at a type of knowledge that is not composed of our sensory capacities' observations of the visible world; nor does it require a retreat to the spoken Word. Instead, as Maximus indicates, contemplation may be understood in terms of Adam's experience since he had been naked in the simplicity of knowledge before falling from the state of blessed existence.[103] Being wise, [Adam] was higher than natural contemplation because of his knowledge. Thus, the first man had nothing between God and himself which could have been accorded to knowledge and could have obscured the future relationship of voluntary love that underlaid his movement toward God. At the final stage of the process of knowing during which the creator and creature are united, human beings do not leave this world; instead, they see it the way God sees. Regarding this process, Maximus writes:

> Through the working out of the commandments the mind puts off the passions. Through the spiritual contemplation of visible realities it puts off impassioned thoughts of things. Through the knowledge of invisible realities it puts off contemplation of visible things. And finally this it puts off through the knowledge of the Holy Trinity.[104] In the Ambigua, Maximus states that the divine presence in the world is manifested through five conceptual categories: being, motion, difference, mixture, and position (οὐσία, κίνησις, διάφορα, κρᾶσις, and θέσις). Being, motion, and difference refer to God himself as creator, providence, and judge, while mixture and position have to do with God's relationship to creation. Natural contemplation of the logoi of creation is realized through these components of divinity. Thus, it is not God's essence that is known during contemplation of the logoi. Insofar as such

---

102. See *Q. Thal.* (Introd.) PG 90 261A. Laga-Steel, CCSG, 41.
103. See *Amb. Io.* (45) PG 91 1356AB.
104. *Car.* I 94.

reflection is focused on divine proceedings in the earthly realm, divine actions in the world are known though such contemplation. Nevertheless, looking beyond the representations and images of sense perception, the mind contemplates the logoi, which have their origin in the divine Logos. These logoi cannot be attained by human beings, but the unity of Logos is seen through the multiplicity of their existence.[105]

When the mind rises toward God, the divinity also changes. Thus, Maximus applies the Aristotelean maxim regarding the identity between the knowing subject and the known object when he writes: "But when [the mind] comes to be in God, it becomes wholly without form and pattern, for in contemplating the one who is simple it becomes simple and entirely patterned in light."[106] In his thoughtful reflections on Maximus, Melchisedec Törönen picks up on this theme:

> The unification of the soul, its union with God, its knowledge of God as Unity, and its conformity to this unity are all reciprocally bound together. The more one detaches one's mind from the multiplicity of the material world, the more the soul becomes unified; and becoming more unified it is drawn closer to God. In this way, the mind's knowledge increases and it is conformed to the object of its knowledge.[107] Although it is within the parameters of the philosophical tradition, Maximus's paradigm of knowing has an original aspect that can be seen in his transformation of each of the components of the threefold structure of knowledge and in his teachings about the logoi. In the first case, Maximus clarifies the terms used to refer to the three stages by specifying their names and defining the spheres of their activities. In addition, he emphasizes the final stage of the process of acquiring knowledge and simultaneously, manages to reveal the unity that lies beyond all of the levels and techniques associated with knowledge. Indeed, in the Ambigua, he states that all three of the soul's motions lead to one movement.

Maximus says that the flesh of the Logos is the logoi of sensible things; the blood of the Logos is the logoi of intelligible things; and the bones of

---

105. Before Maximus, Basil the Great also maintains that the logoi are unattainable by human knowledge.

106. *Car.* 3.97.

107. Törönen, *Union and Distinction*, 76.

the Logos are the logoi of the Divinity—which are beyond any thought.[108] Maximus thus establishes a connection between virtue and the lower levels of contemplation, which are both related to the rational element in the souls of existing things. By referring virtue (and knowledge of it) to the different levels of the logoi, Maximus places praxis and contemplation on the same ontological level, insofar as they are subordinated to theology—which is located above both of them, but, at the same time, holds them in unity.[109]

Thus, Maximus once again underscores the significance of the senses and of the role of sense perception in the process of acquiring knowledge, and thereby specifies the positive value of the body as a whole. Furthermore, he proposes that practicing the virtue is the proper "way of existence" according to "the logoi of things." Maximus develops these themes in Ambigua 10 where he writes:

> But if, however, the Saints are moved by visions of beings, they are not moved, as with us, in a material way principally to behold and know those things, but in order to praise in many ways God, who is and appears through all things and appears through all things and in all things, and to gather together for themselves every capacity for wonder and reason for glorying. For having received from God a soul having mind and reason and sense, so that it can range from the sensible to the intelligible, just as reason ranges from what is inward to what is expressed, and the mind takes that which is capable of feeling into the realm of the intelligible, it is necessary that they should think about the activities of these, so as to apply them not to their own purposes, but to God . . . Instructed by an accurate knowledge of the nature of things, we learn that there are three general ways, accessible to human beings, in which God has made all things. He has constituted it as being, well-being and eternal being—and the two ways of being at the extremes are God's alone, as the cause, while the other one in the middle, depending on our inclination/ gnomi and motion, through itself makes the extremes what they are, properly speaking, for if the middle term is not present and "well" is not added, the extremes are designated in vain, and the truth that is in the extremes cannot otherwise occur to them or be preserved, or even come to be, if the well-being in the middle is not mixed in with the extremes, or rather intended by eternal movement towards

---

108. See *Q. Thal.* (Introd.) PG 90 261B. Laga-Steel, CCSG, 41.
109. *Q. Thal.* (Introd.) PG 90 252AB. Laga-Steel, CCSG, 27.

God.[110] In this representation of the threefold process of spiritual growth that leads to knowledge, Maximus reaffirms the important position occupied by the sensory realm—insofar as the mind does not turn back to its "preexistence." Adopting Dionysius's point of view, Maximus postulates a symbolic type of natural contemplation. In his judgement, this symbolic capacity leads the mind to a knowledge of divine things, which paradoxically compels human beings to reexamine their weakness, not only as a consequence of their sinfulness, but also because human nature is dependent on—and different from—divine nature. The idea that symbolic natural contemplation involves a consideration of nearly all of the symbolic reflections of divine realities which lead to an apophatic understanding of the human capacity for acquiring knowledge of God reflects Dionysius's influence and seems to be yet another rejection of Evagrius's Origenism.

In conclusion, it bears repeating that the movement from the visible realm to knowledge of invisible entities that characterizes the preliminary steps of praxis and contemplation does not necessitate a rejection of the lower stages by higher and more perfect forms of knowledge. On the contrary, these various stages provide a complete picture of the ascent to God. In other words, insofar as they are interrelated and mutually determining, praxis and contemplation reduce the movements involved in acquiring knowledge to a single act of striving toward God in which unity is given priority over difference in the name of the One from whom light and knowledge come.

FAITH

Maximus views faith, hope, and love, which constitute the foundation of Christian life in and from God, in terms of the trichotomic system of knowledge that he inherited from the ancient tradition developed by Plato, Aristotle, Philo, Clement of Alexandria, Evagrius, Origen, and the Cappadocians. The Confessor manages to unify pre-Christian and Christian ideas in his thought.[111] Faith is not opposed to knowledge in Maximus's writings

---

110. *Amb. Io.* (10) PG 91 1116AC. See also trans. by Maximos Constas, On Difficulties, 167.

111. For more discussion of the different parts of the soul and their specific functions, see the section on the relationship between the different levels of knowledge and the various capacities of the soul.

like it was in Origen's work; instead, it is the final stage of practical activity.[112] The same view is shared by Gregory, Philo, and Proclus, who place faith above knowledge. Dionysius similarly describes faith (and mystical contemplation) as "[the] thing that cannot be learned."[113] Faith is not merely the precondition for, or the beginning of, the process of knowledge.

In the Mystagogia, the structure of the soul's motion conceived in relation to reason or logos is described as reason, prudence, action, virtue, faith, and goodness (λόγος, φρόνησις, πρᾶξις, ἀρετή, πίστις, ἀγαθὸν).[114] Contrary to typical expectations, faith does not stand at the beginning of rational activity; instead, it is at the end of the process. The Mystagogia's outline of the soul's various capacities and activities has an eclectic character that brings together Aristotelean, Stoic, and Neoplatonic motifs. Faith is true knowledge of indemonstrable principles, the hypostasis of things that are above mind and reason.[115] Faith and agape, which is the highest of virtues, are at the beginning and end of knowledge.[116] The important point here is that reason possesses faith as potential; faith becomes real only through its own activities (praxis), which actualize the virtues. As Maximus says in the Mystagogia, "faith without works is dead;" only true faith leads to the goodness of God.

Continuing this theme in Question to Thalassius, Maximus declares:

> The mother of the Word is pure faith. After creating faith, the Word becomes the Son of faith, incarnating her in the virtues of practice and in spiritual work. Thanks to this faith, we practice that which is good . . . Because without faith—whose God by nature and Son by grace is the Word—it is impossible to dare to address God in prayer.[117] Here, the question of the relationship between rational activity, praxis, and faith is resolved in the same way that it was in the Mystagogia. As was noted previously, 'the Logos descends in praxis in order to ascend with us in knowledge.'[118] Faith completes the effort to know by providing the starting point of rational activity in the Augustinian sense represented by the words, "I believe

---

112. Von Balthasar, *Kosmische Liturgie*, 339.
113. Dionysius On Divine Names 2.9 PG 3 648B.
114. This paradigm is also discussed in the section on rational knowledge.
115. See *Cap. Gnost.* 1. 9; Thunberg, *Microcosm and Mediator*, 337.
116. See *Amb. Io.* (7) PG 91 1084A 3–4; Lollar, *To See Into the Life of Things*, vol. 2, 228.
117. See *Q.Thal.* (54) PG 90 520B. Laga-Steel, CCSG, 449.
118. See the citation of *Quaestiones et Dubia* at the beginning of the section entitled "Practical Philosophy as Praxis."

in order to understand." Moreover, faith fulfills the knowledge of praxis that the Logos bestows as it realizes its own actuality by springing from God and returning us to him. Maximus points out that in the course of the process of acquiring knowledge, we rediscover ourselves as we seek to return to our Creator.[119] However, God is with us throughout the whole process.

Insofar as the Logos is the origin of faith, it is faith's task to bring us back to the Logos through knowledge of the logoi and by actualizing the virtues that constitute the Logos. Thus, keeping the virtues enables faith to consummate the connection that exists between creatures who are striving to know Goodness and the God who is in the logoi. This is why faith cannot be thought of apart from praxis and contemplation.[120] In Maximus's conception of the soul's capacities, faith and enduring knowledge form one of the five pairs of powers and energies that lead the soul toward the supreme dyad of Goodness and Truth. When human beings fall away from faith, the whole structure of knowledge breaks down. Maximus places faith at the end of the process of knowledge because of the central place that it holds in the lives of human beings who are seeking knowledge. By practicing the virtues, human individuals find their logos, which is in God, or more precisely, they arrive at the logos of well-being, which is the final step in the soul's practical activity and the point at which the good life is achieved.

In one of the scholia related to question 51 of Questions to Thalassius, we read:

> The knowing mind perceives the logoi of things that affirm faith in God, but do not create it. The logoi of creatures are not the beginning of faith because then, the subject of faith would be describable. The thing that can be understood through knowledge is grasped and understood according to its nature and is within the purview of knowledge.[121] In this passage, the basic teachings of faith are identified with the "logoi of things that ... affirm faith in God." In Maximus's work, the virtues are an essential source of knowledge because the Logos incarnates himself in the faithful in a specific way through them since the logoi of the virtues and the logos of well-being have the Logos as their principle and telos. In this regard, Maximus says that through the virtues and the logoi of knowable things, "God, who is ever willing to become

---

119. *Q. Thal.* (35) PG 90 378D–380A. Laga-Steel, CCSG, 238-241.
120. See Matsoukas, *La vie en Dieu*, 214.
121. *Q. Thal.* (51, Scholium 11) PG 90 488C. Laga-Steel, CCSG, (7), 411.

human, does so in those who are worthy."[122] The Confessor also affirms that the Logos is the place where God is made manifest in accordance with the virtues and knowledge and thereby, becomes present in those who are worthy of it.[123] In the same text, Maximus asserts that the true Christian lives according to Christ, which means according to his tropoi (virtues) and logoi (knowledge)—to the extent that this is possible for human beings.[124]

THEOLOGY

Theology: Introductory Remarks

The highest level of the path to knowledge is an important theme in this part of the book by looking at the concept of theology in Maximus's work. It is essential that we examine the various connotations of the term "unknowing," which is often applied to the final stage of knowing. The objective will be to describe the finitude of human cognitive capabilities. This theme corresponds to subsequent reflections on the issue of cataphatic and apophatic cognitive modes. It is not only difficult to arrive at a conception of divinity; it is also a challenge to communicate this experience. As Aristotle Papanikolaou asserts,

> the very being of God as transcendent and immanent, who brings that which is not God into communion with God, demands a theological discourse that is antinomic and keeps in tension apophatic and cataphatic theologies. Since God it that which is 'other' than creation and in this 'otherness' is a being who can be united with creation without absorbing or obliterating it, such a God can only be described in apophatic terms.[125] Insofar as the sphere of theology may be defined as the realm of "unknowing," the entire terminological framework of the cognitive faculties discussed up to this point is inapplicable in this context. According to Maximus, Θεολογία is not just the highest form of knowledge; it is beyond all knowledge that is available to human beings regarding God—who himself is also beyond all knowledge. Long before Nicholas of Cusa, Evagrius uses the phrase "boundless unknowing" to refer to

---

122. *Q. Thal.* (22) PG 90 321B, trans. Blowers-Wilken.
123. See *Q. Thal.* (62) PG 90 657D. Laga-Steel, CCSG, 133.
124. *Q. Thal.* (63) PG 90 680C. Laga-Steel, CCSG, 167.
125. Papanikolaou, *Being with God*, 44.

mystical knowledge of God. The term used to denote this level of knowledge in the writings of Dionysius and Gregory of Nazianzus is "darkness" (γνόφος), which is portrayed as being opposed to the light of knowledge.

This distinction depicts the difference in human experiences of knowledge before and after the fall. In their original state, human beings contemplate the divine logoi directly. They do not need the mediation of cognitive abilities and techniques in order to reach God. Therefore, ignorance before the fall—which is of a different sort than the ignorance that is the focus of the present discourse about knowledge—may be compared to the ignorance of mystical theology that is beyond the discourse which is carried on by discerning human beings. Nevertheless, even though the experiences of sensory and rational activities are surpassed in the ignorance of mystical theology, they leave an imprint and have an impact, insofar as they constitute a compulsory stage in humankind's ascent. The postlapsarian state gives rise to a phenomenon known as "unknowing knowledge," while the original form of knowing is said to be "complete," or "angelic," knowledge.

Of course, there is also a type of unknowing that is the result of falling away from God and of turning away from the path that leads to unity with God. Maximus understands this type of ignorance in an ontological sense—when he describes evil as ignorance of the reason for our existence in Questions to Thalassius and Chapters on Love—and in a gnoseological sense in the letter to John Cubicularius where he portrays unknowing as a vice that involves a falling away from the divine since the essence of virtue is the Logos. Maximus maintains that reason's primary vice is ignorance (ἄgnoia). As a consequence of misusing their will, human beings turn away from God and toward the sensory world. Since this movement depends on decisions made by the will, human beings' rational capacities are as much to blame for the fall as the senses. Therefore, at least one type of unknowing appears to be the result of the misuse of the rational faculty.

Ignorance (ἄγνοια) plays an important role in Maximus's theology. As mentioned above, he reveals the meaning of the term by considering several of its components. In an ontological sense, by distorting the human mind and opening up the sensory realm, ignorance has made divine knowledge completely alien to the human mind, and vice versa. In other words, ignorance has filled the mind with an impassioned knowledge of sensory things that is conditioned by the difference between material and nonmaterial aspects of nature. Yet, ignorance also has a salvific power when it enables the mind to overcome or remain blind to the temptations of the sensory world. In Questions to Thalassius, Maximus uses the word "salvific" to designate this kind of unknowing (τὴν ἕξομεν ἄγνοιαν) where, having moved beyond the burden of the senses and the activities of the discursive mind, human beings are able to contemplate God as he is. Conceived in gnoseological terms, the word "ignorance" refers to a type of super-knowledge that is either beyond discursive thought or has the negative connotations associated with the choice of sensory pleasures that leads human beings to fall away from God and results in their changed status before the deity. It appears that there are two roads that lie ahead of human beings: knowledge and life in God or unknowing and the path to non-being.

THEOLOGY

Maximus also calls theology (θεολογία) theological philosophy, theological contemplation, mystical theology (μυστικὴ θεολογία), and theological science. He uses these designations to denote the third step in the process of attaining knowledge of God—which follows praxis and contemplation. As we have seen, Maximus reformulates inherited conceptions of the different steps of knowing. Thus, contemplation of the *logoi* involves a broad range of methods of knowing that extend from the particular capacities that distinguish the lower levels of the visible world all the way to the intelligible domain. However, theology transcends the sphere of contemplation. It is given by grace, and cannot be attained by human effort.

The realm of theology is beyond nature; it is a supra-natural dimension of knowledge that not only rejects all ties with the senses and reason, but is also detached from the mind; sensible and intelligible entities; flesh and matter; and form, quality, quantity, figure, and time. In other words, theology presupposes a renunciation of the mind, of all images and representations, of all thought and intellectual activities, and, in short, of anything that characterizes the created world. This movement resembles an apophatical way to God whereby God is reached by rejecting everything we think we know.

According to Maximus, theology is the Trinity's self-revelation, and at the same time, it entails contemplating divine life in a participatory way, given that it is possible for human beings to step beyond the limits of human nature. In this second representation of theology—which "originates in experience," but transcends all concepts, images, and representations—human beings become part of divine life in eternal well-being.[126] Knowledge of God that transcends being is not only unattainable for the senses and reason, but also for the mind (νοῦς).[127] Thus, theology surpasses thinking and knowledge, as well as sensory phenomena. It involves "the cessation of the movement of the mind around sensible things."[128] Maximus calls this cessation of every activity of the senses, reason, and the mind "rest."

Papanikolaou similarly states: "Union with God is not knowledge of God as an object but an experience of God, a mystical experience that surpasses all understanding and description."[129] Therefore, theology is a special kind of suprarational knowledge, which is beyond that which is thinkable and, because of that, is inexpressible. This means that "knowledge" is not the right term for this stage of spiritual growth. The sphere of theology is the abode of ignorance, so the whole body of terminology used up to this point to describe human capacities for knowing is inapplicable here. According to Maximus, Θεολογία is not just the highest form of knowledge; it involves a relationship with the God who is beyond every kind of human knowledge.[130]

Maximus uses apophatical epithets inherited from Dionysius to underscore the impossibility of describing this spiritual stage insofar as it is does not belong to the discursive mode of knowing. These include hyperknowledge, supraknowledge (ὑπεργνωκώς), and ignorance (ἄγνοια). The divine Logos is incarnate in the virtues and in natural contemplation, but the third stage of knowledge is characterized by a state of "otherness" or "ignorance" that is the very opposite of the mind's definitive motion. This final stage consummates God's fulfilment by ignorance, while simultaneously not depriving the mind of the experience that it has attained during the first two stages of the process of acquiring knowledge.

Before Nicholas of Cusa spoke of "learned ignorance," Evagrius used the term "infinite ignorance" to refer to mystical knowledge of God. In the works of Dionysius and Gregory of Nyssa, this stage of knowledge is called "darkness" (γνόφος), which is portrayed as being opposed to the light of

---

126. Noble, *Tracking God*, 5.

127. *Amb. Io.* (10) PG 91 1128A.

128. *Q. Thal.* (65) PG 90 756C. Laga-Steel, CCSG, 279.

129. Papanikolaou, "Ontology and Theological Epistemology-Knowledge as Union," 21.

130. *Amb. Io.* (1) PG 91 1036B.

knowledge. Thunberg engages in a detailed analysis of various interpretations of infinite ignorance, or infinite knowledge, as Maximus later calls it.[131] In that work, Thunberg demonstrates the conflict between Evagrius's understanding of infinite ignorance and the darkness of the unknown that is described by Dionysius and Gregory of Nyssa. Maximus speaks of the darkness of the unknown in passages where he tries to unite these two positions, and his reflections on Dionysius's interpretation of the divine darkness that Moses enters during the revelation on Mount Sinai (Exodus 20:21) becomes one of the main themes of the mystical theology of the Orthodox Church. Apophatic theology begins here.[132] The image of Moses turning toward God in the darkness, which first appears in the Corpus Areopagiticum, becomes the key image of the unknowableness of divine nature in the works of the Church Fathers.[133] Maximus develops this theme in Ambigua 10:

> So again Moses followed God who called him, and, passing beyond everything here below, entered into the cloud, where God was, that is, into the formless, invisible, and bodiless state, with a mind free from any relationship to anything other than God. Having come into this state, insofar as human nature is worthy of it, he receives, as a worthy prize for that blessed ascent, knowledge encompassing the genesis of time and nature.[134] In other words, by following God's call, Moses moves beyond everything here and steps into the darkness where God—the imageless, invisible, and incorporeal being—is (Exodus 20:21). There, his mind is free of all attachments to anything but God. Being in the divine darkness—to the extent that human nature merits that—Moses receives, as a fitting reward for his "blessed ascent," knowledge regarding "the genesis of time and nature." Elsewhere, it is said that

> the most penetrating mind converses in silence with itself, and through assiduous perseverance in a discerning contemplation of being, learns, in an inexpressible way, of the wise economy of divine providence, . . . and then, through mystical theology, which in unexpressed delight, confides in the pure mind through prayer, the mind enters into ignorance and, in inexpressible way—as if in darkness—is united with God and, like Moses receiving the tablets

131. Thunberg, *Microcosm and Mediator*, 382–83.
132. Pseudo-Dionysius, *De mystica theologia*, PG 3, 1000–1001.
133. See, for example, Gregory of Nyssa, *De vita Mosis*, PG 44 29–430.
134. Amb.Io.(10) PG 91 117B.

of commandments on Mount Sinai, is drawn inwardly into the dogma of devotion and outwardly into the grace of the virtues... The person who prefers pursuing the virtues to wealth and glory becomes a spiritual Moses.[135] Ignorance

There is a passage in the *Ambigua* that was already mentioned in conjunction with the doctrine of the logoi. This text emphasizes turning toward "darkness," which is presented as a gnoseological category. In addition, it says that

> if we exclude the highest and apophatic theology of the Word, according to which the Word is inexpressible, unthinkable, and is not related at all to the knowable ... and nothing in no way is not part of Him, then the many logoi are the One Logos, and the one, many.[136]

Similarly, Maximus suggests three interpretations of the reflections on Easter in which Gregory of Nazianzus speaks of the initial state of human beings before their fall from Paradise. Specifically, Maximus hypothesizes that the human body had a different composition prior to the fall, and he affirms this "lightness of being."[137] Reflecting on the impassionate and pure existence that is given by grace, Maximus envisions a blessed state of direct knowledge, although he also says that the darkness of the unknown still prevents us from seeing the truth because of the turn of the mind toward the sphere of hesitation.

In his second interpretation, Maximus continues in the gnoseological vein when he says:

> Although being impassionate by grace, he did not allow himself to be misled by passionate images according to pleasure ... And being wise, he is above natural contemplation because of knowledge. Thus the first man did not have anything between him and God that could be known and that obscured their future unity through love with God.[138]

Maximus concludes by describing the differences that characterize human experiences of knowledge before and after the fall. In their primal state, human beings contemplate the divine logoi directly. They do not need the mediation of cognitive capacities and techniques to reach God. Thus, insofar as igno-

---

135. See Gregory of Nyssa, De vita Mosis.

136. *Amb. Io.*(7) PG 91 1081B. See also trans. by Maximos Constas, On Difficulties, 101.

137. To borrow a phrase from Kundera, *The Unbearable Lightness of Being* (1984).

138. See Q. *Thal.* (Introd.) PG 90 253CD. Laga-Steel, CCSG, 31.

rance before the fall is different from that which distinguishes the present discourse of discerning persons, it is identified with mystical theology—which is beyond discourse. Yet, even if the experiences born of sensory and rational activities are transcended in the case of mystical theology, they leave their traces and constitute an obligatory stage in the human ascent. The postlapsarian state gives rise to a phenomenon that is known as "ignorant knowledge," while the primal mode of knowing is said to be complete, or angelic, knowledge.

Of course, there is also a type of ignorance that is the result of falling away from the mode of knowing that leads human beings to unity with God. Maximus primarily regards such ignorance ontologically—when he describes evil as ignorance of the Cause of being in Questions to Thalassius and Chapters on Love—and gnoseologically in the letter to John Cubicularius where he says that ignorance is a vice of the rational soul that falls away from the divine, insofar as the Logos is the essence of virtue.[139] According to Maximus, reason's primary vice is ignorance (ἄγνοια). As a result of misusing their will, human beings turn away from God and toward the sensory world. Since this movement depends on decisions made by the will, human beings' rational capacities are as much to blame for the fall as the senses are. Ignorance is a result of an abuse of the rational faculty.

IGNORANCE AS THE VICE OF THE SOUL

The dynamics that characterize the relationship between ignorance and knowledge constitute one of the main themes of Maximus's gnoseology and anthropology. When ignorance is viewed as a vice, emphasis is placed on the important role that knowledge plays in facilitating self-creating acts that reflect the proper use of free will. Of course, ignorance has a broader meaning.[140] Here, however, the emphasis will be on the interactions that

139. Q. Thal. (Prol.) PG 90 257B. Laga-Steel, CCSG, 35. Car. 3.29; *Maxime le Confesseur, Lettres*, trans. Ponsoye, 30.

140. Ignorance is a term that has a variety of uses in the works of Maximus and other Church Fathers. At the level that is above what can be known, ignorance is the stage of knowledge where the discursive powers of the human mind are no longer use. At this stage, it is not reason, intellect, or even the human will that act; rather, the sense of God's presence, which characterizes mystical contemplation in ecstasy, is operative. The phrase "infinite ignorance" refers to this state of knowing God as mystery. This is a "knowing (learned) ignorance" or "supreme ignorance" (ὑπεραγνώστως), as Maximus calls it in *Chapters on Love*, 3.99.

go on between ignorance and knowledge in the realm of that which can be achieved by human beings. Therefore, I will explore ignorance only in the sense that has to do with falling away from knowledge of God. Insofar as human beings who have been created in the image of God are called to be in communion with him, they are considered to be participants in the divine-human dialogue. As created beings, they bear the divine logoi within themselves and are directed toward the Logos throughout the process of attaining knowledge).

It has already been noted that in the Second Letter to John Cubicularius, Maximus asserts that the primary vice of the rational soul is ignorance (ἄγνοια).[141] Likewise, in The Disputation with Pyrrhus, Maximus quotes a work by Cyril of Alexandria entitled Against Theodoret, which leads him to assert that "nothing natural is involuntary in a rational nature."[142] Therefore, ignorance results from the misuse of the rational capacity—or the human will. As we have seen, Maximus invents the terms "gnomi" and "gnomic will" for the special aspect of the human will that is a unique characteristic of human beings because only they are subject to hesitation.[143] Here, it is important to note that rather than talking about virtues and vices as such, Maximus prefers to speak of the human disposition toward one or the other (ἕξις τῆς ἀρετῆς or ἕξις τῆς κακίας).

According to Maximus, being is given to human individuals by grace; well-being can be attained through human beings' own efforts; and eternal well-being is also given by God through illumination. Thus, the dynamic process of attaining knowledge, which is ontologically grounded in the three modes of being, reveals the interrelationship that exists between created and uncreated nature. The self's openness and the constant movement of the organic entity of body and soul toward Goodness comprise the existence of knowing human beings. As the actualization of naturally given virtues makes unity with the Logos possible, God becomes reachable for human beings, insofar as the whole process of human knowledge that happens through the logoi coincides with the self-revelation of the Logos itself. The progressive nature of human existence means that the constant observance of the virtues and the ever-increasing presence of the Logos in human beings go hand in hand.

---

141. *Maxime le Confesseur, Lettres,* trans. Ponsoye, 30 and Louth, *Maximus the Confessor,* 85.

142. *Pyrr.* PG 91 287A–354B.

143. Ibid.

Human Knowledge According to Saint Maximus

In Maximus's thought, there is a constant tension between different levels of ignorance and different objects of knowledge. This tension is evident in the postlapsarian tropos of human existence where ignorance (ἄγνοια) becomes an unavoidable element of human existence because the Fall conceals the logoi of creation from human sight. Thus, all human "sciences" and insights are ultimately based on ignorance. At the final stage of human perfection that is opened up by the Logos's self-revelation, there is another kind of ignorance—an infinite ignorance—that is the highest form of knowledge. Therefore, I would characterize the aspect of the ascent of human knowledge that is occasioned by the proper use of the human will as a transformation of human ignorance. Human beings in a postlapsarian state of existence must dwell with ignorance as part of their condition; yet, they simultaneously must remake ignorance into a mode of existing in knowledge that is defined by dialogue with the divine Logos.[144]

The mystery of ignorance (ἄγνοια) is an important component of Maximus's thought. As was noted above, Maximus differentiates this notion on several levels. Ontologically speaking, in Questions to Thalassius, it is said that evil is ignorance of the benevolent cause of existence. This ignorance, which bends the mind by bending the mind, has alienated the mind from divine knowledge and conversely, has made human beings passionate about sensible things. In Questions to Thalassius, Maximus calls this type of ignorance "salvific" (τὴν ἕξομεν ἄγνοιαν) since it constitutes an arena where, without the burden of the senses and having moved beyond discursive reasoning, we will be able to contemplate God "as he is" and "to see God face to face."[145] In the gnoseological context, "ignorance" has a rather negative meaning, insofar as it refers to falling away from God because of a preference for sensible pleasures. This choice leads to a transformation of human beings' status before God. At this juncture, there are two ways that lie ahead; that is, knowledge that corresponds to life in God or ignorance that leads to nothingness and nonbeing.

Adam's ignorance and humankind's knowledge before the fall is also a key issue in Maximus's writings and in scholarly literature regarding his work. Maximus says that the Logos restores the "original knowledge" that human beings have before the fall, and van Balthasar's research has led to the following interpretation of Maximus's assertion that before the fall, "nothing obscured the knowledge of God." This statement suggests that there was

---

144. See Dimitrova, "From Logos to 'Dialogos,'" 191–210.
145. *Q. Thal.* (Introd.) PG 90 261C. Laga-Steel, CCSG, 41.

a time when human beings "knew" God.[146] However, Maximus continues that nothing prevented [humankind from being] united with God through the next . . . motion [directed] toward him.[147] Therefore knowledge and motion toward God were given to Adam as potentialities, but he was not able to fulfill them. Thus, according to Maximus, the possibility of Adam's transition from the imperfect knowledge that characterizes his fallen state to knowledge of the initial, pure state is assumed to be possible.

---

146. Von Balthasar, Kosmische Liturgie; Petrov, Максим Исповедник 36.
147. See Q.Thal. (Introd.) PG 90 244A. Laga-Steel, CCSG, 17.

5

Cataphatic and Apophatic Ways of Knowledge

COGNITIVE METHODS

Exploring human capacities for knowledge and examining the processes and techniques of knowing brings us to a question that may mark the beginning of any intellectual activity or cognitive path: That is, how can human beings express their experiences of the divine presence? One of the central pursuits of human knowledge concerns the vital question of how our encounters with God can be shared. Knowing the One who transcends being—and yet at the time same time, is totally immanent—is possible by means of modes of affirmation and negation. Both approaches manifest the limits of human abilities to attain knowledge of the divine essence, insofar as they both begin and end in silence at the point where "God touches the depth of our being, and changes our understanding of what we know by leading us through the darkness of not knowing towards the intimate communion of all things in God."[1]

Designations like "being," "light," and "life" reflect the limits of human nature by affirming the existence of God as such and providing evidence of our inability to transcend the boundaries of our nature. These terms are "(πολυώνυμα), but the other (lower) class of "divine names" are various notions (ἐπίνοιαι) that constitute the (ἑτερώνημα) which describe God ad extra—that is, in terms of his various ways of relating to the world as protector, savior, and so forth."[2] The mode of negation (apophaticism) expresses the

---

1. Noble, *Tracking God*, 78.
2. Demetracopoulos, "Glossogony or Epistemology?" 389.

unattainability of the Creator by creation more accurately than affirmative (cataphatic) statements do. However, according to Maximus, both methods of knowledge have a justifiable place and are of equal value in enabling human beings to reach the knowledge of divinity that is available to them. In the Confessor's estimation, one method confirms that God exists as the cause of all things, while the other mode denies that he exists because of his incomparability as the cause of all things. Discourse about God takes place by means of the contrasting processes of negation (ἀπόφασις) and affirmation (κατάφασις). Only negative (apophatic) knowledge of God is available to human beings, while angels are initiated into positive, cataphatic theology as well. This enables a «negation of negation,» wherein the negation of human knowledge, which is negative with respect to the divine, allows us to take part in affirmative, angelic knowledge of divinity.[3]

The faculties, levels, and techniques of knowledge that have been described have brought us to a couple of important questions that stand at the beginning of nearly every cognitive activity and path to knowledge; that is, how it is possible to express our experience of knowledge and what are the methods of knowing? Maximus says that those who start from divine words that are cataphatically positioned in relation to the visible make the Word flesh because they recognize that God is the reason for everything, while those who begin from divine words that are apophatically detached from visible things make the Word spirit. They view things as if they were in God, and they turn toward God by knowing the supraknowable, which proceeds from that which human knowledge cannot attain.[4] In the Mystagogia, Maximus reflects on this dynamic by declaring:

> In this way [God] can in no way be associated by nature with any being and thus because of his superbeing is more fittingly referred to as non-being. For since it is necessary that we understand correctly the difference between God and creatures, then the affirmation of superbeing must be the negation of beings, and the affirmation of being must be the negation of superbeing.Maximus goes on to enlighten the reader by adding that

> both names, being and nonbeing, are to be reverently applied to him although not at all properly. In one sense they are both proper to him, one affirming the being of God as cause of beings, the other completely denying in him the being which all beings have,

---

3. See Papanikolaou, "Ontology and Theological Epistemology," 9–48.
4. *Th. Ec.* (2) 39 PG 90 1141 D–1144 A.

based on his preeminence as cause. On the other hand, neither is proper to him because neither represents in any way an affirmation of the essence of the being under discussion as to its substance or nature. For nothing whatsoever, whether being or nonbeing, is linked to him as a cause, no being or what is called being, no nonbeing, or what is called nonbeing, is properly close to Him. He has in fact a simple existence, unknowable and inaccessible to all and altogether beyond understanding which transcends all affirmation and negation.[5]

In other words, both ways of speaking constitute equally appropriate means of alluding to God, since the cataphatic perspective affirms that God is the cause of everything, while apophatic emphases deny that God exists because—as the Cause of everything—he is totally incomparable. Yet, both modes of speaking are equally erroneous, insofar as they do not provide knowledge of the essence and nature of the divine apex of existence. Discourse about God is carried out by means of the contrasting processes of negation (ἀπόφασις) and affirmation (κατάφασις). Only "negative" (apophatic) knowledge of God can be attained by human beings, while angels also have access to "positive" (cataphatic) knowledge. This leads to a "negation of negation," wherein renouncing human knowledge that is negative with respect to the divine provides an opportunity for us to participate in an affirmative angelic, knowledge of divinity.

The path of philosophical knowledge involves intellectual work. Understanding and thinking, which are situated in the soul where knowledge of God has its roots, are absolutely a priori for the human mind. Even if the divine essence cannot be known or expressed, it can be experienced. This means that negation is not the same as rejection; instead, it enables an openness to the Other and a readiness to experience the Inexpressible. Describing this experience would entail realizing that our limited nature needs to have an unlimited possibility ahead of it in order to set its goals—which, in turn, would mean recognizing that apophaticism is an inclination or disposition to embrace God's transcending mode of being in our world.

Through knowledge of God, human beings reach true likeness to the ontologically given image of God. The three motions of the soul, which involve the senses, reason, and the mind, correspond to negative theology, affirmative theology, and symbolic theology, respectively. Due to these connections, the relationship between anthropology, cosmology, and

---

5. *Myst.* (1) PG 91 664AC.

knowledge is apprehended. There are important differences between the ways in which Dionysius and Maximus envision the process of acquiring knowledge. In Dionysius's works, the ascent of intelligible entitites is related to the negation of lower levels; thus, the highest stage represents the pure, inexpressible limit of the mind and of the knowledge that is possible for it. However, Knut Alfsvag succinctly notes that "for Maximus apophaticism is shaped by his understanding of the incarnation and resurrection as God appearing from beyond all possibilities."[6] In other words, Maximus uses a different approach which is entails a "passing" (διάβᾰσις). According to him, contemplation presupposes a διάβᾰσις of the senses, which ascend toward the mind with the assistance of reason, while for Dionysius, the ascent from the sensible realm to the intelligible sphere by means of the contemplative mind does not presuppose the ascent of the senses and reason to the mind. In contrast, in Maximus the Confessor, every succeeding level incorporates the previous one. This is how a positive assessment of ontological and gnoseological stages of being are made in the great synthesis of Maximus thought.

---

6. Alfsvag, *What No Mind Has Conceived*, 69.

Conclusion

Human knowledge is a unifying element in a large number of Maximus's writings. Nearly all of his works are centered around the issue of gnoseology, which consequently shapes his hermeneutical system. Thus, central questions regarding Christology, anthropology, and eschatology are clarified by means of his views of knowledge. The creation of human beings in the image of God establishes the beginning of the process of acquiring knowledge. Attaining the likeness of the creator is a key task of human existence, but achieving its completeness and entirety is possible only by returning to the principle that constitutes the meaning of existence and the beginning of everything. In the end, all capacities for knowledge have the telos to turn us back to the beginning and to their source. The Logos (λόγος) is the key component in the relationship between mind and body.

The mind (νοῦς) is the divine capacity that is directed toward the intelligible world and gathers the logoi of things which are disclosed through activity of the senses into the one Logos. The senses (αἴσθησις) are ennobled by the Logos, which directs the mind and "renews" human beings through God's grace, so that they can know God. Maximus maintains that at this point, the motions of knowledge, which take place through the senses, reason, and the mind, give way to one movement. The stages of ascent toward knowledge of God make up the unified activity of the whole constitution of human beings, who recognize themselves and God in the Logos and thus reject "sensual" pleasure because, to draw upon the Confessor's words, life in "spiritual enjoyment" requires a certain disposition to change that is related to personal choice. This understanding affirms the beatitude of those who know the Logos and understand both its meaning and the wisdom of the mind that is eternally directed toward Truth. All of the Church Fathers gauge knowing and understanding in terms of love, although virtue and

Conclusion

praxis are the necessary condition for human growth in gnosis. Even if it is not attained, Truth establishes the limits of human knowledge—which is engaged in an everlasting return to the Beginning.

Bibliography

Alfeev, Il. *Jizn i uchenie St. Grigoria Bogoslova*. St. Petersburg: Aleteia, 2001. [In Russian: Алфеев, Иларион, Жизнь и учение Св. Григория Богослова.]

Alfsvag, K. *What No Mind Has Conceived: On the Significance of Christological Apophaticism*. Leuven: Peeters, 2010.

Allen, P., and Neil Brownen, eds., trans. *Maximus the Confessor and His Companions: Documents from Exile*. Sydney: Oxford Early Christian Texts, 2003.

Anselm of Canterbury. *Four Dialogues: De Veritate*. Bibliotheca Christiana 6. Sofia: Lik, 2002. [In Bulgarian: Анселм Кенърбърийски.Четири диалога, За истината.]

Arch. Sophrony. *Voir Dieu tel qu'I lest*. Perspective Orthodoxe 5. Genève: Labor et Fides, 1984. [In Bulgarian: Арх. Софроний Сахаров. Ще видим Бога, както си е.]

Archiv für mittelalterliche Philosophie und Kultur, Heft 1–15. Sofia: Iztok–Zapad, 1994–2009. [In Bulgarian: Архив за средновековна философия и култура.]

Aristotle. *De Anima*. Sofia: Science and Art, 1978. [In Bulgarian: Аристотел, *За душата*.]

———. *De Anima*. 3rd ed. Books 2, 3. Translation, introduction, and notes by D. W. Hamlyn. Oxford: Oxford University Press, 1977.

———. *Metaphysics*. Sofia: Sonm, 2000. [In Bulgarian: Аристотел, *Метафизика*.]

———. *Nichomahean Ethics*. Sofia: Gal i ko, 1993. [In Bulgarian: Аристотел, Никомахова етика.]

Armstrong, A. H. *The Cambridge History of Later Greek and Early Medieval Philosophy*. Cambridge: Cambridge University Press,1967.

Armstrong, A. H., and Robert A. Markus. *Christian Faith and Greek Philosophy*. London: Darton, Longman & Todd, 1960.

Augustine. "On True Religion." In *Earlier Writings*, selected, translated, and introduction by John H. S. Burleigh. London: Westminster, 1953.

Ayres, L. *Nicaea and Its Legacy: An Approach to Fourth-Century Trinitarian Theology*. Oxford: Oxford University Press, 2004.

Basil the Great. *On the Holy Spirit*. Translated by David Anderson. Crestwood, NY: St. Vladimir's Seminary Press, 1980.

———. *On the Human Condition*. Translated and introduction by Verna N. Harrison. Crestwood, NY: St. Vladimir's Seminary Press, 2005.

Bathrellos, D. *The Byzantine Christ: Person, Nature, and Will in the Christology of Saint Maximus the Confessor*. Oxford Early Christian Studies. New York: Oxford University Press, 2004.

———. *Maximus the Confessor, Jesus Christ and the Transfiguration of the World.* Oxford University Press, 2015.

Blowers, Paul M. "The Dialectics and Therapeutics of Desire in Maximus the Confessor." *Vigiliae Christianae* 65 (2011) 435–51.

———. *Exegesis and Spiritual Pedagogy in Maximus the Confessor: An Investigation of the Quaestiones ad Thalassium.* Notre Dame: University of Notre Dame Press, 1988.

Blowers, Paul, and Robert Wilken Louis. *On the Cosmic Mystery of Jesus Christ: Selected Writings from Maximus the Confessor.* Crestwood, NY: St. Vladimir's Seminary Press, 2003.

Boiadjiev, Tz. *Antichnata filosofia kato fenomen na kulturata.* Sofia: Liubomudrie, 1994. [Бояджиев, Ц. *Античната философия като феномен на културата.*]

———. *Krugovrat na duha.* Sofia: Lik, 1998. [Бояджиев, Ц. *Кръговрат на духа.*]

———. *Nepisanoto uchenie na Platon.* Sofia: Nauka i izkustvo, 1984. [Бояджиев, Ц. *Неписаното учение на Платон.*]

———. *Noshtta prez srednovekovieto.* Sofia: Sofia, 2000. [Бояджиев, Ц. *Нощта през средновековието.*]

Boudignon, Chr. *Maxime le Confesseur était-il constantinopolitain?* Philomathestatos. Leuven, 2002.

Bradshaw, D. *Aristotle East and West: Metaphysics and the Division of Christendom.* Cambridge: Cambridge University Press, 2004.

———. "The Logoi of Beings in Greek Patristic Thought." In *Toward an Ecology of Transfiguration: Orthodox Christian Perspectives on the Environment, Nature, and Creation*, edited by John Chryssavgis and Bruce V. Foltz. Fordham University Press, 2013.

Brownen, N. "The *Lives* of Pope Martin I and Maximus the Confessor: Some Reconsiderations of Dating and Provenance." *Byzantion* 68 (1998) 91–109.

Christou, Panayiotis. *Double Knowledge according to Gregory Palamas.* Από: Π. Κ. Χρήστου, ΘεολογικάΜελετήματα, τ. 3 (ΝηπτικάκαιΗσυχαστικά), Θεσσαλονίκη, 1977.

Constas N. "On Difficulties in Church Fathers, Maximos the Confessor," Dumbarton Oaks, Medieval Library. Vol 1,2. Harvard University Press, 2014.

Cooper, G. A. *The Body in St. Maximus the Confessor—Holy Flesh, Wholly Deified.* Oxford: Oxford University Press, 2005.

———. "Maximus the Confessor on the Structural Dynamics of Revelation." *Vigiliae Christianae* 55 (2001) 161–86.

Corpus Christianorum. Series Graeca. Brepols: Leuven University Press, 1977–2010.

Corrigan, K. *Evagrius and Gregory, Mind, Soul, and Body in the Fourth Century.* London: Ashgate, 2010.

Daley, E. Brian. "Apocatastasis and 'Honorable Silence' in the Eschatology of St. Maximus the Confessor." In *Actes du Symposium sur Maxime le Confesseur*, edited by Felix Heinzer and Christoph Schönborn, 309–39. Fribourg: Éditions Universitaires, 1982.

Dalmais, Irénée-Henri. "Un traité de théologie contemplative: Le 'Comentaire du Pater' de saint Maxime le Confesseur." *Revue d'ascétique et de mystique* 29 (1953) 123–59.

De Andia, Y. *Denys L'Aréopagite—Tradition et Métamorphoses.* Paris: Librairie J. Vrin, 2006.

———. *Denys L'Aréopagite et sa postériorité en Orient at en Occident.* Paris, 1997.

De Libera, A. *La philosophie médievale.* Paris, 1993.

Bibliography

Demetracopoulos, John A. *Glossogony or Epistemology? The Stoic Character of Basil of Caesarea's and Eunomius' Epistemological Notion of* ἐpίnoiaand. English version. Proceedings of the 10th International Colloquium on Gregory of Nyssa, Olomouc, September 15–18, 2004. Edited by Lenka Karfikova and Johannes Zachhuber. Leiden: Brill, 2007.

Dimitrova, N. "From Image to the Likeness." *Christianity and Culture* 2(49) (2010) 37. [Димитрова, От образа към подобието, в Християнство и култура, бр.]

———. "From Logos to 'Dialogos': The Problem of Ignorance and the 'Dialogical' Knowledge According to St. Maximus the Confessor." *Communio Viatorum* IV (2013) 191–210.

———. "The Knowing Man according to St. Maximus the Confessor; or, From Image to the Likeness." In *Christianity and Culture* 2(49) (2010) 37. [In Bulgarian: Димитрова, Невена. „Познаващият човек според св. Максим Изповедник или от образа към подобието." в Християнство и култура, бр. 2.]

Epifanovich, S. L. *Materiali k izucheniu jizni i tvorenii prepodobni Maksima Izpovednika.* Kiev, 1917. [In Russian: Епифанович, С.Л., Материалы к изучению жизни и творений преп. Максима Исповедника.]

———. *Prepodobniat Maksim Izpovednik I vizantijskoto bogoslovie.* Sofia: Omofor, 2008. [In Bulgarian: Епифанович,С.Л., Преподобният Максим Изповедник и византийското богословие.]

Évagre le Pontique. *Traité Pratiqueou le moine.* Vol. 1. Introduction Antoine Guillaumont and Claire Guillamont. Paris: CERF, 1971.

Evdokimov, P. *L'Orthodoxie.* Paris, 1979.

———. *Pravoslavieto.* Sofia: Omofor, 2006. [In Bulgarian: Евдокимов Павел, Православието.]

Farrell, P. J. *Free Choice in St. Maximus the Confessor.* St. Tikhon's Seminary Press, 1987.

Флоровский, Георгий. Восточные отцы Церкви *V-VIII* веков. Москва: АСТ, 2003.

Florovsky, Georges. *The Byzantine Fathers of the Fifth to Eighth Centuries.* Paris: YMCA, 1933.

Garrigues, Miguel J. *Maxime le Confesseur: La charité, avenir divin de l'homme.* Paris: Beauchesne, 1976.

Gersh, S. *From Iamblichus to Eriugena: An Investigation of the Prehistory and Evolution of the Pseudo-Dionysian Tradition.* Leiden: Brill, 1978.

Gilson, Et. *History of Christian Philosophy in the Middle Ages.* Sofia: Sofia University Press, 1994. [In Bulgarian: Жилсон, Ет. Бьонер, Ф. Християнската философия.]

Gregory of Nazianzus. *Five Theological Orations.* Translation and commentary by Ivan Hristov. Sofia: Gal iko, 1994. [In Bugarian: Григорий Назиански, Пет Богословски слова.]

Gregory of Nyssa. *On Soul and Resurrection.* Sofia: Lik, 2001. [In Bulgarian: Григорий Нисийски, За душата и възкресението.]

Grillmeier, Aloys. *Christ in Christian Tradition.* Vol. 1, *From the Apostolic Age to Chalcedon (451)*; vol. 2, *From the Council of Chalcedon (451) to Gregory the Great (590-604).* London, 1995.

Healy, Nicholas J. *The Eschatology of Hans Urs von Balthasar: Eschatology as Communion.* Oxford: Oxford University Press, 2005.

Heinzer, Felix, and Schönborn, Christoph. *Actes du Symposium sur Maxime le Confesseur: Fribourg, 2–5 september 1980.* Fribourg: Éditions Universitaires, 1982.

Bibliography

Heinzmann, R. *Philosophie des Mittelalters*. Stuttgart: Kohlhammer, 1998. [In Bulgarian: Хайнцман, Р. *Философия на Средновековието*.]

Hristov, I. *Bitie I sushtestvuvane v diskusiata za metoda mejdu St. Gregory Palamas I Varlaam*. In *Humanism, Culture, Religion*, 37–49. Sofia: Lik, 1997. [In Bulgarian: Христов, И., Битие и съществуване в дискусията за метода между св. Григорий Палама и Варлаам.]

———. "The Hierarchy of Being in 'Hexaemeron' by Joan Exarch." In *Archiv für mittelalterliche Philosophie und Kultur*, 1:35. [In Bulgarian: Христов, И., Йерархията на битието в „Шестоднев" на Йоан Екзарх.]

———. *Hristianskiat neoplatonizum c korpusa na Areopagitikite* in *Neoplatonism i christianstvo. Gruckata tradicia III–IV vek*, 129–72. Sofia: Lik, 2002. [In Bulgarian: Христов, И., Християнският неоплатонизъм в корпуса на "Ареопагитиките." в Неоплатонизъм и християнство. Гръцката традиция III-VIв.]

Ierodiakonou, K. *Byzantine Philosophy and Its Ancient Sources*. Oxford: Oxford University Press, 2002.

Izbornik. *Svetootechesko nasledstvo*. Sofia: Omofor, 2001. [In Bulgarian: Изборник – Светоотеческо наследство.]

Jeauneau, É. "Jean l›Érigène et les Ambigua ad Iohannem de Maxime le Confesseur." In *Actes du Symposium sur Maxime le Confesseur*, edited by Felix Heinzer and Christoph Schönborn, 343–64. Fribourg: Éditions Universitaires, 1982.

———. "Θεοτόκια grecs conservés en version latine." In *Philohistôr: Miscellanea in honorem Caroli Laga septuagenari*, edited by A. Schoors and P. Van Deun, 399–421. Orientalia Lovaniensia Analecta 60. Leuven: Peeters, 1994.

Kapriev, G. *Byzantica minora*. Sofia: Lik, 2000. [In Bulgarian: Каприев, Георги. *Byzantinicaminora*.]

Kapriev, G. *Byzantine Philosophy*. Sofia: Lik, 2001. [In Bulgarian: Каприев, Георги. Византийската философия.]

Karayannis, V. *Maxime le Confesseur—Essence et* Énergies *de dieu*. Paris: Beauchesne (Theologie historique), 1993.

Kartashev, V. A. *Vselenskie sobori*. Moscow: Eksmo, 2006. [In Russian: Карташев, В. А. Вселенскиесоборы.]

Knežević M., B. Šijaković, eds., Arche kai Telos. Aspects of Philosophical and Theological Thought of Maximus the Confessor, Nikšić 2006.

Knežević M., ed., The Ways of Byzantine Philosophy, Alhambra, CA: Sebastian Press; Kosovska Mitrovica: Faculty of Philosophy, 2015.

Kundera, M. "The Unbearable Lightness of Being." London: Faber & Faber, 1984.

Laga, C. "Maximus as a Stylist in Quaestiones ad Thalassium." In *Maximus Confessor: Actes du Symposium sur Maxime le Confesseur*, edited by F. Heinzer and C. Schönborn, 139–46. Fribourg, 1982.

Larchet, Jean-Claude. *La divinisation de l'homme selon saint Maxime le Confesseur*. Paris: CERF, 1996.

———. *Maxime le Confesseur, médiateur entre l'Orient et l'Occident*. Paris: CERF, 1998.

———. *Saint Maxime le Confesseur (580–662)*. Paris: CERF, 2003.

Lebedev, P. Aleksei. *Istoria vselenskih soborov*. Chast II: Vselenskih sobori VI, VII I VIII vekov. Moscow: Olega Abishko, biblioteka hristianskoi misli, 2004. [In Russian: Лебедев, П. Алексей. История Вселенских Соборов. Часть2: Вселенские Соборы *VI, VII и VIII* веков.]

Bibliography

Léthel, François-Marie, *Théologie de l'agonie du Christ: la liberté humaine du fils de Dieu et son importance sotériologique mises en lumière par saint Maxime le Confesseur*. Paris: Beauchesne,1979.

Lévy, A. *Le créé et l'incréé. Maxime le Confesseur et Thomas d'Aquin*. Librarie Philosophique. Paris: Vrin, 2006.

Lollar, G. J. *To See Into the Life of Things: The Contemplation of Nature in Maximus the Confessor and His Predece*. Vol. 2. Turnhout Brepols, 2013.

Lossky, Vladimir. *The Mystical Theology of the Eastern Church*. Crestwood, NY: St. Vladimir's Seminary Press, 1976. [Лоски Владимир. Очерк върху мистическото богословие на Източната Църква.]

Loudovikos, N. "A Eucharistic Ontology: Maximus the Confessor's Eschatological Ontology of Being as Dialogical Reciprocity." Brookline, Massachusetts: Holy Cross Orthodox Press, 2010.

Loudovikos, N. "Being and Essence Revisited: Reciprocal Logoi and Energies in Maximus the Confessor and Thomas Aquinas, and the Genesis of the Self-referring Subjects" pp 117-146 . Appeared in: Teimos: Aportacoes Filosofica de Leste e Oeste = Theisms: Philosophical Contributions from the East to the West/ ed. Manuel G. Sumares. In: Revista Portuguesa de Filosofia. - Braga. - Volume 72 (2016), Issue 1 [ISBN: 978-972-697-253-2; published by Axioma.]

Louth, A. "Apophatic Theology and the Liturgy in St. Maximos the Confessor." In *Wisdom of the Byzantine Church: Evagrios of Pontos and Maximos the Confessor; Four Lectures by Andrew Louth* (1997 Paine Lectures in Religion), edited by J. Raitt, 34–45. Columbia, MO, 1998.

———. *Maximus the Confessor*. Early Church Fathers. London: Routledge, 1996.

———. "St. Denys the Areopagite and St. Maximus the Confessor: A Question of Influence." In *Studia Patristica* XXVII, edited by Elizabeth A. Livingstone, 166–74. Leuven, 1993.

Lurie, Vadim M. *Istoria vizantiiskoi filosofii*. St. Petersburg: Axiōma, 2006. [In Russian: Лурье, В. М. *Византийская философия. Формативный период*.]

Madden, J. N. "Aisthesisnoera (Diadochus-Maximus)." In *StudiaPatristica* XXIII, edited by Elizabeth A. Livingstone, 53–60. Leuven: Peeters, 1989.

Matsoukas, A. N. *La vie en Dieu selon Maxime le Confesseur: cosmologie, anthropologie, sociologie*. Paris: AXIOS, 1994.

Maximus the Confessor. *The Ascetic Life; The Four Centuries on Charity*. Translated and annotated by Polycarp Sherwood. London: Westminster, 1955.

———. *Ambigua*. Translation by Emmanuel Ponsoye, notes and introduction by Jean Claude Larchet. Paris: Les Éditions du L'Ancre, 1994.

———. *Capitoli sulla carita*. Critical ed. Rome: Studium, 1963.

———. *The Disputation with Pyrrhus of Our Father among the Saints*. Translated by Joseph P. Farell. St. Tikhon's Seminary Press, 1990.

———. *Lettres*. Translated by Emmanuel Ponsoye. Paris: CERF, 1998.

———. "On the Soul." Translated by Georgi Kapriev. In Archiv *für mittelalterliche Philosophie und Kultur*, I (1999) 354–62. [In Bulgarian: Максим Изповедник, За душата,превод: Георги Каприев, в Архив за средновековна философия и култура.]

———. *Selected Writings*. Translated by C. George Berthold, introduction and notes by Jaroslav Ian Pelikan, Irénée-Henri Dalmais. Classics of Western Spirituality. London: SPCK, 1985.

Bibliography

McFarland, I. "Developing an Apophatic Christocentrism. Lessons from Maximus the Confessor." In *Theology Today* 60 (2003) 200–214.

Meunier, B. *Le Christ de Cyrille d' Alexandrie, L'humanité, le salut et la question monophysite.* Paris, 1997.

Meyendorff, J. *Byzantine Theology.* Sofia: Gal iko, 1996. [In Bulgarian: Майендорф, Й. Византийско богословие.]

———. *Byzantine Theology: Historical Trends and Doctrinal Themes.* New York: Fordham University Press, 1979.

Milo, R. D. *Aristotle on Practical Knowledge and Weakness of Will.* The Hague: Mouton, 1966.

Mitralexis, S. *Ever-moving Repose: The Notion of Time in St. Maximus the Confessor's Philosophy Through the Perspective of a Relational Ontology.* Berlin, 2014.

Moore, E. *Origen of Alexandria and St. Maximus the Confessor: An Analysis and Critical Evaluation of Their Eschatological Doctrines.* Boca Raton, FL: Dissertation.com, 2005.

Mueller-Jordan, P. *Typologie spatio-temporelle de l'Ecclesia byzantine: la mystagogie de Maxime le Confesseur dans la culture philosophique de l'Antiquité tardive,* Leiden: Brill, 2005.

Nemesius of Emessa. *On the Nature of Man.* Translation, introduction, and notes by R.W.Sharples and Philip J. Van der Eijk, Liverpool University Press, 2008.

———. За природата на човека. Bibliotheca Christiana 13. София: Лик, 2003.

Neoplatonism i hristianstvo. Chast I. Grutzkata tradicia III-IVv. Sofia: Lik, 2002. [In Bulgarian: *Неоплатонизъм и християнство,* ч. I .*Гръцката традиция* III-VIв.]

Neoplatonism i hristianstvo, Chast II. Vizantiiskata tradicia. Sofia: Lik, 2004. [In Bulgarian: *Неоплатонизъм и християнство,* ч. II. Византийскататрадиция,С.:Лик, 2004.]

Noble I., *The Many Voices of Orthodox Theology in the West in the Twentieth Century,* SVS Press, 2016.

Noble, I. *Tracking God: An Ecumenical Fundamental Theology.* Eugene, OR: Wipf & Stock, 2010.

Noble, I. *Theological Interpretation of Culture in Post-Comunist Context. Central and Eastern european Search for Roots.* London: Ashgate, 2010.

Noble I., *The Ways of Orthodox Theology in the West,* New York: SVS Press, 2015.

Noble I., *Wrestling With the Mind of the Fathers.* New York: SVS Press, 2015.

Opera, Patrologia Graeca, vol. 90–91, edited by J.-P. Migne. Paris, 1850.

Ouspensky, L. "Theology of Icon." Crestwood, NY: St. Vladimir's Seminary Press, 1978.

The Oxford Dictionary of the Christian Church. Edited by F. L. Cross. Oxford: Oxford University Press, 1957.

Papanikolaou, A. *Being with God.* Notre Dame: University of Notre Dame Press, 2006.

———. *Mystical as Political.* Notre Dame: University of Notre Dame Press, 2012.

Papanikolaou, A., and P. Hamalis. "Toward a Godly Mode of Being: Virtue as Embodied Deification." *Studies in Christian Ethics* 26 (2013) 271–80.

Parvis, P., ed. *Studia Patristica* XLII, *Papers presented at the Fourteenth International Conference on Patristic Studies held in Oxford 2003,* 205–9. Leuven: Peeters, 2006.

Pascal, Blaise. *Pensées.* Section 3, "Of the Necessity of the Wager III.233." Translated by W. F. Trotter. Grand Rapids, MN: Christian Classics Ethereal Library, 199[?].

Pelikan, J. *Christianity and Classical Culture: The Metamorphosis of Natural Theology in the Christian Encounter with Hellenism.* Gifford Lectures at Aberdeen, 1993.

Perl, E. D. *Methexesis: Creation, Incarnation, Deification in St. Maximus Confessor.* New Haven: Yale University Press, 1991.

Bibliography

———. *Theophany: The Neoplatonic Philosophy of Dionysius the Areopagite*. Albany: State University of New York Press, 2007.

Petrov, V. V. *Maksim Ispovednik: Ontologia I metod v vizantiiskoi filosofii VII veka*. Moskva, 2007. [In Russian: Петров В.В. Максим Исповедник: онтология и метод в византийской философии VII века.]

The Philokalia. Vol. 2. Translated and edited by G. E. H. Palmer et al. London: Faber & Faber, 1981.

Piret, P. *Le Christ et la Trinité selon Maxime le Confesseur*. Paris: Beauchesne,1983.

Платон. *Диалози*, т. 1-4. С. 1979–1990.

Плотин. *Енеади*. С. 2005.

Прокъл. *Първоосонови на теологията*. С. 1995

Св. ДионисийАреопагит, *За божествените имена*. С., 1996

Св. ДионисийАреопагит, *За небесната йерархия. За църковната йерархия*, С., 2001

Св. Максим Изповедник, Творения, Света гора, Атон, 2002

Святитель Григорий Нисийский, Избранные творения, Изд. Сретенского монастыря, Москва, 2007

Redovic, A. *Gregory of Nazianzus (Or. 29.2) in Maximus the Confessor's Ambigua*. Studia Patristica XXXVII, 250–57. Leuven: Peeters, 2001.

Riou, A. *Le monde et l'Eglise selon Maxime le Confesseur*. Paris: Beauchesne, 1973.

Sherwood, P. *Date-List of the Works of Maximus the Confessor*. Herder (Studia Anselmiana 30), Rome: Orbis Catholicus, 1952.

———. *The Earlier Ambigua of St. Maximus the Confessor and His Refutation of Origenism*, Rome: Orbis Catholicus, 1955.

———. "Survey of Recent Work on St. Maximus the Confessor." *Traditio* 20 (1964) 428–37.

Sidorov, I. A. "Prepodobni Maksim Ispovednik: Epoha, jizn, tvorchestvo." In *Tvorenia prepodobnogo Maksima Ispovednika*., Moskva: Martis God, 1993.]

———. *Tvorenia prepodobnogo Maksima Ispovednika*. Moskva: Martis God, 1993. [In Russian: Сидоров, И. А. Творения преподобного Максима Исповедника.]

Speer, A. "The Certainty and Scope of Knowledge: Bonaventure's Disputed Questions on the Knowledge of Christ." *Medieval Philosophy and Theology* 6 (1997) 25–46.

Srednovekovni filosofi, Chast I. Sofia: Universitetsko izdatelstvo, 1994. [In Bulgarian: *Средновековни философи. Част първа*.]

Staniloae, Dumitru. *Comentaire des Ambigua, St. Maxim le Confesseur, Ambigua*. Translated by Jean-Claude Larchet. Paris: Éditions de l'Ancre, 1994.

Stead, D. J. *The Church, the Liturgy, and the Soul of Man: The Mystagogia of St. Maximus the Confessor*. Still River, MA: St. Bede's, 1982.

Steel, C. "Elementatio evangelica. A propos de Maxime le Confesseur, Ambigua ad Ioh. XVII." In *The Four Gospels*, edited by Van M. Segbroeck, 219–43. Leuven: Leuven University Press, 1992.

———. "Le jeu du Verbe. À propos de Maxime, *Amb. ad Ioh.* LXVII." In *Philohistôr. Miscellanea in honorem Caroli Laga septuagenarii*, edited by A. Schoors and P. Van Deun, 281–93. Orientalia Lovaniensia Analecta 60. Leuven: Peeters, 1994.

———. "Maximus Confessor on Theory and Praxis: A Commentary on Ambigua ad Iohannem VI (10) 1–19." In *Theoria, Praxis, and the Contemplative Life after Plato and Aristotle*, edited by Thomas Benatouil and Mauro Bonazzi, 229–57. Leiden, Boston: Brill, 2013.

Bibliography

———. "The Tree of Knowledge of Good and Evil." In *Iohannes Scottus Eriugena: The Bible and Hermeneutics; Proceedings of the Ninth International Colloquium of the Society for the Promotion of Eriugenian Studies, Leuven and Louvain-la-Neuve, June 7-10, 1995*, edited by Gerd Van Reil et al. Leuven University Press, 1996.

Studia Patristica XXXVII. Papers presented at the Thirteenth International Conference on Patristic Studies, Oxford 1999. Leuven: Peeters, 2001.

Suchla, B. R. *Dionysius Areopagita: Leben—Werk—Wirkung*. Freiburg: Herder, 2008.

Tatakis, B. *Byzantine Philsophy*. Cambridge: Hacket, 1949.

Thunberg, L. *Man and the Cosmos: The Vision of St. Maximus the Confessor*. Crestwood, NY: St. Vladimir's Seminary Press, 1985.

———. *Microcosm and Mediator: The Theological Anthropology of Maximus the Confessor*. Lund: Open Court, 1995.

Tollefsen, Th. T. *Activity and Participation in Late Antique and Early Christian Thought*. Oxford:Early Christian Studies, 2012.

Tollefsen, Th. T. *The Christocentric Cosmology of St. Maximus the Confessor*. Oxford Early Christian Studies. Oxford: Oxford University Press, 2008.

Törönen, M. *Union and Distinction in the Thought of St. Maximus the Confessor*. Oxford: Oxford University Press, 2007.

Toutekov, Svilen. Dobrodetelta zaradi istinata: bogoslovski i aretologicheski osnovi na aretologiata. Veliko Tarnovo: Sintagma, 2009. [In Bulgarian: Тутеков Свилен, Добродетелта заради Истината: богословски и аретологически основи на аретологията.]

———. *Lichnost, obschtnost, drugost*. VelikoTarnovo: Sintagma, 2009. [In Bulgarian: Личност, Общност, Другост.]

Turcescu, L. *Gregory of Nyssa and the Concept of Divine Persons*. Oxford: Oxford University Press, 2005.

Van Deun, P. "Les extraits de Maxime le Confesseur contenus dans les chaînes sur l'Évangile de Matthieu." In *Philohistôr. Miscellanea in honorem Caroli Laga septuagenarii*, edited by A. Schoors and P. Van Deun, 295–328. Orientalia Lovaniensia Analecta 60. Leuven, 1994.

Völker, W. *Maximus Confessor als Mesiter des Geistlichen Lebens*. Wiesbaden: Franz Steiner Verlag SMBH, 1965.

Von Balthasar, H. U. *Kosmische Liturgie, "DasWeltbild Maximus' des Bekenners."* 2nd ed. Switzerland: Johannes Verlag, 1961.

———. "Kosmische Liturgie: Das Weltbild Maximus' des Bekenners." French translation. "Liturgie Cosmic: Maxim le Confesseur," 1947.

Von Schönborn, C. *Sophrone de Jerusalem. Vie monastique et confession dogmatique*. Paris: Beauchesne, 1972.

Weiswurm, A. A. *The Nature of Human Knowledge according to St. Gregory of Nyssa*. Philosophical Studies CXXXVI. Washington: Catholic University of America, 1952.

Williams, J. P. *The Incarnational Apophasis of Maximus the Confessor*. In Studia Patristica XXXVII, *Papers presented at the Thirteenth International Conference on Patristic Studies, Oxford 1999*, edited by M. F. Wiles and E. J. Y. Arnold, 631–35. Leuven: Peeters, 2001.

Williams, N. A. *The Divine Sense: The Intellect in Patristic Theology*. Cambridge: Cambridge University Press, 2007.

Bibliography

Yanakiev, K. Bogut na opita i bogut na filosofiata. Refleksii vurhu bogopoznanieto: Sofia: Anubis, 2002. [In Bulgarian: Янакиев, К. Богът на опита и богът на философията. Рефлексии върху богопознанието.]

——. Filosofski opiti vurhu samotata i nadejdata. Sofia: Orientalia, 2008. [In Bulgarian: Янакиев Калин, Философски опити върху самотата и надеждата, Ориенталия.]

——. Religiozno-filosofski razmishlenia. Sofia: Anubis, 1991. [In Bulgarian: Янакиев К., Религиозно-философски размишления.]

——. Tri ekzistencialno-filosofski studii. Zloto. Stradanieto. Vuzkresenieto. Hristianska kultura vol.6. Sofia: Anubis, 2005. [In Bulgarian: Янакиев К., Три екзистенциално-философски студии.Злото.Страданието.Възкресението. Християнска култура, т.6.]

Zizioulas, J. *Communion and Otherness (Further Studies in Personhood and the Church)*. London: T. & T. Clark, 2006.